CHARACTER CALENDAR

By

SISTER MARY FIDELIS, S.S.N.D.
AND
SISTER MARY CHARITAS, S.S.N.D.

REVISED BY
SISTER MARY CHARITAS, S.S.N.D.

D1715620

ST. AUGUSTINE ACADEMY PRESS
HOMER GLEN, ILLINOIS

NIHIL OBSTAT:

     John A. Schulien, S.T.D.
     Censor librorum

IMPRIMATUR:

     ✠ *Roman R. Atkielski*
     Administrator Diocesanus Milwauchiensis
     Sede Vacante

July 17, 1953

This book was originally published in 1931
by The Bruce Publishing Company.
It was subsequently revised by one of the original
authors in 1953 to reflect changes in the General
Roman Calendar as promulgated in 1954, and to
incorporate other elements of the Liturgical Year.

This facsimile edition reprinted in 2018
by St. Augustine Academy Press.

ISBN: 978-1-64051-075-3

INTRODUCTION
(To the First Edition)

The CHARACTER CALENDAR is an effective utilization of the liturgy in the formation of character. It emphasizes the humanity of the saints and etches sharply a significant aspect of the life of each. It uses the *Imitation of Christ* in its most effective way in spiritual development. Its formulation of ideals is in a language within the ordinary person's appreciation and has a tang of its own. Its homespun directness and even colloquial quality breaks down barriers to action.

This combination of the liturgy, the *Imitation of Christ* of à Kempis, the modern publicity man's technique of slogans, and the Bible will have a great appeal because of its novelty, its freshness, and its practicality. It will have, too, an effectiveness because the material is of such a nature as to look to action, and consequently to form the will.

Such material as this, good every year, could serve as an excellent basis for a practical training in meditation. It would help in prayer. It would become, in very fact, a spiritual exercise. It would help mightily in that spiritual formation of the individual which is the goal of Christian education.

I am glad of the opportunity to commend this "labor of love" of Sisters Fidelis and Charitas, and proud of having had a little to do with it in its preparation.

EDWARD A. FITZPATRICK

FOREWORD TO REVISED EDITION

The CHARACTER CALENDAR was written in three weeks of a busy summer school in 1930. It became immediately popular as it appeared each month serially in the *Catholic School Journal*. In 1931, The Bruce Publishing Company brought out the CALENDAR in its recent form.

But 23 years is a long time in the fast-moving history of the saints and in the progress of a very live and active Church. The more important collaborator, Mother Fidelis, died in 1949.

It is to present the current changes in the liturgical calendar and to reap what profit we can from both the inspiration of their life and their intercession that this revision of the CHARACTER CALENDAR is now presented. Also to satisfy the calls of the original CALENDAR's thousands of friends, for whom may God and His saints and their and our friends be thanked.

THE SURVIVING AUTHOR

Purification, 1953
Chicago, Ill.

CONTENTS

CONTENTS

Jan. 1. THE CIRCUMCISION OF OUR LORD

This is the day on which the Infant Christ was given the name of Jesus formally.

The Lord said to me: Thou art My Son; this day have I begotten Thee. — *First Nocturn*

What a great thing it is to love Jesus. — *Imitation: Book III*

IDEAL: Our Lord was not obliged to submit to this painful fulfillment of the law, but He was showing us how to live as true followers of His; and as such He does not expect us to question whether we are strictly obliged or not when the omission might give bad example.

TODAY: You think the whole of a new year is before you. It is not. Only this moment is yours. Make this moment holy, and each moment, one at a time as you receive it from God to live, and you will find that that is all it takes to become the saint God expects you to be, for sanctity consists in doing God's will one moment at a time.

SLOGAN: New Year resolution: I want to do what God asks of me NOW.

Jan. 2. MOST HOLY NAME OF JESUS
(When January 1 is Sunday, Monday, or Tuesday; otherwise on Sunday between January 1–6)

How fitting it is that this feast should follow immediately upon the feast commemorating His reception of the Name!

In the Name of Jesus every knee shall bend. — *Epistle*

Let Thy holy Name be blessed. — *Imitation: Book III*

1

IDEAL: Abraham Lincoln is the Emancipator; Henry Clay, the Compromisor; Babe Ruth, the King of Swat; each one named for what he did. Jesus means Saviour; and that is precisely what He has done and continues to do for you individually.

TODAY: St. Paul said that whether we eat or drink or no matter what we do, we ought to do it in the Name of Christ Jesus. Our Lord Himself said: "If you ask the Father anything in my Name, He will give it to you." Well, so what?

SLOGAN: No name so sweet; to the penitent, no name so mild. — *St. Bernard*

Jan. 3.   ST. GENEVIEVE, Virgin
(Within the Octave of St. John)

When St. Germanus was passing through the district of Nanterre, near Paris, he took particular notice of a little shepherdess, and predicted her future sanctity. This was but the beginning of unusual events in the life of St. Genevieve. She became an angel of mercy, was unjustly persecuted, procured corn for Paris during the siege, turned away the threatening Huns, and became adviser to King Clovis.

Because of truth, and meekness, and justice, thy right hand shall conduct thee wonderfully. — *Gradual: Psalm 10*

Thou alone art good, just, and holy; Thou canst do all things; Thou givest all things; Thou fillest all things leaving only the sinner empty. — *Imitation: Book III*

IDEAL: Perhaps if a little girl tending sheep by the wayside tried to tell you a few things or to give you a bit of sound advice, you would be inclined to wonder at her daring. Yet see how truly great she became and how much the nation owes her.

TODAY: Watch yourself. Are there not some people whom you take very much for granted as being your decided inferiors? This is how you can tell. Do you ever think or say, when certain people criticize what you do, "Who does he think he is?" You are despising a person like that and thinking very much better of yourself; that is pride. Be careful of it; it is an ugly trait and destroys that resemblance to your Mother you wanted so much.

SLOGAN: Said the old Quaker to his wife:

"And all the world's a little queer,
But thee and me, dear,
And even thee's a little queer."

Jan. 4. ST. TITUS, Bishop
(Within the Octave of the Holy Innocents)

St. Titus, the well-beloved disciple of St. Paul endured the fatigues of numerous and distant voyages on land and sea to bring the Gospel to different nations. Despite hardship and labor, he lived to be ninety-four.

The harvest indeed is great, but the laborers are few. Pray therefore the Lord of the harvest to send forth laborers into His harvest. — *Gospel: Luke 10*

Keep thyself as a pilgrim and a stranger upon earth, that hath no concern with the business of the world. Keep thy heart free and lifted up to God, for thou hast not here a lasting city. — *Imitation: Book I*

IDEAL: You probably know very little about St. Titus. But he must have been a very fine man for he was one of the most intimate friends of St. Paul. That says it all, does it not?

TODAY: When people see boys and girls associate with you, are they inclined, perhaps, to say, "So-and-so can't be worth much if he goes with that person?" The thing, of course, that really matters is this: What kind of companion are you for yourself? You know what Shakespeare says: "To thine own self be true; then it must follow as the night the day: thou canst not then be false to any man."

SLOGAN: Going much with wolves soon teaches one how to howl.

Jan. 5. ST. SIMON STYLITES
(The Vigil of the Epiphany)

A sermon on the eight beatitudes awakened in St. Simon a desire for evangelical perfection. He mortified his body in an almost superhuman manner. He spent 37 years on the top of a pillar, exposed to heat and cold, day and night, adoring the majesty of God.

Who shall ascend into the mountain of the Lord: or who shall stand in His holy place? — *Prime: Psalm 23*

Study, therefore, so to live now, that in the hour of death thou mayest be able rather to rejoice than to fear. Learn how to die to the world, that then thou mayest begin to live with Christ. — *Imitation: Book I*

IDEAL: When you read the peculiar method of penance this saint chose, were you inclined to smile and think him just a bit queer? Will you take the time to think today of how ever so much more foolish are the things we do to satisfy the world? Think of how people have their eyebrows plucked, for instance.

TODAY: Public penance is very well for saints, but for us who are still only beginners, it is much safer to practice interior penances that no one sees but God. If you are in the habit of stopping for a drink each time you pass the fountain, don't do it just this one day.

SLOGAN: Be a fool, then, for Christ's sake.

Jan. 6. THE EPIPHANY OF OUR LORD

The word "Epiphany" means "manifestation." As at Christmas time it is the mystery of a God who makes Himself visible, but it is no longer only to the Jews that He shows Himself, but to the Gentiles.

And behold the star, that they had seen in the East, went before them until it came and stood over the place where the Child was. And when they saw the star they rejoiced exceedingly. And entering into the house, they found the

Child with Mary His Mother and falling down they worshipped Him. And opening their treasures, they offered Him gifts, gold, frankincense, and myrrh. — *Gospel: Matthew 2*

For thus also Thy saints, O Lord, who now exult with Thee in the kingdom of heaven, during life awaited in faith and much patience the coming of Thy glory. What they believed, I believe; what they hoped, I hope for; and whither they are arrived, I trust that I also, through Thy grace shall arrive. — *Imitation: Book IV*

IDEAL: Had you lived at the time of the appearance of the wonderful star, you would not have hesitated one minute, would you? You would probably have left your work or play at once to travel a thousand miles to see the Infant Christ.

TODAY: Just across the way, perhaps a few blocks from your own home, perhaps on your way to school, lives the same, the very same, Little Christ; and He sends you a star every day by way of an inspiration to come in, for He has something for you. And you?

SLOGAN: I rejoiced at the things that were said to me, we shall go into the house of the Lord.

(This feast is important enough to be celebrated through six weeks here or before Advent.)

Jan. 7. ST. LUCIAN, Martyr
(Within the Octave of the Epiphany)

St. Lucian was a priest who devoted his time to charitable works and to the study of the Sacred Scriptures. In this latter work he did much to prepare the way for St. Jerome, who gave us the Latin translation of the Bible called the "Vulgate." He died in prison, happy that he was able to give his life as a small measure of return for the priceless gift of faith.

Blessed is the man that endureth temptation: for, when he is tried, he shall receive the crown of life, which God hath promised to them that love Him. — *Lauds*

He labored abundantly for the edification of others, as

much as lay in Him, and as much as He could; but He could not prevent being sometimes judged and despised by others. — *Imitation: Book III*

IDEAL: Nobody knows that St. Lucian did much toward inspiring St. Jerome for the great work of translating the Bible; St. Jerome is generally given that credit alone.

TODAY: Does it make any difference to you if someone else gets the credit for the fine things you have done, or that you have made possible? Try to be satisfied that God knows; for, really, when you go about asking for honors and attention, people despise even the actual good you have done. Have you noticed that?

SLOGAN: Not to us, O Lord, but to Thy name be glory.

Jan. 8. ST. APPOLLINARIS, The Apologist

Very little is known about this saint except such things as may be learned from his writings and those of his contemporaries. One of his best works is his apology for the Christian religion.

O ye priests of the Lord, bless the Lord; O ye holy and humble of heart, praise God. — *Introit: Daniel 3*

Thou wilt never be interior and devout unless thou pass over in silence other men's affairs, and look especially to thyself. — *Imitation: Book II*

IDEAL: He wrote a book in defense of the Church. That is all. And we dismiss the thought of the saint from our mind when the day is over. Why? Because the world does not acclaim him loudly. But that is no indication of true greatness; there was a time when Christ said to this saint: "Well done, thou good and faithful servant, enter thou into the joy of the Lord."

TODAY: Keep impressing on your own mind day by day the thought that nothing counts but God's approval.

SLOGAN: Naught but Thyself, O Lord, naught but Thyself.

Sunday Within the Octave of the Epiphany. THE HOLY FAMILY

Though the primary purpose of our dear Lord's coming to earth was to show us how to be individually holy, this feast is dedicated to the Holy *Family*. Christ realized, as His life illustrates so beautifully, the fact that the family, as the beginning of things, must possess the spirit of true holiness.

O Lord Jesus, make those whom Thou dost refresh with the heavenly sacrament, to imitate continually the example of Thy Holy Family. — *Postcommunion*

Nothing, therefore, ought to give so great a joy to one that loveth Thee as the accomplishment of Thy will. — *Imitation: Book III*

IDEAL: Our dear Lord said, "My meat is to do the will of My Father" and "Whoever does the will of My Father in Heaven, he is my brother and sister and mother." If you wish to make yours a holy family, there is only one thing to do, one method of achieving your goal; that is to do the will of God NOW. Do it!

TODAY: Do not look to what you will do by and by to become holy. You may not be living by and by. You may no longer be living at the end of this day. Surely there is coming a day whose end you will not see. This moment is all. The Holy Family lived a very simple life; the nearest neighbors did not realize that they lived next door to the Holy Family. The members of the Holy Family did nothing extra in their home in Nazareth. They just did God's will perfectly, every moment, as God the Father expects it of us. This is the only way of arriving at holiness; there is no other way.

SLOGAN: "All the way to Heaven is Heaven; because He said, 'I am the Way.'" — *St. Catherine of Siena*

Jan. 9.   SS. JULIAN and BASILISSA, Martyrs
(Within the Octave of the Epiphany)

This saintly married couple converted their beautiful home into a hospital. They assisted personally in serving the sick. St. Basilissa died a natural death; St. Julian was martyred.

Thy saints shall flourish like the lily, O Lord, and be as the odor of balsam before Thee. — *Gradual*

O pleasant and delightful service of God, which maketh a man truly free and holy. — *Imitation: Book III*

IDEAL: When we think of saints, we ordinarily think of them as bishops or religious or at least as people who spent much time in prayer. These two saints were husband and wife who lived each day as perfectly as possible.

TODAY: Saints are people who spend the whole day in prayer. You must do the same. How? Make the intention each morning to do all that day for the greater honor and glory of God; make the Sacred Heart League intention. Of course, see to it that your work during the day is at least not a disgrace to be offered to God.

SLOGAN: All for the greater honor and glory of God.

Jan. 10.   ST. WILLIAM, Archbishop
(Within the Octave of the Epiphany)

St. William reluctantly accepted the dignity of archbishop. As archbishop he redoubled his austerities saying that now he had to do penance for others as well as for himself. He always wore a hair shirt under his religious habit.

I have laid help upon one that is mighty, and have exalted one chosen out of My people; for My hand shall help him. — *Matins: Fifth Responsory*

For the just man will not be troubled, whatever happeneth to him from God. — *Imitation: Book III*

IDEAL: How do you accept honors and compliments? Do

you feel deep down inside that, well, it is coming to you? What if people outside knew you as God who sees your innermost conscience knows you, do you suppose they would ever walk on the same side of the street with you?

TODAY: You thought while you read the above, "I don't think I am any worse than the rest of them, and, anyway, I wouldn't think of doing some of the things I have seen others do." That is pride; you are exalting yourself and despising others.

SLOGAN: He that exalteth himself shall be humbled.

Jan. 11. ST. THEODOSIUS
(Within the Octave of the Epiphany)

The long life of this holy man was filled with self-sacrificing charity for others. The poor, the sick, the unfortunate found in him a constant friend. Those who were associated with him felt that he walked in the presence of God.

This the people saw and understood it not, neither laid they this up in their minds, that the grace of God and His mercy are with His saints, and that He hath respect unto His chosen. — *Matins: Second Lesson*

By day they labored, and much of the night they spent in prayer; though while they labored, they were far from leaving off mental prayer. — *Imitation: Book I*

IDEAL: You know St. Paul's lovely epistle on charity, do you not? That has reference particularly to love of God, but we are told too, "He that saith he loves God and loveth not his fellow men is a liar."

TODAY: Do your friends readily turn to you for kindness? Do you readily "sponge" on others, or are you considerate of the feelings of others even if you yourself are often imposed upon?

SLOGAN: Amen, I say to you, as long as you did it for one of these, the least of My brethren, you did it for Me.

Jan. 12.   ST. AELRED, Abbot
(Within the Octave of the Epiphany)

St. Aelred left the royal court of Scotland to follow the call of God in the monastic life. He entered the severe Cistercian Order. Throughout his life his associates found in him a sympathetic friend. His special devotion was the Passion of Christ.

Beloved of God and men, whose memory is in benediction. He made him like the saints in glory, and magnified him in the fear of his enemies, and with his words he made prodigies to cease. — *Epistle: Book of Ecclus.*

In like manner, do not be inquisitive or dispute concerning the merits of the saints: who is more holy than another, or who greater in the kingdom of heaven. — *Imitation: Book III*

IDEAL: This saint left an earthly court for the immediate service of his King; became a member of the imperial bodyguard, as it were.

TODAY: Make a special visit or two to the church today; when you go in, tell our Lord you have come to do sentinel duty before His tent. Try to assure Him that you are honored — as indeed you are — to be allowed to stand before Him.

SLOGAN: I have chosen to be an abject in the courts of my God, rather than to dwell among thousands.

Jan. 13.   ST. VERONICA OF MILAN
(We continue keeping the Epiphany to this day.)

When St. Veronica became concerned about her lack of education, the Blessed Virgin appeared to her and taught her three lessons: purity of intention, abhorrence of murmuring or criticism, daily meditation on the Passion. Through practice she learned these lessons and became a saint.

Who would deny that this is a life which hath come down

from heaven, seeing it is a life whereof it is not easy to find an example before God came down to dwell in a body of clay. — *Second Nocturn: Sixth Lesson*

I am accustomed to visit My elect in two manners of ways; namely, by trial and by consolation. And I daily read to them two lessons: one to rebuke their vices, and the other to exhort them to the increase of virtue. — *Imitation: Book III*

IDEAL: You notice that one of the three lessons taught this saint by our Lady herself was abhorrence of criticism.

TODAY: When you are about to say something unkind of anybody, will you remember that you are on the verge of injuring the reputation of one of our Lord's friends? Besides, to say an unkind thing about another proves you a coward of the deepest dye. You are afraid to say this thing to the person concerned and you are not big enough to control an instrument not three inches long.

SLOGAN: With my little bow and arrow, I killed Cock Robin.

Jan. 14. ST. HILARY, Bishop

St. Hilary was an intrepid defender of the divinity of Christ. Because of his uncompromising stand on the side of truth he was banished from France. During the time of his exile he composed the learned works on the Blessed Trinity which earned for him the title of "Doctor of the Church."

Neither do men light a lamp and put it under a measure, but upon the lampstand so as to give light to all in the house. Even so let your light shine before men in order that they may see your good works and give glory to your Father who is in heaven. — *Gospel: Matthew 5*

He to whom I speak will quickly be wise and will profit greatly in spirit. — *Imitation: Book III*

IDEAL: When this man was banished from France, he wasted no time pitying himself, as you notice. He went right at something else.

TODAY: Learn to make the best of things. There are certain

experiences that you must live through, anyway; you might as well gain merit by being resigned to God's will. Then, nothing ever happens that does not suit you.

SLOGAN: Not my will, but Thine be done.

Jan. 15. ST. PAUL, The First Hermit

This saint was very rich and highly educated. During the persecution of Christians he went to the desert, trusting that Divine Providence would supply his temporal needs. His confidence was not misplaced. He lived to be 90 years old, subsisting on the simple diet of food to be found on an oasis. He spent his time in penance and prayer.

The just shall flourish like the palm tree; he shall grow up like the cedar of Libanus; planted in the house of the Lord, in the courts of the house of God. — *Introit: Psalm 91*

Oh, how great is the abundance of Thy sweetness, O Lord, which Thou hast hidden for those that fear! But what are Thou to those that love Thee? What to those that love Thee with their whole heart? — *Imitation: Book III*

IDEAL: An example of the kind of man of whom the world says, "He buried all his talent becoming a monk," this St. Paul arrived at sanctity in the directly opposite manner to his namesake, the Apostle of the Gentiles.

TODAY: Different people have different natures — different dispositions, that is; but each person has the correct disposition for sanctity; all that is necessary is for the individual to use what gifts he has in doing his several duties well, one at a time.

SLOGAN: Be ye perfect as your heavenly Father is perfect.

Jan. 16. ST. MARCELLUS, Pope and Martyr

St. Marcellus reigned during the troublesome days of the persecution of the Christians by Maxentius. For nine months this Pope was in the power of the tyrant who ill-treated him and made him do the work of slaves. Rescued by the

Christians and kept in concealment for some time, he was again seized and put to a lingering death.

The enemy shall have no advantage over him, nor the son of iniquity have power to hurt him. — *Gradual*

It is a great honor, a great glory, to serve Thee, and to despise all things for Thee. — *Imitation: Book III*

IDEAL: Get a copy of the life of this saint today and read it; you will find it interesting to note in what peculiar fashion he earned his heavenly crown, though he had been a pope.

TODAY: A few days ago, you were given as slogan to "Be a fool for Christ's sake." This saint was. Shakespeare told us that we mortals are fools all, and we know it anyway, so let us be Christ's fools, and do our daily "stunts" for Him; He pays us with heaven for our service, regardless of our awkwardness, if only we have *wanted* to do well, and tried to.

SLOGAN: Take my heart, Lord; who but You would want it, knowing it as You do? — *Mother Loyola's Communion Prayer*

Jan. 17. ST. ANTHONY, Patriarch of Monks

Hearing at Mass the words, "If thou wilt be perfect, go, sell what thou hast, and give to the poor," this saint gave away his vast possessions and retired to the desert where he lived on bread and water. The devil attacked him in visible form. The saint defied him with the words: "I fear you not; you cannot separate me from the love of Christ."

He was excelled by none in watchfulness and self-restraint. He surpassed all in long-suffering, meekness, tenderness, lowliness, perseverance, and continual study of the Holy Scriptures. — *Second Nocturn: Fifth Lesson*

Look upon the lively examples of the Holy Fathers, in whom shone real perfection and the religious life, and thou wilt see how little it is and almost nothing that we do. — *Imitation: Book I*

IDEAL: In order to escape from the dangers of the world, this saint left his home and went to live in the desert. When the devil tried to tempt him to sin, he kept close to God in prayer, and knew the devil could not harm him so long as he remained a friend of God.

TODAY: You have heard little boys boast, "I ain't scared of nuthin'," and you have smiled at their foolishness. If you heard a person say, "I'm not afraid of polio or the flu," you would know that person to be wrong. Since our soul is so much more important than the body, does it not seem worth while to try to escape the devil?

SLOGAN: Watch and pray that ye enter not into temptation. — *Our Lord*

Jan. 18.   ST. PETER'S CHAIR AT ROME

In making Rome mistress of the world, Divine Providence was preparing all things for the spread of Christianity. St. Peter saw that the capital of the world's empire was a strategic point from which might radiate the beneficent influence of the Gospel. It was at Rome, therefore, that he established his pontifical chair.

Thou art the Shepherd of the sheep, and the Prince of the Apostles, and unto thee hath God given all the kingdoms of the world. Therefore unto thee hath He given the keys of the kingdom of heaven. — *Third Responsory*

Watch and pray, that ye enter not into temptation, saith the Lord. — *Imitation: Book III*

IDEAL: Perhaps you know people who can trace descent of their family back through several hundred years, and can boast of great women and men who are their ancestors. What are a few hundred years, and a few great mortals in the ancestral line? As a Catholic, you may boast of a family that goes back all the way to Christ!

TODAY: The Church Unity Octave begins today. Pray especially for the gift of faith for all men, and for a strengthening of your own that you may be a Christopher to others.

SLOGAN: Thy Kingdom come!

Jan. 19. SS. MARIUS, MARTHA, AND COMPANIONS

(St. Canute, King of Denmark, is commemorated.)

The Persian nobles, Marius and Martha, came with their sons, Audifax and Abachum, to Rome to visit the tombs of the Apostles, SS. Peter and Paul. They were thrown into prison and finally put to death for their faith.

Let the just feast, and rejoice before God, and be delighted with gladness. — *Introit of the Mass*

Who then is the best off? Truly he that is able to suffer something for the love of God. — *Imitation: Book I*

IDEAL: Would you note that these holy people came out of Persia away back in the year A.D. 270? We do not today normally think of Persia as being a Catholic country. And yet the earth of that country, too, has been moistened with the blood of saints.

TODAY: It is very smart to pray for the country from which the saint of the day came; surely, in heaven, the saints do not lose their interest in their native land.

SLOGAN: Somewhere each soul lives on forever, in light or in darkness.

Jan. 20. SS. SEBASTIAN and FABIAN

St. Sebastian was one of the finest of Roman soldiers, an intrepid fighter and a stranger to fear. Condemned to be shot by the archers for being a Christian, he faced death unflinchingly and was left for dead. However, he was nursed back to health by the Christians, later to die a martyr, beaten to death with clubs.

St. Fabian was chosen pope when, during the meeting of the council, a dove flew into the chamber and sat upon his shoulder. This was taken as a miraculous sign. For sixteen years he ruled before he was martyred.

God is glorious in His saints, wonderful in majesty, doing wonders. — *Gradual*

Thou must pass through fire and water before thou come to refreshment. — *Imitation: Book I*

IDEAL: One is naturally attracted to a man who has physical prowess, athletic ability, and with all that is also a splendid type of gallant manhood. Of such kind was St. Sebastian, the kind of saint you would like, and could not help it.

TODAY: If you have not already done so, get a copy of *Fabiola* and read it today. Watch for an opportunity to see the movie. If you think you have a great deal of courage, see if you can say "no" when you should.

SLOGAN: Better is he that ruleth himself than he that taketh cities.

Jan. 21. ST. AGNES, Virgin and Martyr

St. Agnes was only twelve years old when she was told to offer incense to the gods or be prepared to die. Many of those who witnessed the torture of this mere child were moved to tears. After sentence of death was passed, she stood erect for a moment in prayer, and then bowed her neck to the sword.

Let us keep with joy and gladness, the feast of this most saintly maiden, let us call to mind the holy passion of the blessed Agnes: in her thirteenth year she conquered, losing death and finding life, because she loved the only Giver of Life. — *First Responsory*

If whole armies should stand together against me, my heart shall not fear. The Lord is my Helper, and my Redeemer. — *Imitation: Book III*

IDEAL: This lovely young saint, beautiful, wealthy, withstood the attacks of the judges who thought to win her over by threats or flattery. When offered a wealthy young prince in marriage, St. Agnes responded with her beautiful bridal hymn, "He has placed a seal upon my countenance," etc.

TODAY: Choose St. Agnes for your patroness today. The Church has assigned her especially as an ideal for youth. Pray to her particularly for the grace of keeping your soul looking like your Mother's as closely as possible.

SLOGAN: Keep my soul like thine, my Mother.

Jan. 22. SS. VINCENT and ANASTASIUS

Both of these saints suffered the most excruciating pains rather than deny their faith. After St. Vincent had been tortured he was put into prison where the angels consoled him and told him his end was near.

Come ye blessed of My Father, inherit the kingdom! I will render unto you a reward of your labors. — *Eighth Responsory*

Here, therefore, men are tried, as gold is in the furnace. — *Imitation: Book I*

IDEAL: St. Vincent was roasted to death. You can scarcely imagine a death like that. Perhaps you sometimes think you are making a very great sacrifice for your faith when you rise for an early Mass or walk several blocks through deep snow and a cold wind. Balance your spirit of sacrifice with that of St. Vincent.

TODAY: Sacrifice is measured by love. Do you love God sufficiently to control an uncharitable tongue today? You will know tonight.

SLOGAN: Thou hast made our hearts for Thee, O Lord.

Jan. 23. ST. RAYMOND OF PENNAFORT

This saint was born at Barcelona in Spain, a country which has given the Church a great many saints through the years. Born in 1175 he lived for one hundred years in spite of great penance and mortification. When the king tried to prevent his leaving the court, Raymond spread his cloak on the water and sailed away.

The law of God is in his heart. — *Introt of the Mass*

Son, lift up thy heart to Me in Heaven and the contempt of men will not grieve thee. — *Imitation: Book III*

IDEAL: You find it a little hard to believe that this saint might have ridden over the sea on his cloak? St. Peter walked right on the unfrozen surface without anything but his two feet. Our Lord said something one day about having faith as large as a mustard seed. Perhaps your faith needs enlarging.

TODAY: St. Raymond was the kind of man who had the courage of his convictions. "Know you're right and then go ahead" might have been his motto. Not bad; it puts sand under your wheels so that you do not slip.

SLOGAN: Know you're right — then go ahead. But — know you're right!

Jan. 24. ST. TIMOTHY, Bishop and Martyr

St. Timothy was a friend and disciple of St. Paul. He was a close companion and fellow worker with St. Paul on many of the latter's missionary travels. As Bishop of Ephesus he received two letters from St. Paul which bear his name. He was stoned to death. Novena for the feast of the Purification begins today.

Follow after justice, godliness, faith, charity, patience, mildness. Fight the good fight of faith; lay hold on eternal life, whereunto thou art called, and hast confessed a good confession before many witnesses. — *Epistle of St. Paul to Timothy 6*

In Me the love of thy friend ought to stand; and for Me is he to be loved whoever he be, that appeareth to thee good and much to be loved in this life. — *Imitation: Book III*

IDEAL: St. Paul called him "my beloved son Timothy." Have you ever read *Paul, Hero and Saint?* Read it today, if you want the story of two real live heroes.

TODAY: The main reason for the success of men like today's saint was their willingness to work regardless of whether they got a great deal of attention from men or not. Will you try to impress it ever so deeply on your own mind that the only worth-while regard is that of God?

SLOGAN: Write it on your heart that God's love only is worth striving after.

Jan. 25. THE CONVERSION OF ST. PAUL

St. Paul was born at Tarsus. While on his way to Damascus to persecute the Christians, a light from heaven suddenly shone around him and struck him to earth. He heard a voice saying: "Saul, Saul, why persecutest thou Me?" And he said: "Who art Thou, Lord?" And the Lord said: "I am Jesus whom thou persecutest; it is hard for thee to kick against the goad."

> Lead us, great teacher, Paul, in wisdom's ways,
> And lift our hearts with thine to Heaven's high throne;
> Till faith beholds the clear meridian blaze,
> And, sunlike, in the soul reigns charity alone.
>> *First Vespers, Hymn*

Give all for all; seek nothing, call for nothing back; stand purely and with a full confidence before Me, and thou shalt possess Me. — *Imitation: Book III*

IDEAL: And conversion it was. What wilt thou have me to do? was the submissive question of the man under his horse's feet. How do you act when you are met with some sudden affliction? Do you ever permit yourself the thought, "What have I done that I should be so afflicted?" Ought we not rather to wonder that things go so well with us when we are so altogether undeserving?

TODAY: Ask St. Paul today to obtain for you what we all need and so seldom ask for, common sense.

SLOGAN: What wouldst Thou have me do?

Jan. 26. ST. POLYCARP, Bishop and Martyr

St. Polycarp was a disciple of St. John. After a long life devoted to God and His Church, he was arraigned before the proconsul and ordered to curse Christ and go free. Polycarp answered: "Eighty-six years I have served Him, and He never did me wrong; how can I blaspheme my King and my Saviour?" At the stake he thanked God for letting him drink of Christ's chalice.

Whosoever shall confess Me before men, him will I also confess before My Father. — *Lauds: First Antiphon*

Then is he weary of longer life; and wisheth death to come, that he may be dissolved, and be with Christ. — *Imitation: Book I*

IDEAL: At the age of eighty-six this dear saint was burned to death in the amphitheater for his faith. The deeds we consider so very heroic in our own life dwindle away when we think of what some real heroes have done.

TODAY: You may never be called on to give up your life in martyrdom, but you are asked daily to endure little inconveniences patiently. Get into the habit of believing that everything that happens is a special gift of God meant to advance your sanctity.

SLOGAN: Every hour comes with some little faggot of God's will fastened upon its back.

Jan. 27.   ST. JOHN CHRYSOSTOM

On account of the golden stream of his eloquence, this saint is called by the Greeks, "the golden-mouthed." He was a lawyer and a man of the world of much eminence, before he turned his great intellect and wonderful industry to the study of things sacred. He died in exile with these words on his lips: "Glory be to God for all this."

Let those that put their trust in Thee, rejoice: Let them ever shout for joy, because Thou dwellest in them: Let them also that love Thy name be joyful in Thee. For Thou wilt bless the righteous. — *Matins, Psalm 5*

Speak, Lord, for Thy servant heareth. I am Thy servant; give me understanding, that I may know Thy testimonies. Incline my heart to the words of Thy mouth; let Thy speech distill as the dew. — *Imitation: Book III*

IDEAL: Chrysostom means golden-mouthed. He received his name on account of his lofty eloquence. He spoke "in season and out of season" for the furtherance of God's glory. Have you ever wondered what title would best suit your tongue?

TODAY: If you have ever made a retreat, you know how easy it is to be good when you do not speak. St. James, as you know, says that he that offends not with his tongue is a perfect man. Watch yourself for one day and keep account how many times you fail in the proper use of your tongue.

SLOGAN: But the tongue is a fire, a world of iniquity.

Jan. 28. ST. PETER NOLASCO

St. Peter spent all the money he possessed in delivering Christians from captivity. He was one of the cofounders of the Order of Our Lady of Mercy.

O God who, after the example of Thy charity, didst divinely teach holy Peter to render Thy Church fruitful in a new progeny for the redemption of the faithful; grant through his intercession, that being loosed from our sins we may enjoy perpetual liberty in our heavenly country. — *Collect*

"Hope in the Lord," saith the Prophet, "and do good, and inhabit the land, and thou shalt be fed with the riches thereof." — *Imitation: Book I*

IDEAL: This very busy man was asked in a vision by God to help found a religious order for the ransom of captives. That would take a great deal of time, but he managed it very nicely, chiefly because he loved God so much that he didn't feel he was working extra at all.

TODAY: Do you ever say, when asked to do a kindness, "Well, really, if I had time," etc.? Think of your fellow men as "other Christs" when they ask you a favor and you will scarcely refuse them anything within the bounds of right principle.

SLOGAN: Amen, I say to you, as long as you did it for one of these, the least of My brethren, you did it for Me.

Jan. 29. ST. FRANCIS OF SALES

This saint took the degree of Doctor of Laws, both Civil and Ecclesiastical, at Padua, with much distinction. Though by nature hot-tempered, he became the gentlest of saints. By meekness and kindness he converted 72,000 Calvinists. "You can catch more flies," St. Francis used to say, "with a spoonful of honey than with a hundred barrels of vinegar."

O God who, in order that souls might be saved, didst will that blessed Francis should become all things to all men; fill our hearts, we beseech Thee, with that charity which is sweet; so that, guided by his teaching, and having part in his merits, we may attain unto everlasting happiness. — *Collect*

He that hath true and perfect charity seeketh himself in nothing, but only desireth God to be glorified in all things. — *Imitation: Book I*

IDEAL: This hot-tempered man gained such control of himself that even intentional provocation could not disturb his serenity. He labored among the most stubborn of Calvinists and converted over 70,000 of them through his imperturbable meekness.

TODAY: Do you find it hard to keep cool? St. Francis proves what can be done. Keep a record that only you shall see of how many times you are impatient this morning, how many times this afternoon, and keep that up for a week and see how much you can improve in that time.

SLOGAN: Learn of Me for I am meek and humble of heart.

Jan. 30. ST. MARTINA, Virgin and Martyr

St. Martina was a Roman maiden arrested while at prayer, put to the torture, and beheaded. Though put to death at Ostia, her relics were transferred to Rome where a large church was erected in her honor and where each year she is venerated with great solemnity.

After her shall virgins be brought to the King. — *Gradual*

Command the winds and storms; say to the sea: Be still; to the north wind, Blow thou not: and there shall be a great calm. — *Imitation: Book III*

IDEAL: It does seem that God might have protected St. Martina at least while she was at prayer. But, no matter what men may do to us physically, there is no way in which anybody, anybody at all, can reach our soul, except through our own free will. There every man (and woman) is king in his own castle.

TODAY: With St. Teresa of Ávila, let nothing disturb you; God alone suffices and God never changes. You can always be absolutely sure of Him. Trust Him.

SLOGAN: Trust God and you'll never walk alone.

Jan. 31. ST. JOHN BOSCO, Confessor

Here is a man of our own time, died in 1888, not 70 years ago. He was a delightful boy, a charming young man, and is today an endearing and jolly good-natured saint as he was all through his life.

God gave him wisdom and understanding exceeding much, and largeness of heart as the sand that is on the seashore. — *Introit*

All their desire tended upward to the things everlasting. — *Imitation: Book I*

IDEAL: Never was there a saint so careful to get all the joy out of every moment of life as St. John Bosco. He enjoyed life and living to the utmost, and believed in helping others to get as much fun out of every experience as possible. He enjoyed what is called the "liberty of the Children of God."

TODAY: There is no reason why you and I cannot have as good a time or even better than St. John Bosco. If we make our purpose in life to do God's will as perfectly as we can at THIS moment, we may depend upon God to take care of us, for we have a wonderful Father and a most loving Mother.

SLOGAN: Cast thy care upon the Lord, and He will have care of thee.

SEPTUAGESIMA

Septuagesima comes somewhere between the last days of January and the early part of February. It is the seventieth day before Easter, as its Latin name indicates. Years ago, when Catholics had less of other things to do besides saving their souls — and were conscious of the obligation to do so — the fasting of Lent began on this seventieth day. We have merely the names remaining to us today and the special liturgy of the day, along with the violet vestments. The Sundays follow in succession: Septuagesima, Sexagesima, Quinquagesima, and Quadragesima, the latter being actually the first Sunday of Lent as we reckon Lent today.

Possibly it has been wise to introduce us gradually into the holy season of Lent, Holy Mother Church being indulgent with us, her children, even as was her Founder, who would not "crush the bruised reed nor quench the burning flax."

Feb. 1. ST. IGNATIUS, Bishop and Martyr

St. Ignatius was a disciple of St. John. Given his choice between apostasy or death, he chose the latter, rejoicing in the fact that he was soon to merit the martyr's crown. He was devoured by wild beasts in the Roman amphitheater.

I am the wheat of Christ; may I be ground by the teeth of beasts, that I may be found pure bread. — *Communion*

Learn to suffer in little things now, that then thou mayest be delivered from more grievous sufferings. — *Imitation: Book I*

IDEAL: Tradition says that this saint was the little child whom our Lord set in the midst of the Apostles the time He said, "Unless you become as this little child, you shall not enter the kingdom of heaven."

TODAY: We often think we would be martyrs, too, for Christ. How much inconvenience can we endure for Him without complaint? The weather is too cold, the teachers are too cross, our parents are too strict, etc. And we think we could have wild animals eating us while still alive! Today, we will not complain that we froze an ear last winter and now have chilblains, etc.

SLOGAN: It is easy to give advice from a safe port. — *Schiller*

Feb. 2. THE PURIFICATION OF THE BLESSED VIRGIN MARY

The Blessed Virgin, wishing to obey the Mosaic law, had to go to Jerusalem forty days after the birth of Jesus to offer the prescribed sacrifice. Mothers were to offer a lamb or, if their means did not allow, two doves or pigeons. She took

25

with her the Infant Jesus. The Candlemas procession recalls the journey of Mary and Joseph to the temple.

Novena for the feast of Our Lady of Lourdes begins today.

This day the Blessed Virgin Mary presented the Child Jesus in the temple; and Simeon, filled with the Holy Ghost, took Him up in arms, and blessed God forever and ever. — *Antiphon at the Magnificat*

Oh, when shall it be fully granted me to be free, and to see how sweet Thou art, O Lord my God! — *Imitation: Book III*

IDEAL: At the moment in which the holy man Simeon pronounced the prophecy "set for the fall and rise of many" did the little Heart of the Saviour suffer a pang at thought of you or did it beat faster with delight?

TODAY: Our dear Lady's suffering was accentuated today at the expectation of the "sword that should pierce" her heart. It was our fault. We must be so certainly her faithful children today that we assure her such intense anguish has not been in vain.

SLOGAN: This child is set for the fall and for the rise of many in Israel.

Feb. 3.   ST. BLAISE, Bishop and Martyr

St. Blaise, in his earlier years, was a noted physician. In the practice of medicine he saw so much of the miseries of life that he decided to devote himself to the healing of souls as well as bodies. One time a distracted mother whose child was dying, choked by a bone which had stuck in his throat, begged the saint's intercession. The child was relieved by the prayers of the saint.

This is the priest whom the Lord hath crowned. — *Gradual*

Know for certain that thou must lead a dying life; and the more a man dieth to himself, the more doth he begin to live unto God. — *Imitation: Book II*

IDEAL: You are so familiar with the special ceremony of this day that you know the story of St. Blaise very well. He is a patron against diseases of the throat. Has it occurred to you how very holy a thing your throat is, through which has passed so often the most holy Body of Christ?

TODAY: You would be shocked and pained beyond endurance should the garbage man dump his load in your church. Why? Because the church is God's dwelling place. What of your body, your tongue, your throat? Resolve today that never will any language defile your mouth that would not pass in favor in the hearing of Christ.

SLOGAN: Place Thyself as a seal upon my lips!

Feb. 4. ST. ANDREW CORSINI

Born at Florence, St. Andrew was consecrated to the Blessed Virgin from his birth. In his youth this saint led a rather dissolute life but through the prayers of his mother and the grace of God he saw the folly of his ways and became a Carmelite.

> Grant then that we, O gracious God,
> May follow in the steps he trod;
> And freed from ev'ry stain of sin,
> As he hath won, may also win. — *Lauds: Hymn*

So that when we have read and searched all, let this be the final conclusion, that "through many tribulations we must enter the kingdom of God."

IDEAL: Like so many of the saints, St. Andrew owes his sanctity after God to his mother, who prayed for him without ceasing until he was converted from his careless life.

TODAY: One of the easiest things in the world to do is to say pretty things about mother or to wear a carnation on her day or to bring her a gift bought with her money from time to time. Today, resolve to live so that your very life may be a gift of thanks to your mother.

SLOGAN: It is easier to say than to do.

Feb. 5. ST. AGATHA, Virgin and Martyr

In the midst of dangers and temptations St. Agatha served Christ in purity of body and soul, and she died for the love of chastity. To this day Christ has shown His tender regard for the body of this virgin. Her body is still incorrupt. On several occasions her veil saved the people of Catania during an eruption of Mt. Etna.

But the foolish things of the world hath God chosen, that He may confound the wise, and the weak things of the world hath God chosen, that He may confound the strong. — *Epistle: St. Paul to the Corinthians*

He is truly great who hath great charity. He is truly great who is little in his own eyes, and counteth for nothing all the heights of honor. — *Imitation: Book I*

IDEAL: This lovely young girl gave her life rather than sully a soul she had tried to keep very pure and closely like our Lady's. With St. Agnes she is a patroness of youth for the preservation of virtue.

TODAY: Pray to St. Agatha today for courage and prudence against the temptations that are bound to come to you on your way through life that you may bring your soul to God's judgment seat as pure and undefiled as hers.

SLOGAN: Blessed are the clean of heart for they shall see God.

Feb. 6. ST. TITUS, Bishop and Confessor
(St. Dorothy, Virgin and Martyr, is commemorated. Look her up!)

A great friend and disciple of St. Paul, Titus lived to be 105, and he lived a very strenuous life at that; and we thought we had discovered the secret of long life in our century. We are about eighteen centuries too late.

Behold a great priest who in his days pleased God. — *Epistle*

Son, commit thy cause to Me always; I will dispose of it well in its due season. — *Imitation: Book III*

IDEAL: Read the Epistle of St. Paul to Titus. It is that of a teacher trainer to a teacher-in-service. St. Paul had, of course, studied in the best schools, but the Holy Spirit, on whom he relied so much, knows something about educational psychology too.

TODAY: It would be worth while remembering that the advice of St. Paul to Titus was for the latter's flock of newly converted pagans. Note the substantial nourishment those early Christians were expected to digest. We do not even understand it too well.

SLOGAN: If you trust in the Lord, He will sustain you.

Feb. 7. ST. ROMUALD, Abbot

St. Romuald entered a monastery to do penance for a murder his father had committed. He became a monk and founded the Order of Camaldolese.

God worked miracles by him both during his life and after his death, and likewise gave him the gift of prophecy. Like the Patriarch Jacob, he saw a ladder reaching from earth to heaven, and men in white garments ascending and descending upon it, in whom he marvelously knew were represented the monks of the Camaldolese Institute, of which he was the founder. — *Matins: Sixth Lesson*

From a pure heart proceedeth the fruit of a good life. — *Imitation: Book III*

IDEAL: Doing penance for a crime his father committed was largely responsible for making this saint very holy.

TODAY: If you have not already adopted the practice, do so by offering or asking our Lady to offer the Precious Blood of her Son to the Heavenly Father that one mortal sin may be prevented this night. Do that each evening.

SLOGAN: He that shall convert one sinner from his evil way, shall save his own soul from death.

Feb. 8. ST. JOHN OF MATHA

At St. John's first Mass an angel appeared, dressed in white, with a red and blue cross on his breast, and his hands reposing on the heads of a Christian and a Moorish captive. In company with St. Felix of Valois, he founded the Order of the Holy Trinity for the rescue of captives.

Those that he planted in the house of the Lord, shall flourish in the courts of the house of our God.

Son, thou oughtst not be turned back, nor presently cast down, when thou hearest what is the way of the perfect; but be drawn the more onwards toward its lofty heights, or at least aspire ardently for their attainment. — *Imitation: Book III*

IDEAL: By a vision God called this saint to the service and salvation of Christian captives. Through an angel, he was asked to take up this work. God calls you to the same service, not as extensively as St. John, of course, but He calls you just the same through your prayers.

TODAY: If there is not existing an organization to aid the missions at your school, perhaps you could do something by way of asking to have one organized. While waiting for developments, look up in *America* the name of a destitute mission and send them something that means personal sacrifice to you and an advantage to them.

SLOGAN: Clothe the naked; feed the hungry; instruct the ignorant. — *Works of Mercy*

Feb. 9.   ST. CYRIL OF ALEXANDRIA

St. Cyril was a formidable opponent of the heresiarch Nestorius, who denied that the Blessed Virgin was the Mother of God. St. Cyril suffered much but in the end truth triumphed and St. Cyril received the honor due him.

May Thy saints, we beseech Thee, O Lord, everywhere rejoice us: that while we recall their merits, we may feel their patronage. — *Secret*

And if thou arrive at an entire contempt of thyself, know that then thou shalt enjoy an abundance of peace, as much as is possible in this thy earthly sojourn. — *Imitation: Book III*

IDEAL: One would say that this saint had notions of his own; and he did and he stood by them. But when he was told by the Holy See to relent from his severity with the heretics, he obeyed at once.

TODAY: Have convictions! Do things because you think they are right, but be willing to change your methods of procedure when those who should know tell you to do so. Think this over today: how many of the things you do by daily routine are done because they are right?

SLOGAN: Know you're right; then go ahead. But — know you're right!

Feb. 9. ST. APOLLONIA and the MARTYR OF ALEXANDRIA (Commemorated)

St. Apollonia was arrested during a persecution of Christians. After having her teeth torn out, she was burned at the stake. While her body was reduced to ashes, her soul was borne into the glory of heaven.

And Thou hast delivered me, according to the multitude of the mercy of Thy name, from them that sought my life, and from the ages of afflictions which compassed me about; from the oppression of the flame which surrounded me, and in the midst of the fire I was not burned. — *Epistle: Eccles.*

Fear God, and thou shalt not be afraid of the terrors of man. — *Imitation: Book III*

IDEAL: Possibly you have had a tooth extracted some time in your life, and you remember the painful sensation. Our saint today had her teeth struck out with a heavy iron hammer and forced down her throat. We could scarcely endure a thing like that, but it did not kill her, for she was finally martyred by being burned alive.

TODAY: People pray to St. Apollonia when they have a toothache or are about to have some serious work done on their teeth. It is well to remember this. Today, when somebody complains to you that he has a bad headache or a toothache or some other ache, sympathize with him and don't say, "If you knew the bad headache I had yesterday," etc.

SLOGAN: An empty barrel makes the most noise.

Feb. 10. ST. SCHOLASTICA

St. Scholastica was a twin sister of St. Benedict. She founded a community of women near Monte Casino. One day when St. Benedict refused to prolong his visit with her, she bowed her head in prayer and a terrible storm arose so that St. Benedict could not return.

O God who didst cause the soul of the blessed Scholastica to enter heaven in the form of a dove, to show the way of innocence, grant us, by her prayer and merits, to live so innocently that we may deserve to arrive at eternal joys. — *Collect*

I am accustomed to visit my elect in two manners of ways — namely, by trial and by consolation. — *Imitation: Book III*

IDEAL: When St. Scholastica asked her saintly brother, St. Benedict, that he write out some rule of life for her since she wished to become a saint, he answered her letter three times in succession with these words "Will it!"

TODAY: That seems simple enough: to *will* to be a saint and thus to be one. But — if you are on one side of a street and you will to be on the other, you know what you do, do you not? You walk over to the other side. Draw your own conclusions. Pray to St. Scholastica for light to know how she went about becoming a saint.

SLOGAN: Whatever you do, do with your might;
Things done by halves are never done right.

Feb. 11. THE APPARITION OF OUR BLESSED LADY OF LOURDES

From February 11 to July 16, 1858, the Blessed Virgin came down eighteen times from heaven and showed herself to Bernadette Soubirous in the cave of the rock at Massabielle. On March 25, she said to the little shepherdess: "I am the Immaculate Conception." The Virgin of Lourdes is clothed in a robe and veil as white as snow; she wears a blue girdle and on her bare feet rests a golden rose.

Arise my love, my beautiful one, and come; my dove in the clefts of the rock, in the hollow places of the wall. — *Gradual: Song of Solomon*

Give Thyself to me and it is enough; for without Thee no comfort is of any avail. — *Imitation: Book IV*

IDEAL: Have you ever noticed what very simple unassuming people Heaven always chooses for great tasks? Note little Bernadette Soubirous, for instance. It should prove to you that what really counts and alone is worth while is that we be pleasing to God; and the one way to please God is to do one's duty well.

TODAY: You need no special prompting to do things today to honor our Lady, not when you are trying each day to pattern your life as closely as possible after hers.

SLOGAN: To honor the Mother is to glorify her Son.

Feb. 12. THE SEVEN HOLY FOUNDERS OF THE SERVITE ORDER

From the mouth of little children these saints received the name of "Servants of Mary." Illustrious by their birth, they became still more so by the salutary influence of their order in France, Germany, and Poland.

The just sang to Thy holy Name, O Lord, they praised with one accord Thy victorious hand. For wisdom opened the mouth of the dumb, and made the tongues of infants eloquent. — *Introit: Wisdom 10*

The saints that are the highest in the sight of God are the least in their own eyes; and the more glorious they are, the more humble they are in themselves. — *Imitation: Book II*

IDEAL: Don't you think it a beautiful arrangement to have these holy founders on the day following our Lady's feast?

They founded an order that is devoted to honor Mary especially.

TODAY: Find out something today about the founder of the order to which your teachers belong.

SLOGAN: They that lead many unto justice shall shine as the stars of heaven.

Feb. 13.   ST. CATHERINE OF RICCI

At the age of thirteen, St. Catherine entered the Third Order of St. Dominic. Her special attraction was to the Passion of Christ. She received the sacred stigmata, the wound in the left side, and the crown of thorns.

God hath chosen her, and forechosen her. He hath made her to dwell in His tabernacle. — *Matins: Verse and Answer*

Oh, how wise was that soul that says: My mind is solidly established in and grounded upon Christ. — *Imitation: Book III*

IDEAL: St. Catherine received the impression of the wounds of our Saviour much as St. Francis of Assisi did.

TODAY: Look up some material on Theresa Neumann of the present day. The fact that such extraordinary manifestations are being made is evidence that our Lord wishes us to honor His Passion more than we do. Make your plans now for saying the Way of the Cross each day during Lent.

SLOGAN: We adore Thee, O Christ, and bless Thee, because by Thy holy cross Thou hast redeemed the world.

Feb. 14.   ST. VALENTINE

St. Valentine was a holy priest in Rome who brought help and comfort to the martyrs during the persecution. To abolish the heathen custom of boys drawing girls' names in honor of their goddess Februata Juno, several zealous pastors substituted the names of saints in billets given on this day.

Grant, we beseech Thee, O almighty God, that we who keep the birthday of the blessed martyr Valentine may be

delivered by his prayers from all the ills that hang over us.
— *Collect*

Write, read, sing, lament, keep silence, pray, bear adversities manfully: eternal life is worth all these, and great combats. — *Imitation: Book III*

IDEAL: So much disagreeable nonsense has been attached to the observance of this day that St. Valentine cannot be honored by some of it. However, if you can make someone happy or even make them laugh heartily over a valentine today, that is not out of place entirely. Be very careful, though, that there be no possibility of offense.

TODAY: We send a valentine to those we love. You'll not forget today, then, to send a little valentine by way of an ejaculation or an act of mortification to our Lord and another to His Mother and a little plain one to St. Joseph and a rather elaborate one to your guardian angel. They will probably tell each other about getting them from you but they'll not be jealous.

SLOGAN: I love them that love me. (And the saints do.)

Feb. 15.   SS. FAUSTINUS and JOVITA, Martyrs

These saints were brothers, born of a noble family of Brescia. They were zealous teachers of the Christian religion. Accused of being Christians they suffered indescribable tortures. Nevertheless the great power of their faith made them more than conquerors, shining even as gold tried in the furnace.

Theirs is a brotherhood indeed, whose tie no storms availed to sever: together they followed the Lord in the shedding of their blood. Together they set at naught the royal place; together they attained unto the kingdom of heaven. — *Eighth Responsory*

Ought not all painful labors to be endured for everlasting life? — *Imitation: Book III*

IDEAL: Accused of being a Christian sounds like accused of being good. In the days of the persecutions, however, it was criminal to be a Christian; that is, it was not in compliance with the law.

TODAY: You may at some time in your life be in the company of people who sneer at the idea of abstaining from meat on Friday, etc. What will you do about it? But you cannot have the strength and courage for great things if you have not acquired strength bit by bit through little things.

SLOGAN: Trifles make perfection; but perfection is no trifle.

Feb. 16. ST. ONESIMUS, Disciple of St. Paul

This saint was a slave to Philemon who was converted to the faith by St. Paul. Onesimus robbed his master and fled. Providentially he met St. Paul who converted him and sent him back to Philemon with a letter of recommendation. Philemon pardoned him and sent him back to St. Paul whom he served with great fidelity.

This is he who loved not his life in this world, and is come into an everlasting kingdom. And he is numbered among the saints. — *Third Responsory*

Be grateful then for the least, and thou shalt be made worthy to receive greater things. — *Imitation: Book II*

IDEAL: Through Philemon to whom St. Paul wrote a letter, Onesimus was a disciple of St. Paul. St. Paul naturally attracted all to himself because he made it a purpose of his life "to become all things to all men that he might win them to Christ."

TODAY: Live so this day that someone may be forced to think: "If that is what the Church does for a person, I want to be a Catholic."

SLOGAN: I became all things to all men that I might win them for Christ.

Feb. 17. ST. FLAVIAN, Bishop and Martyr

The life of this bishop was a continuous struggle against heretics and heresies. In defense of the faith, St. Flavian suffered mental and physical torture. He sealed his faith with his blood.

> By the virtue of thy prayer,
> Let no evil hover nigh;
> Sin's contagion drive afar:
> Waken drowsy lethargy.

Who, then, is the best off? Truly he that is able to suffer something for the love of God. — *Imitation: Book I*

IDEAL: The saint could be very meek and mild when he was attacked personally; but when the teachings and the rights of the Church were concerned it was an entirely different matter, and the prestige and the power of the heretics made no difference to St. Flavian.

TODAY: We speak of people like St. Flavian as persons who have the courage of their convictions. Resolve today to learn your history as well as possible, and whenever you have an opportunity read the *Sunday Visitor* through. It would be an excellent idea to make a scrapbook of clippings from the *Sunday Visitor*. You might even ask your teacher to inspect your scrapbook from time to time.

SLOGAN: One of the best defenses of the Church today is a practical Catholic who knows his religion.

Feb. 18. ST. SIMEON, Bishop and Martyr

St. Simeon, son of Cleophas and of Mary, who was so closely related to the Blessed Virgin as to be called her sister, became Bishop of Jerusalem after the Apostle St. James.

And he who does not carry his cross and follow Me cannot be My disciple. — *Gospel: Luke 14*

For even our Lord Jesus Christ Himself was not for one hour of His life without the anguish of His passion. "It behooved," said he, "that Christ should suffer, and rise from the dead, and so enter into His glory." — *Imitation: Book II*

IDEAL: St. Simeon was rather closely related to our Lady. Do you think that a great honor? It is; but yours is greater;

you are her child; Jesus is your brother. Before He died He as much as willed her to us. You would have been shocked if our Lady's relatives had not been good. We say, "They should be saints."

TODAY: Has your mother at home ever chided you with "You're a disgrace to the family"? We do not always do credit to our self-sacrificing parents, it is true, but try today to be a credit, too, to your Mother and your Brother.

SLOGAN: Make my heart like Thine, sweet Lord!

Feb. 19. ST. BARBATUS, Bishop

St. Barbatus was one of the most eloquent preachers of his day. Despite slanders and persecutions of various kinds, he continued to preach the word of God. His untiring efforts were crowned with success.

Who, dost thou think, is the faithful and prudent servant whom his master has set over his household to give them their food in due time? Blessed is that servant whom his master, when he comes, shall find so doing. Amen I say to you, he will set him over all his goods. — *Gospel: Matthew 24*

But they that follow Thee, by the contempt of worldly things and the mortification of the flesh, are found to be wise indeed; for they are translated from vanity to truth, from the flesh to the spirit. — *Imitation: Book III*

IDEAL: Are you easily dissuaded from doing your duty by the critical comment of others? This saint pursued his teaching in spite of anything that was said or done to hinder him.

TODAY: If you have not already done so, read either, or both, *Heart of a Man* and *Shepherd of the North* by Richard A. Maher, for thrilling stories of men who did their duty because it was right.

SLOGAN: Love God; then, do as you please. (Ask your teacher to explain this slogan to you.)

Feb. 20. ST. EUCHERIUS, Bishop

In order to raise money for war, Charles Martel often stripped the churches of their revenue. St. Eucherius reproved these encroachments with so much zeal that Charles banished him to Cologne. The saint was received into this city with great rejoicing. Charles ordered him taken to Liége. Here the governor was so charmed with the saint that he made him his chief almoner.

By his manly chastity, by his sternly noble temperance, by the graceful courtesy which marked him, he drew all men's love to God. — *Matins: Fifth Lesson*

My God and my all! To one that understandeth sufficient is said; to one that loveth, to repeat it often is delightful. — *Imitation: Book III*

IDEAL: Martel, the Hammerer of heretics, in spite of all the good he had done for the Church, could not infringe on the rights of that Church, while St. Eucherius was about.

TODAY: One of the greatest difficulties in the world today is the readiness with which people will yield to any demands for money. Would you? What do you think, for instance, of men who accept great sums of money to deceive the government? Would you do it?

SLOGAN: Honesty is the best policy.

Feb. 21. ST. SEVERIANUS, Bishop and Martyr

Because he refused to accept the Eutychian heresy, St. Severianus was seized, dragged out of the city, and martyred.

> Martyr of unconquered might,
> Follower of the Incarnate Son!
> Who, victorious in the fight,
> Hast celestial glory won. — *Lauds: Hymn*

Lift up, therefore, thy face to heaven; behold I and all My saints with Me, who in this world have had a great conflict, now rejoice, are comforted now, are now secure, are now at rest; and they shall for all eternity abide with Me in the kingdom of My Father. — *Imitation: Book III*

IDEAL: These persecutors did the saint a great favor when they put him to death; they sent him to heaven by the shortest possible route.

TODAY: The Little Flower of Jesus, St. Thérèse, became a saint by seeing in everything that happened to her an opportunity for growing in merit before God. As long as we must endure certain disagreeable situations anyway, we might as well be philosophic and "fool the devil" and let those very hardships help us to heaven.

SLOGAN: To them that love God all things work together unto good.

Feb. 22.   ST. PETER'S CHAIR AT ANTIOCH

Before St. Peter went to Rome he founded the See of Antioch, the capital city of the East at that time. Realizing that Rome was a better center, geographically and politically, St. Peter left Antioch and went to Rome.

In the honor which is this day paid to the inauguration of the first Bishop's throne, an honor is paid to the office of all bishops. — *Matins: Sixth Lesson*

Let all exercises of tribulation become lovely and most desirable to me for Thy name's sake; for to suffer and to be afflicted for Thee is very healthful for my soul. — *Imitation: Book III*

IDEAL: A fisherman with no education, but with intense love of God, and continually striving to make himself more and more like his Master, St. Peter saw with an inspired eye what would be to the advantage of the Church.

TODAY: Students sometimes are afflicted with the notion that they know so much better than their elders what is proper and what should and what should not be done, etc. Are you such? Pray for some of St. Peter's simple faith today.

SLOGAN: Lord that I may see!

Feb. 23. ST. PETER DAMIAN

Orphaned at an early age, St. Peter was treated so cruelly by his elder brother that a younger brother sent him to the University of Parma where he acquired great distinction. He was adviser to seven popes in succession and was sent on the most delicate and difficult missions.

In the midst of the congregation did the Lord open His mouth and filled him with the spirit of wisdom and understanding. — *Eighth Responsory*

I am He that in an instant elevateth the humble mind to comprehend more reasons of the eternal truth than if anyone had studied ten years in the schools. I teach without noise of words, without confusion of opinions, without ambition of honor, without strife of arguments. — *Imitation: Book III*

IDEAL: A poor abused orphan, St. Peter Damian became one of the most brilliant students at the University of Parma. Later he was called upon by seven popes in succession to help them in important decisions. Best of all, and most important, he became a saint.

TODAY: Persons who continually lament that they have no chance and they wish this and they hope that, never get anywhere. Do as St. Ignatius suggested, "Pray as if all depended upon God alone, and work as if all depended upon you alone."

SLOGAN: He who only hopes is hopeless.

Feb. 24. ST. MATTHIAS, Apostle

St. Matthias was elected to fill the place of Judas. The saint was above all remarkable for his mortification of the flesh.

He sanctified him in his faith and meekness, and chose him out of all flesh. And He gave him commandments before His face, and a law of life and instruction, and He exalted him. — *Epistle: Book of Wisdom*

Be fond of inquiring, and listen in silence to the words of the saints; and let not the parable of the ancients be displeasing to thee, for they are not uttered without cause. — *Imitation: Book I*

IDEAL: After the fall of Judas from his place, another man was to be chosen to fill up the number, and the lot fell upon Matthias. That looks like chance, does it not? To the eyes of men, it was, but really it was God's will.

TODAY: If you have ever been told or have reason yourself to believe that you have a vocation to a higher life, do not throw away to the world the most precious of your endowments, youth and virtue; let your offering to God be entire. Say an extra prayer each day for the grace to know what God has intended for your lifework; begin today.

SLOGAN: You have not chosen Me, but I have chosen you.

Feb. 25. ST. TARASIUS

In the midst of the court and in its highest honors, St. Tarasius led a life like that of a religious man. As Patriarch of Constantinople he was a model of perfection to clergy and laity. He was prayerful and abstemious and fearless of opposition when he knew that he had the side of justice and truth.

This is the wise and faithful steward, whom his lord setteth over his family: to give them their measure of wheat in due season. — *Communion*

A good life maketh a man wise according to God, and giveth great experience. — *Imitation: Book I*

IDEAL: Regardless of what others did in the court in which he lived, Tarasius set his own standards and lived his own life. That is a very hard thing for young people to do in our day more than at any other time perhaps.

TODAY: Just because twenty thousand people of your age are doing wrong, their doing it does not make it right. Be independent, too independent to be a "tag-along" when there is question of wrongdoing or infringing the least bit on your principles.

SLOGAN: Be ye steadfast and immovable.

Feb. 26.   ST. PORPHYRY, Bishop

In spite of physical ailments. St. Porphyry visited the holy places every day. Following divine inspiration he sold his property and gave the proceeds to the poor. In reward God restored him to perfect health. He became a priest and was intrusted with the relics of the True Cross.

Let Thy priests, O Lord, be clothed with justice, and let Thy saints rejoice: for Thy servant David's sake, turn not away the face of the anointed. — *Introit*

I have received, from Thy hand, the Cross; I will bear it, and bear it even unto death, as Thou hast laid it upon me. — *Imitation: Book III*

IDEAL: God always rewards almost immediately those who, like the widow in the Gospel, give much of their little in alms to God. Suppose that our Lord came about your street and held out His hand, for alms, and you had a dime you were on your way to spend for ice cream; what would you do?

TODAY: Do not say, "If I had about a million dollars, I'd give a few thousand to have the church decorated or to build a new one or to help some poor missionaries." You don't need a million. If you have little give of that, but cheerfully, appreciating the honor of being allowed to assist God with His own gift to you.

SLOGAN: Almsgiving pays the largest rate of interest on the investment.

Feb. 27.   ST. GABRIEL OF OUR LADY OF SORROWS, Confessor

St. Gabriel is a young saint of the times, born in 1838, died in the second year of our Civil War. Our Lady directed him from early youth into the Passionist Order where he died with the reputation of great holiness at twenty-four years of age.

I write to you, young men, because you are strong and the word of God abides in you. — *Epistle of the feast*

If thou couldst empty thy heart of every creature, Jesus would willingly fill it. — *Imitation: Book II*

IDEAL: This charming young saint took literally the facts in the history of the Passion, and was overwhelmed with so much love from God that he could think of nothing else. He devoted himself as a dutiful squire to the service of his Queen, the Sorrowful Mother.

TODAY: Regardless of your age, choose St. Gabriel as your patron to redeem and secure the youthfulness of your soul, and ask for his intercession to "become as a little child."

SLOGAN: In my heart each wound renew of my Saviour crucified.

Feb. 28. SS. ROMANUS and LUPICINUS, Abbots

In the forests of Mt. Jura, St. Romanus found a spot that satisfied his desire for solitude and for gardening. He spent his time working, reading, and praying. His brother Lupicinus joined him and he in turn was followed by others. Together they built a monastery.

The just shall flourish like the palm tree: he shall grow up like the Cedar of Libanus. — *Gradual*

He that seeketh anything else but simply God, and the salvation of his soul, will find nothing but trouble and sorrow. — *Imitation: Book I*

IDEAL: Gardeners, indeed, these two holy men cultivated herbs for the sick and flowers in their own souls for God. Gardeners, who did their gardening well and became saints in the doing. If you are doomed to drive a truck all your life or to wash dishes, drive your truck well and wash your dishes thoroughly; make the good intention, be content; love God and your neighbor; you'll be a saint.

TODAY: If you have a Ford and the neighbors have a Cadillac, be glad that it costs less to keep up a Ford and that it gets one through places where a Cadillac could not venture.

SLOGAN: Rather want what you have than try to have what you want.

Feb. 29. ST. OSWALD, Bishop

Desirous of correcting the carelessness that had developed among the monks of a certain monastery, St. Oswald encouraged devotion to our Lady in a very special manner, by which means the monks soon became as fervent again, as once they had been.

> Gentle was he, wise, pure, and lovely-hearted,
> Sober and modest, ever foe to strife. — *Vespers*

It is no small thing to dwell in monasteries and to live there without complaint, and to persevere faithfully even unto death. — *Imitation: Book I*

IDEAL: Through devotion to our Lady, St. Oswald did the greatest service to the Church. You cannot love our Lady and lead a careless life; you must give up one or the other.

TODAY: When you have special difficulties with algebra or with penmanship or with a history examination, do the best you can and ask our Lady to make the respective subject stick fast in your mind. She never forsakes those who do their own part and then call on her.

SLOGAN: It has never been heard that anyone who fled to thy protection was left unaided. — *St. Bernard*

SHROVE TUESDAY

In the days of faith, Catholics went to confession on this day in preparation for the spending of a good Lent, and then they made merry with their friends by participation in wholesome fun.

Graciously hear our prayers, we beseech thee, O Lord, and unloosing the bonds of sin, guard us from all adversity. — *Collect*

Two things especially help to great amending: for a man to withdraw himself with violence from such things as nature is viciously inclined to, and fervently to labor for the good that he most needeth. — *Imitation: Book I*

IDEAL: What was once a day of innocent enjoyment upon which the Saviour could look with pleasure has become in so many cases a day of riotous carousing and sinfulness. It is for us, passively, to refrain absolutely from anything that might mean added offense to the Divine Majesty, and actively, to arrange for the harmless amusement of others, particularly of those for whom we may be responsible.

TODAY: Be conscious of a very real effort all day to make reparation to the Suffering Saviour whose Passion we are so soon to consider very definitely for forty days. Make Him feel that He may look at least to you at any time during this day and find your thoughts occupied with Him.

SLOGAN: Now is all the land made desolate because no one thinketh in his heart.

ASH WEDNESDAY

The ashes used on this day are obtained by burning the palms of the preceding year's Palm Sunday. Though intended primarily to remind the faithful of death, they bring out also the significance of the transitory nature of temporal glory.

Let us amend and do better those things in which we have sinned through ignorance, lest the day of death take us unaware and we cry for a time to atone. — *From the Blessing of the Ashes*

Have a mind ever on thine end, and that time lost never cometh again. — *Imitation: Book I*

IDEAL: Years ago in Europe there was a plague, called the Black Death. As soon as a person showed that he had symptoms of the disease, he knew that in but a few hours he would be a corpse. Would it frighten you to have a physician tell you today that "You have all the symptoms of the Black Death"? The ashes which the priest places on your forehead today are a quarantine sign; but there is no telling how much sooner than a few hours after the sign has been placed there, you may meet death.

Today: Much as you may revolt against the idea, take some time this morning to realize the reality of death and its dreadful uncertainty; then, resolve to spend this Lent so that you could die with reasonable assurance on Holy Saturday evening. You may go before that, so it is well to be ready.

Slogan: Man, remember thy last end and thou shalt never sin!

EMBER DAYS IN LENT

The Wednesday, Friday, and Saturday after the first Sunday in Lent are ember days. The ember days occur four times during the year, immediately before the beginning of each season. The precise origin of this custom is somewhat obscure, though it is thought by some authorities to be traceable to the similar custom in the days of Moses. Be that as it may, the purpose in the mind of the Church at the time of their introduction in the sixth century and since, has been that these be days of prayer and penance to entreat the blessing of God upon the approaching season. The Sacrament of Holy Orders is conferred during the Ember Days, and for the young Levites the Church asks us to pray fervently. It is so characteristic of the Church thus to provide at the same time for ministry to our temporal and to our spiritual wants. We serve our own interests if we implore the blessings of Heaven upon the fruits of earth and upon the dispensers of the fruits of Redemption.

EMBER DAYS IN SUMMER

The Wednesday, Friday, and Saturday after Pentecost.

EMBER DAYS IN FALL

The Wednesday, Friday, and Saturday after September 14.

EMBER DAYS IN WINTER

The Wednesday, Friday, and Saturday after December 13.

MARCH

March 1. ST. ALBINUS, Bishop

As a monk St. Albinus was a living example of his rule. His soul seemed so perfectly governed by the spirit of Christ that he seemed to live only for Him. As Bishop of Angers he was indefatigable in his zeal for the glory of God. Honored by the world and even by kings, he was never affected by vanity.

Who, dost thou think, is the faithful and prudent servant whom his master has set over his household to give them their food in due time?

Look upon the lively examples of the holy Fathers, in whom shone real perfection and the religious life, and thou wilt see how little it is, and almost nothing, that we do. — *Imitation: Book I*

IDEAL: At thirty-five this man was chosen to be abbot of a large monastery, but it made no difference in his modesty nor in his practice of mortification.

TODAY: Keep a close guard on yourself and see if you have the habit of turning your head this way and that either to see all that is going on or to see if anybody is looking at you. Perhaps you would scarcely think it, but that is usually an indication of a kind of silly vanity. Keep looking straight ahead of you.

SLOGAN: Keep your powder dry and fire straight ahead. — *Advice given to one of our presidents*

March 2. ST. SIMPLICIUS, Pope

St. Simplicius reigned during a stormy period in the history of the Church. The West was in the hands of barbarian hordes; the East was torn by heresy. No sacrifice was too great for this Pontiff in his effort to restore peace and unity.

48

Thou art a priest forever according to the order of Melchisedech. This is the priest whom the Lord hath crowned.

We ought rather to choose to have the whole world against us than to offend Jesus. — *Imitation: Book II*

IDEAL: When Rome was besieged by barbarians, this Pope set about doing "good to his enemies" as our Lord had said we should, and converted many to Christianity. When the East also made inroads on Rome, he did the same there, thus turning the efforts of the Evil One against himself.

TODAY: When you are tempted today to "fly off the handle," walk very slowly and do not talk at all; or take out your books very deliberately and say to the Tempter: "Not this time, if you please."

SLOGAN: Make of yourselves a pleasing sight before angels and men.

March 3. ST. CUNEGUNDIS, Empress

To prove her innocence this saint walked over red-hot plowshares in the presence of her husband, St. Henry. Upon the death of St. Henry she became a nun in a monastery which she herself had founded. She was an example to all of humility and kindness. The poor and the sick were special objects of her solicitude.

She hath put out her hand to strong things, and her fingers have taken hold of the spindle. She hath opened her hand to the needy, and stretched out her hands to the poor. — *Epistle: Proverbs 31*

They renounced all riches, dignities, honors, friends, and kindred; they hardly took what was necessary for life; it grieved them to serve the body even in its necessity. — *Imitation: Book I*

IDEAL: This sweet, retiring saint was an empress of the Roman empire. After her husband's death, she became a religious, her greatest desire being to humble herself and be everybody's servant as our Saviour had been.

TODAY: Genuine Christian charity is the loveliest courtesy you can have. Be just as attentive as you can to the wants of others today, to your parents and teachers most of all, and note how good it makes you feel tonight.

SLOGAN: Everyone that doth not renounce all that he possesseth cannot be My disciple.

March 4. ST. CASIMIR, King

In an atmosphere of luxury, this young prince fasted, wore a hair shirt, slept upon the bare earth, prayed by night, and watched for the opening of the church doors at dawn. His love for our Blessed Lady is expressed in a beautiful hymn. Numberless miracles testify to his sanctity.

Being made perfect for a short space, and full of piety and good works, he foretold the day of his own death, and gathering around him a choir of priests and monks, he rendered his soul into the hands of the God whom they were praising upon the fourth of March in the year of our Lord 1482, the twenty-fifth of his own age. — *Matins: Sixth Lesson*

O Lord, my God, Thou hast created me to Thine own image and likeness, grant me this grace, which Thou hast shown to be so great, and so necessary to salvation, that I may overcome my most corrupt nature which draweth me to sin and to perdition. — *Imitation: Book III*

IDEAL: The life of this saint is so fascinating, so charming, that you must read it in its entirety. You have a *Pictorial Lives of the Saints* at home; read it there or ask for the copy in your school library.

TODAY: Notice how very lovely the influence of our Lady is on the saints especially devoted to her. There is a certain gallantry that nothing else can give about those who love our Lady very truly.

SLOGAN: Queen of all Saints, pray for us.

March 5. SS. ADRIAN and EUBULUS

These two saints were on their way to visit Christian friends when they were apprehended and asked where they were going and what their errand was. Upon admitting that they were Christians, they were first tortured and then cruelly put to death.

Yea, though I walk through the valley of the shadow of death, I will fear no evil: for Thou art with me. — *Psalm 22*

Many follow Jesus to the breaking of bread; but few to the drinking of the chalice of His passion. — *Imitation: Book II*

IDEAL: These two men were most cruelly martyred for their faith. Adrian was partly eaten by a lion, but not killed. One shudders to read such things; but the love of these men for our Lord was so great that they were happy for the opportunity to do something to show their gratitude.

TODAY: If it rains on your way to school or is slushy underfoot, be glad to have an opportunity to offer something to God in atonement for your past sins. If anybody treated us in the manner that we respond to all God's great kindness, we would not permit him near us another moment.

SLOGAN: More suffering, my Saviour, give me still more suffering. — *St. Lidwina*

March 6. SS. PERPETUA and FELICITAS, Martyrs

St. Perpetua had just become a mother and St. Felicitas was on the point of becoming one when they were arrested at Carthage during the persecution of Severus. When the judge told them that they were condemned to the wild beasts, they were transported with joy.

Filled with the mystical joys which are the objects of our desires, grant us, we beseech Thee, O Lord, to obtain by the intercession of Thy holy martyrs Perpetua and Felicitas the everlasting effects of what we do in life.—*Postcommunion*

But they that love Jesus for Jesus' sake, and not for the sake of some consolation of their own, bless Him no less in tribulation and anguish of heart than in the greatest consolation. — *Imitation: Book II*

IDEAL: Both these saints were mothers of a family, and each had a very sweet little child when they were thrown into prison. Though an appeal was made to each to save her life for the child's sake by offering incense to the gods, they refused, thus withstanding the appeal of what is considered the strongest incentive in the world.

TODAY: Our Lord has said, "He that loveth father or mother more than Me is not worthy of Me," which means that not anything in the world is to be preferred to God. If you stop to consider for just a moment some of the very contemptible things you have at times preferred to God, it will make you very humble and should make you very contrite.

SLOGAN: My God and my All. — *St. Francis*

March 7. ST. THOMAS AQUINAS

As a young man St. Thomas determined, in spite of family opposition, to enter the Dominican Order. He so completely conquered the demon of impurity that he was exempt from all temptation. Aided by a supernatural light, his intelligence sounded the depths of divine mysteries.

I wished, and understanding was given me; and I called, and the spirit of wisdom came upon me; and I preferred her before kingdoms and thrones. — *Epistle: Book of Wisdom*

Blessed is the man who for love of Thee, O Lord, abandoneth all things created; who offereth violence to nature and through fervor of spirit crucifieth the concupiscence of the flesh; that so with a serene conscience, he may offer to Thee pure prayers and become worthy to be admitted among the choir of angels, having excluded himself both exteriorly and interiorly from all the things of earth. — *Imitation: Book III*

IDEAL: This splendid type of manhood, this glorious light of the University of Paris, this triumphant conqueror of himself, this angel of purity attributed all his wondrous learning to the crucifix.

TODAY: You must know the life of this excellent student. Get a copy of his biography; if you begin reading, you'll not be able to stop until you have finished. He is an inspiration. Take your missal and read through the liturgy of Corpus Christi; St. Thomas composed it. You cannot help loving this saint enthusiastically and wanting to be like him.

SLOGAN: Thou hast written well of Me, Thomas; what wouldst thou? Nothing but Thyself, dear Lord, nothing but Thyself!

March 8. ST. JOHN OF GOD

This saint was rather wild until he was forty. Then filled with remorse he made amends by selling holy pictures and books at a low price, by ministering to the sick, by working and begging for the poor. In a vision our Lord told him how acceptable his work was.

O God, who didst cause blessed John, when burning with love for Thee, to walk unscathed through flames, and who didst by his means enrich Thy Church with a new religious order: grant, that his merits pleading in our behalf, our evil passions may, to the everlasting healing of our souls, be burned up in the fire of our love of Thee. — *Collect*

He that hath true and perfect charity seeketh himself in nothing, but only desireth God to be glorified in all things. — *Imitation: Book I*

IDEAL: John was rather advanced in years when he felt the call of God; but when he heard the call, he went home, sold his goods, entered the religious order, and became a saint. There was dispatch in his method of doing things.

TODAY: If you are going to be a saint some day; if you are going to begin to spend a good Lent next week; if you are going to make up your mind tomorrow, you will never be any greater saint than you are now, perhaps less so. Do it now.

SLOGAN: Today I begin. — *St. Ignatius*

March 9.   ST. FRANCES OF ROME

The parents of St. Frances overruled her desire to become a nun, and she was married at the age of twelve to Ponziano, a Roman noble. During the forty years of their married life they never had a disagreement. Her guiding principle, to quote her own words, was: "A married woman must leave God at the altar to find Him in her domestic cares." She constantly lived in the visible presence of her guardian angel.

O how lovely and glorious is the generation of the chaste. — *Matins: First Antiphon*

The nature of thy Beloved is such that He will not admit of a rival; but He will have thy heart for Himself alone and sit as King upon His throne. — *Imitation: Book II*

IDEAL: This charming saint enjoyed the visible presence of her guardian angel. No one knew how very intensely St. Frances suffered all the while mentally from temptations of the devil, which her angel helped her overcome.

TODAY: The fact that St. Frances could see her angel did not mean that he was present at her side any more than your angel is always with you. Think about that today and get into the habit of being conscious of his presence always. You resolved last October, you recall, to say little prayers to your angel from time to time each day.

SLOGAN: Dear angel, ever at my side,
To light, to guard, to rule and guide.

March 10.   THE FORTY MARTYRS OF SEBASTE

The forty martyrs were soldiers quartered at Sebaste in Armenia. When their legion was ordered to offer sacrifice, they refused. As a result they were exposed on a frozen pond. One of them weakened and threw himself into a tepid bath; but their guard, touched by the grace of God, took his place and there were still forty martyrs.

The just cried, and the Lord heard them; and delivered them out of all their troubles. — *Introit*

Whoever findeth Jesus findeth a good treasure — yea, a good above every good. And he that loseth Jesus loseth much — yea, more than the whole world. — *Imitation: Book II*

IDEAL: These were forty men who refused to offer sacrifice to the gods. One of their number crept from the frozen pond into the warm bath near by and died immediately while one of the attendants rushed out to take his place and keep the number forty intact.

TODAY: Your class intends to make this day as nearly perfect in the final record as possible. You will not be the one to spoil the record by slipping up ever so slightly on the requirements of your particular group.

SLOGAN: In unity there is strength.

March 11. ST. EULOGIUS, Martyr

As head of the ecclesiastical school at Cordova, St. Eulogius won the hearts of all by his humility, mildness, and charity. Seized by Moors, he was thrown into prison and beheaded for his faith.

> Loosened from the fleshly chain
> Which detained thee here of old,
> Loose us from the bonds of sin,
> From the fetters of the world. — *Lauds: Hymn*

Our merit, and the advancement of our state, consists not in the having of many sweetnesses and consolations; but rather in bearing great afflictions and tribulations. — *Imitation: Book II*

IDEAL: While this martyr was being led out to execution, one of the guards struck him a blow on his face. At once Eulogius turned the other cheek to receive another blow.

TODAY: Trying to get even is a mark of savagery; do you do it? Watch yourself today or the next time somebody does what seems to you an injustice to you.

SLOGAN: An offense was intended or it was not; if it was, you lower yourself to get even; if it was not, forget it.

March 12.   ST. GREGORY THE GREAT

St. Gregory gave his wealth to the poor, turned his home into a monastery, and became a perfect monk. Elected successively abbot, cardinal, and supreme pontiff, he was one of the greatest popes the Church has ever had. He is one of the four great Latin Fathers.

He was the author of many books, and Peter the Deacon declared that he often saw the Holy Ghost in the form of a dove when he was dictating them. It is a marvel how much he spoke, did, wrote, and legislated, suffering all the while from a weak and sickly body. He worked many miracles. — *Matins: Sixth Lesson*

He doth much who loveth much. He doth much who doth well what he hath to do. — *Imitation: Book I*

IDEAL: Member of a saintly family, Father of the Church, a brilliant student, this saint seems to have had all the advantages that help toward starting out right in life, but you know from the example of many saints that it depends on one's good will much more than on heredity and environment.

TODAY: Count your blessings. Thank God you are a Catholic, that you have an opportunity to attend a Catholic school, that you were born after the time our Lord lived on earth, that you are not blind, that you can walk.

SLOGAN: Thou hast blessed us, Lord, far beyond our deserts.

March 13.   ST. EUPHRASIA, Virgin

St. Euphrasia dedicated her life to God in the convent at the age of seven. When she became of age she ordered her vast estate to be sold and divided among the poor. In order to overcome temptation she often performed painful penitential labor, as sometimes to carry heavy stones from one place to another.

The Lord is the King of virgins. O come, let us worship Him. — *Matins: Invitatory*

O sacred state of religious servitude, which maketh men equal to angels, pleasing to God, terrible to the devils, and commendable to all the faithful. — *Imitation: Book III*

IDEAL: This little saint wanted to be in a convent from the time she was seven years old. Her mother lived near a large convent and Euphrasia was allowed to live with the Sisters. She became a great saint, doing the humblest tasks, and feeling, as she should have, that her least service was service in the immediate house of God.

TODAY: There will come a time when you no longer have a mother or father whom you can assist; then you will regret the many opportunities you missed when you might have lightened their burden. Do all you can for them now, even before they ask you. *See* with your eyes.

SLOGAN: I love you, mother, said little John
And, forgetting work, his cap went on,
And he was out in the garden swing
Leaving his mother the wood to bring.

March 14. ST. MAUD, Queen

St. Maud was the wife of Henry, king of Germany. While her husband was engaged in extending his kingdom, she spent her time in visiting and comforting the sick, in serving and instructing the poor, and bringing succor to prisoners.

Who can find a virtuous woman? For her price is far above the rarest merchandise. The heart of her husband doth safely trust in her, so that he shall have no need of spoil. She will do him good and not evil all the days of her life. — *Matins: First Lesson*

He that hath true and perfect charity seeketh himself in nothing, but only desireth God to be glorified in all things. — *Imitation*

IDEAL: Maud was the daughter of Theodoric. Being very wealthy she had great means of assisting the poor. Nothing pleased her more than to carry food and medicines to the poor, sick, and ailing.

TODAY: Perhaps there is somebody ill in your neighborhood who would love to have you read a story to him or talk pleasantly a while to cheer him up. Perhaps you could go to the hospital and inquire if you may visit someone there who has not friends to come and make the long hours pleasant. Your turn may be coming soon, you know.

SLOGAN: Do as you would be done by.

March 15.   ST. ZACHARY, Pope

St. Zachary was a man of singular meekness and goodness. Devoted to his people, he risked his life that they might be spared. His fervor in saying Mass inspired all present with devotion.

Who shall ascend into the mountain of the Lord? or who shall stand in the holy place? He that hath clean hands and a pure heart. — *Matins: Psalm 23*

A great thing is love — a great good every way; which alone lighteneth all that is burdensome, and beareth equally all things that are unequal. — *Imitation: Book III*

IDEAL: Now that we are getting on in Lent, with Easter in the near distance, what progress have we made? Are we merely "holding in" now on certain things that we will permit ourselves again, immediately Lent is over?

TODAY: The very best fast, as you know, is fast from sin to which we are all obliged and always. You seem not to be suffering particularly from the little penances you are practicing now; why not keep up some of them even after Lent is over?

SLOGAN: Only with God do we count our hours.

March 16.   SS. ABRAHAM and MARY

Fifty years St. Abraham spent in a hermitage. The bishop of Edessa ordained him priest, though the saint felt that he was entirely unworthy of so great an honor. After his ordination he was sent to an idolatrous city that had refused to accept Christianity. Relying on fasting and prayer, rather than on preaching, he brought every citizen to baptism. Among those he led to sanctity was his niece Mary.

Novena for the feast of the Annunciation begins today.

Hearken unto the voice of my cry, my King and my God; for unto Thee will I pray. — *Matins: Psalm 5*

Son, thou art never secure in this life; but as long as thou livest spiritual weapons are always necessary for thee. — *Imitation: Book III*

IDEAL: These were uncle and niece who lived a life of seclusion in the desert. Even in the desert, alone and away from the rest of the world, Mary committed a great sin, for which she did severe penance the rest of her life.

TODAY: Mary's fall should prove to us that we are, after all, each our own greatest difficulty. Pray today then for perseverance in God's grace.

SLOGAN: Give me grace to keep Thy grace
        And grace to merit more. — *Mother Loyola*

March 17. ST. PATRICK, Apostle of Ireland

This holy bishop put to such profit the talents he had received from God that he became the father of all his people and that Ireland has preserved for him, after thirteen centuries, an ardent and tender devotion which nothing has been able to weaken. March 17 is a national day and a holyday of obligation in Ireland.

They say that it was his custom to repeat every day the whole Book of Psalms, together with songs and hymns, and 200 prayers; that he bent his knees in worship 300 times every day. — *Matins: Sixth Lesson*

Love feeleth no burden, thinketh nothing of labors, would willingly do more than it can, complaineth not of impossibility, because it conceiveth that it may and can do all things. — *Imitation: Book III*

IDEAL: Some say St. Patrick was French, others that he was Scotch; but whether French or Scotch, the Irish have all reason to be proud of their patron. The important thing, however, is: Has the dear saint good reason to be proud of you?

TODAY: Live so that when you blush with pride at mention of St. Patrick, your neighbors need not say: "Are you a Catholic? I never knew that." *Live* by your faith.

SLOGAN: Not everyone who says to me, "Lord, Lord," shall enter the kingdom of heaven; but he who does the will of My Father in heaven shall enter the kingdom of heaven.

March 18.   ST. CYRIL OF JERUSALEM

St. Cyril, in giving instruction to converts preparing for baptism, arranged the first systematic exposition of the Christian religion. He was chosen Bishop of Jerusalem and witnessed Julian's futile attempt to rebuild the Temple.

Look down with favor, we beseech Thee, O Lord, upon the spotless Victim we offer up to Thee: and grant that by the merits of blessed Cyril, Thy confessor and bishop, we may ever strive to receive it into a heart undefiled. — *Secret*

For at too great a hazard doth he stand who casteth not his whole care on Thee. — *Imitation: Book III*

IDEAL: Cyril lived at the time that Julian the Apostate tried to rebuild the Temple at Jerusalem. Cyril was not disturbed. "God's word will not fail," he said and calmly looked on the efforts of the deluded emperor. You know the tragedy of the attempt.

TODAY: The Ten Commandments are God's word. They are as true and as binding in 1961 as they were when given amid thunder and lightning on Mt. Sinai, and don't let anybody ever convince you otherwise.

SLOGAN: Heaven and earth shall pass away, but My words shall *not* pass away.

March 19. ST. JOSEPH

The Church always honors St. Joseph with Mary and
Jesus, especially during the Christmas season. Let us imitate the purity, humility, the spirit of prayer, and meditation
of St. Joseph.

> Death brings to other saints their rest;
> Through toil they win the victor's place; —
> Thou, happier, like the angels blest,
> Alive hast seen God face to face. — *Vespers: Hymn*

By two wings is man lifted above earthly things, viz., by
simplicity and purity. — *Imitation: Book II*

IDEAL: The Scriptures make one single statement regarding the character of this great, great saint, "Joseph was a
just man." Few people knew him, and even they spoke of
him only as the carpenter. Do you see what it all comes to
again? Nothing matters except what God thinks of us.

TODAY: Pray for three graces from St. Joseph every day
of your life: personal love for Jesus and Mary, union with
God in your daily work, a happy death.

SLOGAN: Help us, Joseph, in our daily strife
E'er to live a good and holy life.

March 20. ST. WULFRAN, Archbishop

St. Wulfran resigned his bishopric after two years and
became a humble missionary. Through prayer St. Wulfran
saved the life of a man who was to be sacrificed to the
gods by hanging. After this miracle his prestige was firmly
established among the pagans.

They that sow in tears shall reap in joy. They go forth
weeping sowing their seed; they shall doubtless come again
rejoicing, bringing their sheaves with them. — *Vespers: Psalm
125*

To walk with God within, and to be bound by no affection
from without, is the state of the interior man. — *Imitation:
Book II*

IDEAL: By a miracle, St. Wulfran saved a man from being offered in sacrifice to the gods, and then saved the man's soul for God in heaven.

TODAY: A story is told in the life of this saint, of a pagan who jokingly put off his conversion until later. When that "later" time came, this man sent for a priest to talk over his possible conversion, but before the priest could reach him, the man was dead. Some people tell us that constant thought of death would make us morose; but, if we are to be morose at all, it is better before death than after.

SLOGAN: Death shall come like a thief in the night.

March 21.   ST. BENEDICT, Abbot

St. Benedict went to school in Rome. Frightened by the wickedness of young people, he fled to the desert of Subiaco. After spending three years in a cave, he attracted crowds by his virtue. The great Roman families sent their children to him and he founded in the mountains twelve monasteries.

Some months before he departed this life, Benedict fore-warned his disciples on what day he was going to die; and he ordered his grave to be opened six days before he was carried to it. — *Matins: Sixth Lesson*

Many are His visits to the man of interior life, and sweet the conversation that He holdeth with him: plenteous His consolation, His peace, and His familiarity. — *Imitation: Book II*

IDEAL: This is the brother of St. Scholastica. He was accustomed to visit his holy sister once a year to talk over affairs concerning their advance in holiness. Feeling that she was to die the night of his last visit, she begged him to stay a bit longer, but he refused since according to his rule, his time was up. St. Scholastica played a little trick on him by praying for a storm which came down in such fury that her brother had to stay. That night, St. Scholastica died.

TODAY: Perhaps you have the mistaken notion, too, that

saints are necessarily gloomy people who are always praying from a prayer book or doing extraordinary penance, never smiling, or playing tricks on one another. That is a grave mistake. A saint is a person who does God's will as well as he reasonably can. You can be a saint right this minute, today.

SLOGAN: I *can*; I MUST; I WILL.

March 22. ST. CATHERINE OF SWEDEN
(When April 4 falls in Holy Week, the feast of St. Isidore is kept on March 22.)

St. Catherine was the daughter of St. Brigid. Even as a child she was remarkable for her love of God. She was married to Egard, a man of great virtue. By a holy emulation they encouraged one another in doing good. St. Catherine accompanied her mother on pilgrimages and practices of devotion and prayer.

Come, O My chosen one, and I will establish My throne in thee, for the King hath greatly desired thy beauty. — *First Responsory*

I confess, therefore, my unworthiness; I acknowledge Thy bounty; I praise Thy goodness; and I give Thee thanks for Thy exceeding love. — *Imitation: Book IV*

IDEAL: This dear saint was a member of a very holy family. She did her duty day for day, nothing extraordinary, just her duty, but she did it extraordinarily well; that made the difference.

TODAY: Now that Lent is advancing so rapidly to its close, make up for lost time, though really that cannot be done. All you can do now is to make extra efforts to counterbalance the opportunities you have let slip by without using them to advantage.

SLOGAN: Time lost is lost forever.

March 23. ST. VICTORIAN and COMPANIONS, Martyrs

St. Victorian was governor of Carthage with the Roman title of proconsul. After the king had issued his edicts against the Christians, he offered Victorian wealth and honor if he would renounce his religion. Victorian made a generous renunciation of this offer. This infuriated the king, and Victorian paid the price with his blood.

By all the praise Thy saints have won;
By all their pains in days gone by;
By all the deeds which they have done;
Hear Thou Thy suppliant people's cry. — *Lauds: Hymn*

Blessed is that man who for Thee, O Lord, abandoneth all things created. — *Imitation: Book III*

IDEAL: Victorian was a very wealthy magistrate whom the king loved for his fidelity; but when the edicts against the Christians were published, Victorian refused to carry them out. For this he was most cruelly tortured and put to death.

TODAY: We admire persons who are courageous enough to say "no" at the right time. During Lent you may have many an occasion to do just that. There are many things that are not wrong to do during Lent, but our permitting ourselves the indulgence is a bad example to people about us.

SLOGAN: Even so let your light shine before men, in order that they may see your good works and give glory to your Father in heaven.

March 24. ST. GABRIEL, Archangel

With a feeling of holy reverence, St. Gabriel came to the Virgin who from all eternity had been chosen to be the Mother on earth of Him of whom God is the Father in heaven. In the words inspired by the Most High he said: Hail, full of grace, the Lord is with thee: blessed art thou among women.

Now in the sixth month, the Angel Gabriel was sent from God to a town of Galilee, called Nazareth, to a virgin betrothed to a man named Joseph, of the house of David: and the virgin's name was Mary. — *Gospel: Luke 1*

Being grounded and established in God, they can by no means be proud. — *Imitation: Book II*

IDEAL: Just before the lovely feast of the Annunciation, comes this feast of Gabriel who brought to us from heaven the message of our approaching salvation and taught us the *Hail Mary.*

TODAY: Say the *Hail Mary* as devoutly as possible today. Try to be conscious of the presence of an angel at your side as much of the time as you can. You recall how you were accustomed to make room for him when you were small. At least, make room for him in your thoughts today.

SLOGAN: Ever this day be at my side.
To light, to guard, to rule and guide.

March 25.   THE ANNUNCIATION OF THE BLESSED VIRGIN MARY

Today the Church recalls the greatest event in history, the Incarnation of our Lord. On this day the Word was made flesh, and has united to Itself forever the humanity of Jesus.

O God who wast pleased that Thy Word should take flesh, at the message of an angel, in the womb of the Blessed Virgin Mary, grant to Thy suppliants, that we who believe her to be truly the Mother of God, may be helped by her intercession with Thee. — *Collect*

Let nothing appear great, nothing valuable or admirable, nothing worthy of esteem, nothing high, nothing truly praiseworthy or desirable, but that which is eternal. — *Imitation: Book III*

IDEAL: How shall we ever be able to thank our Lady for pronouncing the single word "Fiat" (Be it done), the answer she sent back to heaven that she would be the Mother of the Saviour?

TODAY: Make a special visit to our Lady's statue today; let it help you to think of our Lady. Close your eyes and pray from your heart whatever your heart dictates. Certainly no one else can tell you what to say to her today when your heart must fairly burst with love and gratitude and praise of your heavenly Mother.

SLOGAN: Behold the handmaid of the Lord; be it done unto me according to Thy word.

March 26.   ST. LUDGER, Bishop

St. Ludger was the apostle of Friesland. He was accused to Charlemagne of wasting his income and neglecting the building of churches. The saint was at his prayers when the summons came to appear at court. St. Ludger finished his prayers and then reported to the king. Upon being reprimanded for his delay, St. Ludger explained that though he entertained the highest regard for his king, he owed greater respect for his God. Charlemagne dismissed him with honor.

Blessed is the man that doth meditate in the law of the Lord: his delight is therein day and night, and whatsoever he doeth shall prosper. — *Matins: First Antiphon*

Speak, then, O Lord, for Thy servant heareth; for Thou hast the words of eternal life. — *Imitation: Book III*

IDEAL: When uncertain what to do about certain matters, Ludger took his difficulty to the Holy See to be certain he was not teaching or acting contrary to the doctrines of the Church.

TODAY: Do you readily submit your judgment to those who have more experience than you, or do you assume the attitude of those who "know it all"? Unless they should tell you to commit sin (which never happens), it is always wise to obey the counsels of your elders.

SLOGAN: Experience holds an expensive school, but fools will learn in no other.

March 27. ST. JOHN DAMASCENE, Confessor and Doctor

St. John was raised up by God to defend the veneration of images, at a time when the Emperor Leo the Isurian endeavored to destroy it. Accused of betraying the Caliph of Damascus, he was condemned to have his right hand cut off. But his hand was miraculously restored, for he promised the Blessed Virgin that he would use it in writing her praises. He kept his promise.

Thou hast held me by my right hand, and by Thy will Thou hast conducted me, and with Thy glory Thou has received me. — *Introit: Psalm 72*

In Thee, therefore, O Lord, do I place all my hope and my refuge; on Thee I cast all my tribulation and anguish; for I find all to be weak and inconstant whatever I behold out of Thee. — *Imitation: Book III*

IDEAL: Ordered by the persecutors to have his right hand struck off, St. John prayed our Lady to heal him and he would use his hand to write her praises. The hand was miraculously healed, and St. John kept his promise.

TODAY: When you next pray for something that you want very badly, if you will do something that means sacrifice to yourself and does honor to God, you will feel how much more readily your prayer is heard.

SLOGAN: Shall we ever be asking and give nothing in return?

March 28. ST. JOHN CAPISTRAN

St. John was chosen by God to deliver Europe from Islam. Supported by the noble Hungarian, John Hunyades, he enrolled 70,000 Christians. These improvised warriors had no other arms but forks and flails. By their bravery John obtained the victory of the Cross over the Crescent.

I will rejoice in the Lord; and I will joy in God my Jesus; the Lord God is my strength. — *Introit*

Thou art my hope, my confidence, my comforter, and in all things most faithful. — *Imitation: Book III*

IDEAL: Through the prayers and following the suggestion of St. John, 12,000 hostile hordes were turned away from the city without bloodshed.

TODAY: Tennyson says: "More is wrought by prayer than this world dreams of." It is said of St. Teresa that she converted by her prayers as many souls as St. Francis Xavier baptized, and we are told he baptized a million. If you have a real desire to be a missionary right now and want to help to spread God's kingdom, do as much as you can now by prayer.

SLOGAN: More things are wrought by prayer than this world dreams of. — *Tennyson*

March 29. SS. JONAS, BARACHISIUS, and COMPANIONS

During the reign of King Sapor of Persia, these saints were seized and subjected to the most cruel tortures for their faith. When told to obey the king and to worship the gods, they replied that it was more reasonable to obey the immortal King of heaven and earth than a mortal prince.

> Courage was theirs which no mocking nor threatening
> Daunted, nor all the inventions of cruelty
> Broke, when the conquerors, strong under agony,
> Crushed the power of the torturer. — *Matins: Hymn*

Nothing is more acceptable to God, nothing more salutary for thee in this world, than to suffer willingly for Christ. — *Imitation: Book II*

IDEAL: It is some time now since we have had a feast of a group like today. There were eleven of them; like a football team with two co-captains, one of whom was St. Jonas. They would not "throw the game" for any price, but gave their lives willingly for their faith.

TODAY: Perhaps during Lent, after you have been particularly good for a week or two, you felt you had a right to a little digression. There is no obligation to the little voluntary penances you undertake, as you know; but it does prove you just a little coward, does it not, if you cannot hold out against yourself for six weeks, when you are supposed to be governing yourself for a lifetime?

SLOGAN: He that perseveres *to the end,* he shall be crowned.

March 30. ST. JOHN CLIMACUS

While still young, St. John had achieved such a reputation for learning that he was called the Scholastic. He gave up what promised to be a brilliant career and retired to a solitude on Mt. Sinai. Other young men came to him, for whom he founded a monastery and wrote *Climax, or Ladder of Perfection.*

He that hath clean hands and a pure heart, who hath not lifted up his soul unto vanity, nor sworn deceitfully unto his neighbor, he shall receive a blessing from the Lord. — *Matins: Psalm 23*

I am He that in an instant elevateth the humble mind to comprehend more reasons of the eternal truth than if anyone had studied ten years in the schools. — *Imitation: Book III*

IDEAL: This is the fourth saint in succession by the name of John. He had a very, very bright mind and a splendid opportunity to make a name for himself, but he left all to become a monk in the desert; he was sixteen at the time he entered the desert.

TODAY: The monks said of St. John that there never was a more docile monk than he. Sometimes when students are especially bright, they get the mistaken notion that they know more than their parents. That very fact betrays ignorance.

SLOGAN: Fools rush in where angels fear to tread.

March 31.   ST. BENJAMIN, Deacon and Martyr

During the persecution of Christians in Persia, St. Benjamin was imprisoned for a year. An ambassador, after having promised that St. Benjamin would not speak of religion to the courtiers, obtained his release. But Benjamin refused to be bound by a promise to which he had never given his consent. He was cruelly tortured to death.

Whosoever shall confess Me before men, him will I confess also before My Father. — *Lauds: First Antiphon*

Because if thou die with Him, thou shalt also live with Him; and if thou art His companion in suffering, thou shalt also be His companion in glory. — *Imitation: Book II*

IDEAL: The story of the martyrdom of St. Benjamin is too terrible to record. He died after over a year of constant inhuman torture.

TODAY: The last day of March and tomorrow is All Fools' day, as you know. Whether anybody else fools you or not, look back over the past long month of wonderful days and see if you have perhaps fooled yourself. If you have reason to think you have done well, thank God for it and make April a banner month.

SLOGAN: There is no standing still in the spiritual life; not to advance is to go back.

PASSION SUNDAY

This Sunday is called Passion Sunday for the reason that Holy Church — and it is supposed all her faithful children — concentrates more than ordinarily upon the sufferings of our Saviour. The crucifix and the statues are covered, partly to remind us that we should seclude ourselves from the world and retire with our Saviour who "hid Himself from" His enemies after the raising of Lazarus from the dead.

For if the blood of goats and of oxen being sprinkled sanctify such as are defiled, how much more shall the blood of Christ cleanse our conscience from dead works. — *Epistle*

Jesus hath many lovers of the realm of Heaven, but few bearers of His cross. — *Imitation: Book II, 11*

IDEAL: When one is conscious of having deeply grieved a very dear friend, one scarcely thinks in words. Though our very best Friend whom we have thus grieved is very willing Himself to forget the offense, we should not be so ready to forget that we owe Him endless reparation and gratitude.

TODAY: If we really mean what we say when we say to our Lord, "I am sorry," let us prove it by avoiding every willful transgression of His Law even in points that we ordinarily count as trivial.

SLOGAN: My iniquity is ever before mine eyes. — *Psalms*

SORROWFUL MOTHER

There are two feasts to honor our Lady's sorrows. This one during Passion Week should call to mind the compassion of the Sorrowful Mother, i.e., the share she had in the Passion of our Saviour.

> For his people's sins' remission
> She beheld each wide incision
> By the blood-stained lashes bared. — *Stabat Mater*

Love is a great thing, a great good in every wise; it alone maketh light every heavy thing, for it beareth burden without burden. — *Imitation: Book III*

IDEAL: Never a son had such a Mother; never a mother had such a Son. He had done only good all His life; and what a death was His! We cannot begin to fathom our Lady's grief at her Son's suffering.

TODAY: Think about it as you go about your work today, and let your heart dictate proper action.

SLOGAN: Oh, all you who pass by the way, attend and see if there be any sorrow like unto my sorrow.

PALM SUNDAY

On this day palms are blessed. You will notice as you read your Missal that the blessing of the palms is much like a

Mass in itself. In the early days of the Church there were two Masses, one for the blessing of the palms, the other after the procession.

He humbled Himself, becoming obedient unto death, even the death of the cross. For which cause God also exalted Him, giving Him a name which is above all names. — *Epistle*

It is a great thing for a man to stand under obedience and live under a master, and not be at his own liberty. — *Imitation: Book I*

IDEAL: Palm Sunday is the best example in history of the value of human praise. And how well our Lord understood and what effort He made to warn us against putting any faith in most of it. See the tears in His eyes as He looks over Jerusalem — and He thought of us, too, in that sweeping glance — and hear Him say, "If thou hadst known in this thy day!"

TODAY: Will you try to make the second part of the sentence written of our Lord in this journey untrue in your case at least this week: "And looking upon the city, *Jesus wept.*" And will you try to make it untrue each time an angel records "And looking into N. N.'s city, Jesus——"?

SLOGAN: And looking over the city, Jesus wept.

SPY WEDNESDAY

Wednesday in Holy Week is sometimes known as Spy Wednesday for the reason that an old tradition has it that it was on Wednesday Judas made his final arrangements for the betrayal.

But He was wounded for our iniquities, He was bruised for our sins. — *Epistle*

There is no other way to life but the way of the holy cross. — *Imitation: Book I*

IDEAL: Every sin is first in the thought. It is there the Spy Wednesday takes place. If we would see to it that there be no Spy Wednesday, there would never be a Good Friday in the life of our soul.

TODAY: Surely with the figure of our Saviour as the *Ecce Homo* so vividly before us these days, it cannot be difficult to pledge our word that never shall there be a Spy Wednesday again in our life, but always Easter Sunday and the forty days following.

SLOGAN: Lord, Thou knowest all things; Thou knowest that I love Thee.

HOLY THURSDAY

At no point in the life of our Lord does He reveal so convincingly the aspect of the lover of men as on this day. Note only some of the expressions "My little children," "With desire I desired to eat this Pasch with you before I die." The name Maundy Thursday is a corruption of the Latin word *Mandatum* which is the first word of the antiphon recited at the washing of the feet, a custom still observed with great solemnity by many bishops on this day in memory of our Saviour washing the feet of the disciples.

Know you what I have done to you? — *Gospel*

Prepare for Me an upper room furnished and I will eat the Pasch with thee. — *Imitation: Book IV*

IDEAL: In the Old Testament the prophet had written of our Lord, "My desires are to be with the children of men." Like a very loving father — and who could ever love as our Lord does? — our Saviour seemed to be unable to tear Himself away from us on this, His last night on earth in visible human form. Surely, He had no reasons from our side to be thus attached to us; but from His side, ah, from His side, it was because of His "heart burning with love for men," even though He was to receive from many of them "naught but coldness and neglect." And because He could not bear to leave us really, He made the promise, "Behold I am with you even to the consummation of the world," and He fulfilled that promise immediately with "This is My body."

TODAY: Will you not spend as much time as possible in adoration and reparation before the repository today? And even when your work prevents you from being actually in the presence of our Saviour in His Eucharistic guise, will you make a very definite effort to keep your mind occupied with the thought of the events we commemorate during these last three days of the holiest week of all the year? You know how very much our Lord was afflicted with the thoughtlessness of His disciples; there is a real cry for sympathy in His plaintive words to Peter: "Could you not watch one hour with Me?" On this one day, He must have no reason to say that to you. It is so tremendous a privilege — though our Lord never makes us feel that — to be allowed to say to the King of heaven and earth, to our Creator, "I love You." By the words He spoke and by the things He has done, our Lord makes us feel that we are doing Him kindness when we say "yes" to His plea, "Son, give Me thy heart."

SLOGAN: I rejoiced at the things that were said to me. We shall go into the house of the Lord.

GOOD FRIDAY

Be as recollected as possible on this day when you arise in the morning. Follow the ceremonies of the Mass of the Pre-Sanctified very closely, and if you are fortunate enough to belong to a parish or to be near to one where the Tre Ore services are conducted, be sure to attend and make the meditations and say the prayers with the priest. Three hours may seem a long time to spend in actual prayer and contemplation, but can you even think of the agony of hanging from nails driven through hands and feet for that length of time? It is unthinkable, and when we remember all the torments, not only of body but also of soul, that our Saviour endured before those three awful hours, we are almost rendered numb at the very thought. All through the services, and all through the day, hear the suffering Saviour calling to you, "O My people, what have I done to you?" Then, resolve with all the power of will you can muster that there shall be an Easter Sunday in your life and always thereafter Eastertide.

HOLY SATURDAY

Only if you have spent the holy season well; only if you have made reasonable effort during the past forty days, will you feel especially happy today, and your heart will sing out in the joyous Alleluia that seems veritably to escape from the celebrant's lips at the Mass.

EASTER SUNDAY

One is well-nigh suffocated with the joy that comes of the realization that "He is risen as He said." Holy Week is depressing; as we walk the Way of the Cross with our Saviour, we feel crushed at the thought that it is to end in the death of the Beloved of our souls, and in a death most cruel and horrible. Also, it comes home so very forcibly — or it should — that we have been the cause of all this; and, because we are really repentant, and would love to undo it all, the twelfth station seems so brutally inexorable. But today! today the Risen Christ Himself overtakes us with the "All hail! I have risen and I am with you." Divine Lover that He is, He would almost make us feel that He has kept us waiting until this third day and would do all in His power to make amends for our grieving. No sign in His look that these wounds, that shine so gloriously now, are ignominious reminders of what we have cost Him; no sign to indicate that ever there was any fall from grace in His sight; no sign that He thinks of "sins that were red as scarlet" but only of souls made "whiter than wool." And for all this, there is an explanation. It is this: this risen Saviour is Jesus, and He loves us.

ASCENSION DAY

Because we are so selfish and because our faith is so weak, Ascension Day does not strike us as a particularly happy feast. Of course, we are glad that Jesus is to make His triumphal return to the right hand of the Father, but, oh, we should love to have Him in His visible form abiding with us still as He walked about with the disciples especially during these forty days after the Resurrection. But, how much wiser and how infinitely more loving His plan to be with us, all of us, each of us, "all days even to the consummation of the world!" And if we really love Him as much as we protest, He has given a very definite task by which we may prove our words by deeds. "Going therefore, teach ye all nations!" We need not get into a pulpit to do that — not all of us need to; our lives preach far more loudly than any words ever could, just what our sentiments are regarding the coming of Christ's kingdom on earth.

SOLEMNITY OF ST. JOSEPH

This feast of St. Joseph as patron of the universal Church occurs on the Wednesday in the third week after Easter.

The God of thy father shall be thy helper, and the almighty shall bless thee with the blessings of Heaven above. — *Epistle*

Take no heed of the shadow of a great name, nor of the praise and friendship of many. — *Imitation: Book II*

IDEAL: Whom God trusted to the extent of making him the guardian of His own son and His Blessed Mother, shall we not trust with our little wants?

TODAY: St. Joseph is very good to people who make special effort to imitate the sweet simplicity his divine Foster Son valued so highly; but he is very good also to those of us who are not quite so deserving for the reason that he is enough like his Foster Son to make a great deal of allowance; and he must when he knows we use so little sense sometimes.

SLOGAN: St. Joseph, patron of the universal Church, pray for us.

April 1. ST. HUGH, Bishop

The blessing of God rested visibly on the labors of this saint. As Bishop of Grenoble, he transformed his whole diocese. Relying on the Pope's tacit consent, he resigned his bishopric and retired to a monastery. But the Pope put him under obedience to resume his duties as bishop. Some time before his death he lost his memory for everything except his prayers.

Well done, thou good and faithful servant, thou hast been faithful over a few things. I will make thee ruler over many things; enter thou into the joy of thy Lord. — *First Responsory*

The greatest saints shunned the company of men when they could, and chose rather to live unto God in secret. — *Imitation: Book I*

IDEAL: St. Hugh was especially privileged by God from his early childhood. He had very holy parents and so he grew up in great love of God. In obedience to the Holy See, he became a bishop later but begged to be released from the burden that he might spend his last year in solitude and retirement.

TODAY: Do you crave being in the "limelight"? If you happen to be in a group today that is discussing the topic on which you have some information you would love to give, just look on and say nothing unless you are asked, and if you are asked an opinion, try to give it with the air of "you could all teach me a great deal" in your tone.

SLOGAN: A fool's heart is on his tongue.

April 2. ST. FRANCIS OF PAULA, Confessor

When thirteen years of age, St. Francis retired into the

desert and led such a holy life that numerous disciples soon came to place themselves under his guidance. He then founded the order to which in his humility he gave the name of Minims, the least in the house of God.

In his words there was a wonderful charm; he kept his virginity always inviolate; he was so great a lover of lowliness that he used to call himself the least of all. — *Second Nocturn: Fifth Lesson*

O Lord, I have called upon Thee, and have desired to enjoy Thee, and am prepared to reject all things for Thy sake. — *Imitation: Book III*

IDEAL: At the tender age of thirteen, St. Francis entered the desert to live a hermit's life. It was not unusual in those days for young men to go into the desert when still quite young.

TODAY: It is certainly unfair to think that we would begin serving God when we are old. Give to God your love from a young heart, serve Him with the enthusiasm only young people have. The Apostles whom our Lord chose were comparatively young men, all of them. Our Lord loves young people, because they are so awake to His wants, so eager to serve One whom they love. Those who return His love are nearest Him. Get on the inside row!

SLOGAN: As the twig is bent, the tree's inclined. — *Pope*

April 3. ST. RICHARD OF CHICHESTER

As Bishop of Chichester, St. Richard showed himself a zealous shepherd of souls. The strict economy of his own household enabled him to give abundant alms. He had great charity for the sick and the poor. He often excused the debts of those who owed him money.

At the point of death he caused an image of Christ suffering to be brought to him, and commended his soul to his Redeemer. — *Matins: Sixth Lesson*

Love often knoweth no measure, but groweth fervent above all measure. — *Imitation: Book III*

IDEAL: A successful farmer, then a learned priest, then a bishop, finally chancellor to the king, Richard was all kindness to those in need, but stood like a wall against the king when the latter encroached on the rights of the Church.

TODAY: St. Richard had lived so careful a life that people came to feel that when Richard was doing a thing, it was right. Do your classmates ever think of you in such terms? For instance, when there is question of a movie, and they are not so certain whether the picture is good morally or not, does your going or not going mean to them that it is good or otherwise, because you are the kind of person who has high standards and lives up to them?

SLOGAN: So let your light shine before men.

April 4.   ST. ISIDORE, Archbishop

Lowly, meek, merciful, careful to restore the laws of Christianity and the Church, unwearied in establishing the same by his word and by his writings, St. Isidore shone in all graces. He founded monasteries and colleges. He himself taught in the latter.

Thou hast made him a little lower than the angels. Thou hast crowned him with glory and honor, and madest him to have dominion over the works of Thine hands. — *Matins: Psalm 8*

Dart forth Thy lightning, and disperse them: shoot Thy arrows, and let all the phantoms of the enemy be put to flight. — *Imitation: Book III*

IDEAL: St. Isidore was a bishop, during which time he wrote a book on what a bishop should be and how he should live, all of which the saint himself practiced.

TODAY: When you write your English today, or when you chance to say that you feel you owe so much to your good parents and to your school, just check up on yourself, and see how much of that you really mean. Actions speak much louder than words.

SLOGAN: If to do were as easy as to know what to do, we had long since become saints.

April 5.   ST. VINCENT FERRER

Every day St. Vincent fasted. He preached every day and refused no one his holy and just advice. He often laid his hands on the sick and they recovered. He cast out unclean spirits, and made the deaf to hear, the dumb to speak, and the blind to see.

Lord, Thou deliverest unto me five talents; behold, I have gained five more. — *First Responsory: Verse*

Principally, therefore, refer all things to Me; for it is I that have given thee all. — *Imitation: Book III*

IDEAL: St. Vincent was a great preacher; the topic of his sermon was most often, "Arise, ye dead, and come to judgment." By impressing upon the mind of his hearers the thought of the coming judgment, he brought about many conversions.

TODAY: Suppose an angel were to tell you this morning that tonight at seven you would be called away by death, what would you do? You may be called before that time, or very shortly after; in any case, it is well worth your while to be ready. "Thou shalt not know at what hour I will come to thee." — *Apoc. 3:3*

SLOGAN: Watch therefore, for you do not know at what hour your Lord is to come.

April 6.   ST. CELESTINE, Pope

St. Celestine's reign is noteworthy for the condemnation of the heretic Nestorius. It was St. Celestine who sent St. Germanus to Britain and St. Paladius to Scotland. Many authors of the life of St. Patrick say that the apostle likewise received his commission to preach to the Irish from St. Celestine.

Let all those that put their trust in Thee rejoice, O Lord, for Thou hast blessed the righteous; Thou has compassed

him with Thy favor as with a shield. — *Second Nocturn:
Second Antiphon*

Study, therefore, so to live now, that in the hour of
death thou mayest be able rather to rejoice than to fear.
— *Imitation: Book I*

IDEAL: St. Celestine was a pope whose whole reign was a
continual combat against heresy, but the saint was undaunted,
his only object being truth and right.

TODAY: When about to do or not to do certain things,
never let the thought "What will people say?" influence your
decision. The only thing that ever counts is "What is right
in this case and what will God think?"

SLOGAN: Know you're right; then go ahead.

April 7.   BLESSED HERMAN JOSEPH

Blessed Herman Joseph was devoted to the Blessed Virgin
in a very special manner. As a child, he spent much of his
playtime in the church near the statue of the Blessed Virgin
where he received many favors. Once our Lady took an
apple from Herman which he offered her in pledge of his
love. His companions called him Joseph because of his love
for Mary.

> Thy suppliant people, through the prayer
> Of the blest saint, forgive;
> For his dear sake Thy wrath forbear
> And bid our spirits live. — *Lauds: Hymn*

By two wings is man lifted above earthly things; viz., by
simplicity and purity. — *Imitation: Book II*

IDEAL: This dear young saint is too charming for words.
You know the story of his bringing an apple to the Infant
Jesus, do you not, and our Lady reaching down to accept it?

TODAY: Read the life of this sweet and simple saint; you
will like it certainly. Try to establish in your own life a
personal relation with our Saviour and His Blessed Mother.
Of course, you cannot see them when you go in to talk

things over with them; but you cannot see your mother either when you speak to her by telephone, can you?

SLOGAN: Lord, I believe; help Thou my unbelief.

April 8.   ST. PERPETUUS, Bishop

St. Perpetuus had a great veneration for the saints, and respect for their relics, adorned their shrines, and enriched their churches. As Bishop of Tours he labored by zealous sermons and wholesome regulations to lead souls to virtue.

I will come into Thine house: I will worship toward Thine holy temple in Thy fear. — *Second Nocturn: Psalm 5*

I am the Rewarder of all the good, and the mighty Prover of all the devout. — *Imitation: Book III*

IDEAL: The principal devotion of this saint was to the relics of the saints. He enlarged the church of St. Martin to accommodate the many worshipers.

TODAY: We venerate anything that George Washington ever used or touched, and rightly so. Read very carefully in your *Catholic Worship* the portion on "Veneration of Relics"; you should be well informed on such topics that you may give intelligent answers to inquiring non-Catholics.

SLOGAN: Know you not that you are the temples of the Holy Ghost?

April 9.   ST. MARY OF EGYPT

Mary of Egypt was a public sinner for seventeen years. She went on a pilgrimage to Jerusalem and with the crowd was about to enter the church where the True Cross was kept. An invisible force prevented her from entering. Touched by the grace of God, she admitted her sinfulness, entered the wilderness, and did penance.

Favor is deceitful and beauty is vain: a woman that feareth the Lord, she shall be praised. — *Prime: Chapter*

To be without Jesus is a grievous hell; to be with Jesus a sweet paradise. — *Imitation: Book II*

IDEAL: When still quite young, Mary left her father's home that she might live a life of sin without restraint. At a festive celebration held in a certain church, Mary wished to enter the church with the rest but was held back. The realization of her sinfulness dawned upon her and she lived a strict life of penance to her death.

TODAY: Mary of Egypt was converted by turning in prayer to our Lady. Our Blessed Mother never forsakes anyone who has recourse to her, and when turning to her in prayer, strive to live as our holy Mother would have us live. If you have not adopted the practice already, make it a life's habit to say the *Hail Mary* three times each day.

SLOGAN: Blessed is he that watcheth daily at My gates.

April 10.   ST. BADEMUS

St. Bademus founded a monastery in Persia. He led his religious on the path of perfection in all sweetness, prudence, and charity. To crown his virtue, God permitted him to be taken prisoner and tortured for his faith. He was beheaded.

I will liken him unto a wise man who built his house upon a rock. — *Vespers: Antiphon*

In the Cross is salvation; in the Cross is life; in the Cross is protection from enemies. — *Imitation: Book II*

IDEAL: As Bademus waited for martyrdom a traitor to the faith was admitted into his cell to dispatch him with a sword. Bademus was so patient to the several wounds inflicted by the unfortunate fellow Christian that persons standing about were moved to acknowledge the beauty and power of his faith.

TODAY: Open-minded non-Catholics will be moved to inquire into your faith far more on account of your good example than for any other reason. It is a dreadful responsibility to have on one's soul to have discouraged even one soul's conversion by our bad example.

SLOGAN: Nor knowest thou what argument, thy life to a neighbor's creed has lent. — *Emerson*

April 11.   ST. LEO THE GREAT

When the terrible Attila, "The Scourge of God," was at the gate of Rome, St. Leo went out to meet him and prevailed upon him to turn back. Attila later admitted that he saw two venerable personages on each side of the Pope and, impressed by these, he had withdrawn.

He hath made him a blessing unto all nations, and hath established His covenant upon his head. — *Second Responsory*

In all this, I beseech Thee, let Thy hand govern and teach me, that I may in no way exceed. — *Imitation: Book III*

IDEAL: When this Pope read his message at the general council, the assembled bishops cried out in one voice, "Peter has spoken through Leo."

TODAY: Do you readily acknowledge greatness in others? Do you like to hear others praised? Do you ever want to say some unkind thing when you hear another praised? When someone else is praised in your presence, are you quite willing to add another favorable compliment? Search out your mode of thinking under this head today.

SLOGAN: Lord that I may know Thee; that I may know me; that I love Thee and despise myself. — *St. Augustine*

April 12.   ST. JULIUS, Pope

Like so many other popes at that time, St. Julius labored all his lifetime to exterminate heresy. He struggled against the Arians despite their threats against his life.

Thy Martyr, he ran all valiantly o'er
A highway of blood for the prize Thou hast given.
— *First Vespers*

Such a one is conqueror of himself, and lord of the world, the friend of Christ, and an heir of heaven. — *Imitation: Book II*

IDEAL: Like many of the early bishops, St. Julius fought a constant battle for the faith against the Arians in 352.

TODAY: Do you get a thrill when you think that you are a member of a family that dates back to 352 and even back to the first century? And, oh, to have our Lady for mother, Christ for brother, God for father, and heaven for home! As you walk about today, keep saying prayers of thanksgiving in your heart all the while.

SLOGAN: My soul doth magnify the Lord. — *Magnificat*

April 13. ST. HERMENEGILD, Martyr

Hermenegild, though an Arian, married a Catholic and became a convert. His father on hearing the news had him imprisoned. On Easter Day an Arian priest entered his cell and offered him pardon if he would receive communion from him. Hermenegild refused and knelt with joy for the death stroke.

Then shall the just stand with great constancy against those that have afflicted them and taken away their labors. — *Epistle: Book of Wisdom*

Oh, how many and grievous tribulations did the Apostles suffer, and the martyrs, and confessors, and virgins, and all the rest who resolved to follow the steps of Christ. — *Imitation: Book I*

IDEAL: The son of a heretical father, Hermenegild became a Christian and was in consequence put to death upon the order of his own father, for whom the martyr prayed even when dying. His prayer converted his father, who strove to do what he could to bring his kingdom back to the true faith.

TODAY: The prayer of the dying St. Stephen gave to the world the glorious St. Paul; the prayer of Hermenegild was instrumental in bringing a kingdom to the faith. Pray for the conversion of sinners, even if you never know the definite persons who have been converted by your prayers; you will meet them in heaven.

SLOGAN: He that shall convert one sinner from his evil ways, shall save his own soul from death.

April 14.   ST. JUSTIN, Martyr

As a pagan philosopher, St. Justin examined the pagan philosophical systems and found only error and false wisdom. Then he examined the word of the crucified God and became a Christian. He became celebrated especially by two Apologies which he had the courage to address to the persecuting emperors.

Thou hast crowned him with glory and honor, O Lord. And madest him to have dominion over the works of Thy hands. — *Matins: Verse and Answer*

Jesus Christ alone is singly to be loved; for He alone is found good and faithful above all friends. — *Imitation: Book II*

IDEAL: When Christ promised that the "gates of hell would not prevail against the Church," that promise was God's own promise. You note that always, when persecution arises, there are great leaders in the Church who defend the Church's cause and lead her children to safety.

TODAY: Pray for perseverance in your faith. We are told that we must earn this latter grace; that God grants it to those only who ask it.

SLOGAN: Lord, increase our faith.

April 15.   ST. PATERNUS, Bishop

St. Paternus founded monasteries and built churches for the greater glory of God. When some false brethren created a division of opinion about him among the bishops of the province, St. Paternus preferred to retire rather than afford any ground for dissension.

This is the faithful and wise steward, whom the Lord setteth over His family. — *Secret*

In silence and quiet the devout soul maketh progress, and learneth the hidden things of Scripture. — *Imitation: Book I*

IDEAL: Rather than cause dissension among the bishops, Paternus preferred to go into solitude.

TODAY: When somebody says a certain thing happened last Tuesday when you *know* it was on Monday, do you keep on insisting until you have your way? Philosophize! What is the difference? In nonessentials, the wiser man always gives in. Be wise!

SLOGAN: Saying a thing is when it is not, never makes it be.

April 16.   EIGHTEEN MARTYRS OF SARAGOSSA

St. Optatus and seventeen others were martyred on the same day. On this day the Church also celebrates the feast of Encratis. In order to escape marriage, this saint fled from her father's house to Saragossa where the persecution was hottest. She was seized and put to death.

As gold in the furnace hath the Lord tried His chosen ones and received them forever as burnt offerings. — *Second Antiphon*

He is gone before thee, carrying His cross, and He died for thee upon the cross, that thou mayest also bear thy cross and love to die on the cross. — *Imitation: Book II*

IDEAL: This is the first group we have had in April. Teachers speak sometimes of this or that class as "that splendid crowd of such and such a year." So very much depends upon the leader in a class.

TODAY: If you know from past experience that you are not a leader, then be a good follower, that is, know whom to follow. If you can be a leader, lead your group to fine and noble things as these saints today were led.

SLOGAN: I am a part of all I have met.

April 17.   ST. ANICETUS, Pope and Martyr

Though St. Anicetus did not shed his blood for the faith, he suffered and endured untold dangers. He preserved his flock from heresy and brought comfort to those in pain.

Novena for the feast of Our Lady of Good Counsel begins.

Amen, amen, I say to you, that you shall weep and lament, but the world shall rejoice; and you shall be sorrowful, but your sorrow shall be changed into joy. — *Gospel: John 16*

For He manifestly exhorts His disciples that follow Him and all that desire to follow Him, to bear the cross saying: "If any man will come after Me, let him deny himself and take up his cross and follow Me." — *Imitation: Book II*

IDEAL: This saint gave his life for Christ very near the day on which we commemorate our Saviour's death. He had only shortly before helped to establish a fixed time for the keeping of Easter.

TODAY: We should all be copies of Christ. Could anybody trace resemblances in you? Would anybody, not knowing, guess from your actions that you are even a Catholic?

SLOGAN: Imitation is the highest form of compliment.

April 18.   ST. APPOLLONIUS, Martyr

This saint was a noted Roman citizen who became a Christian. A slave reported his conversion to the emperor. St. Appollonius was ordered to give up his religion or sacrifice his life and fortune. The saint courageously rejected these terms of safety and was beheaded.

If any man serve Me, him will My Father, who is in heaven, honor. — *Lauds: Antiphon*

Whoever is not willing to suffer all things, and to stand resigned to the will of his Beloved, is not worthy to be called a lover. — *Imitation: Book III*

IDEAL: Another martyr! There is a veritable halo of martyrs about Easter time, when we keep the greatest feast of the year, the resurrection of the King of Martyrs.

TODAY: Oh, to belong to the bodyguard of the King! To have Him point me out in the crowd about and say, "I want you in My immediate personal guard of men." Could you have the heart to say, "Perhaps later on"?

SLOGAN: I want to be a soldier in the force of Christ, my King.

April 19. ST. ELPHEGE, Archbishop

When the Danes sacked the city of Canterbury, St. Elphege was carried off in expectation of a large ransom. St. Elphege would not permit his people to raise the ransom money but preferred to remain in prison rather than deprive the poor of the little they had. In fury the Danes put him to death.

For lo, the wicked bend their bow, they make ready their arrows in the quiver, that they may privily shoot at the upright in heart. — *Matins: Psalm 10*

Let the least be to thee as something very great, and the most contemptible as a special favor. — *Imitation: Book III*

IDEAL: St. Elphege was taken prisoner and when his friends wished to raise money to buy his freedom, he chose rather to remain in a dungeon than to impoverish still more the poor.

TODAY: The poor are easily imposed upon. When someone tells you of how cleverly he fooled this or that person and "they never knew it," if you have not courage enough to express your contempt, at least, do not show your approval; and — don't ever do the same.

SLOGAN: Oppression of the poor — a sin crying to heaven for vengeance.

April 20. ST. MARCELLINUS, Bishop

St. Marcellinus preached the Gospel with great success in the neighborhood of the Alps. By his example as well as by his earnest words he won many of the heathens for Christ. Burning with zeal for the glory of God, he sent Vincent and Domninus to preach the faith in those parts he could not reach.

This is he who wrought great wonders before God, and the whole earth is full of his teaching. May he pray for all people, that their sins may be forgiven unto them! — *Sixth Responsory*

Consider each thing as flowing from the Sovereign Good and therefore all must be returned to Me, as to their origin. — *Imitation: Book III*

IDEAL: Are you amused at the variety of names of the different saints? Just as varied as the names are the saints themselves. You see, they were people just like ourselves, and no two of us are just alike either, nor will we be alike when we are finished saints.

TODAY: A saint? One who does his duty as God wishes him to do it. A saint may be a farmer, student, druggist, clown in a circus, teacher, priest, Sister, hermit, merchant, lawyer, ferryman, cobbler, policeman, fireman, anything. One thing — to do his duty as well as he reasonably can for God.

SLOGAN: I would be a saint. — *St. Scholastica*

Will it. — *St. Benedict's answer*

April 21.　ST. ANSELM, Archbishop of Canterbury

The life of this bishop was a constant struggle against the king of England in defense of the rights of the Church. Accused of disloyalty to the king, he replied: "If any man pretends that I violate my Faith to my King because I will not reject the Holy See of Rome, let him stand forth, and in the name of God I will answer him as I ought." No one took up the challenge and all present sided with the saint.

O right excellent teacher, light of the Holy Church, St. Anselm, blessed lover of the Divine Law, pray for us to the Son of God. — *Antiphon*

Let there be nothing great, nothing high, nothing pleasant, nothing acceptable to thee but only God Himself, or what comes from God. — *Imitation: Book II*

IDEAL: As far back as 1109 St. Anselm was teaching Latin to members of the English court and introducing them to the literature of the Greeks and Romans.

TODAY: You know how much you despise people who show off when they think they know a little more than those about them. Profit by their example and do not do the same, particularly with your own parents; be very careful never to pretend superiority if you are getting a better education than they have. You understand you would not be able to read if it were not for your good parents looking after your education and keeping you alive.

SLOGAN: Honor thy father and mother that it may be well with thee.

April 22. SS. SOTER and CAIUS, Popes and Martyrs

By the sweetness of his discourses, St. Soter comforted all persons with the tenderness of a father, and assisted the indigent with liberal alms, especially those who suffered for the faith. Caius, whose relics are kept in the sanctuary of St. Sylvester at Rome, governed the Church a century later and was put to death in 296.

O ye saints and righteous, rejoice in the Lord. Alleluia! God hath chosen you for His own inheritance. — *Vespers*

For divine charity overcometh all, and enlargeth all the powers of the soul. — *Imitation: Book III*

IDEAL: Each of these saints was a pope and gave his life for his faith. But you know what Sir Galahad said: "If I shall lose my life, I shall find it," meaning that if one gives one's physical life for the cause of God, one finds eternal life.

TODAY: Have you ever heard your father, perhaps, or your older brother talking about different employers in town and saying, "He's a fine boss, he pays his men well"? And everybody likes to work for such an employer. No employer on earth pays as high wages as God does. For the least service, He has Himself promised "a hundredfold." Work for Him only, regardless of who your intermediate foremen are.

SLOGAN: Thousands at His bidding speed o'er land and sea without fail.

April 23. ST. GEORGE, Martyr

In his youth, St. George chose a soldier's life, and soon obtained the favor of Diocletian. But when the emperor began to persecute the Christians, St. George rebuked him and threw up his commission. He was in consequence tortured and beheaded. As years rolled by, St. George became a type of successful combat against evil, the slayer of the dragon, the darling theme of camp and story.

Lord, Thou hast compassed him with favor as with a shield. — *Vespers*

Everyone, therefore, should be solicitous about his temptations, and watch in prayer, lest the devil find opportunity to catch him; who never sleepeth, but goeth about, seeking whom he may devour. — *Imitation: Book I*

IDEAL: Since St. Sebastian, this is the first outstanding soldier saint we have had. And don't you admire a fearless soldier when he is at the same time a *man,* that is, one who fights successfully the battles in his own soul? St. George is always represented slaying a huge monster.

TODAY: Pray to St. George for power against temptation, and learn to know that it is not the number of stripes on your sleeve that mark your distinction as a soldier, but the victories your angel chalks up won on your own private battlefield.

SLOGAN: His strength was as the strength of ten because his heart was pure. — *Tennyson, of Sir Galahad*

April 24.   ST. FIDELIS OF SIGMARINGEN, Martyr

St. Fidelis was at first a lawyer and took so much interest in the poor that he was called "the advocate of the poor." He became a Capuchin. He had a tender love for the Mother of God. After a sermon delivered at Sevis, he was attacked by Calvinists and stabbed to death.

Precious in the sight of the Lord is the death of His saints. — *Third Responsory*

Rare indeed is a faithful friend who will persevere in all the pressing necessities of his friend. — *Imitation: Book III*

IDEAL: The mayor of a city for a time, this saint became a Capuchin and begged that he might be sent among those who would, in return for his service, give him the palm of martyrdom, for he wished to die for Christ whom alone he loved. His wish was granted and he was stabbed to death.

TODAY: Fidelis means faithful, and such this saint was. Have you ever noticed how well nicknames fit the person to whom they are given? What name would fit you best? Be honest with yourself. If your guardian angel who is with you all day were to be unkind enough to name you rightly, what would he call you?

SLOGAN: Come, thou good and faithful servant, enter into the joys of thy Lord!

April 25. ST. MARK, Evangelist

St. Mark, the disciple of St. Peter, is one of the four Evangelists, who wrote, under the inspiration of the Holy Ghost, an abridgment of the life of Jesus. His narration begins with the mission of St. John the Baptist whose voice was heard in the desert; he is represented with a lion at his feet.

O God, who didst exalt blessed Mark, Thy evangelist, by the grace of preaching the Gospel, grant, we beseech Thee, that we ever profit by his erudition, and be defended by his prayer. — *Collect*

Thanks be to Thee, O Lord Jesus, Light of eternal Light, for the table of Holy Doctrine, which Thou hast ministered to us Thy servants, the Prophets and Apostles, and other teachers. — *Imitation: Book IV*

IDEAL: Did you see the picture "King of Kings"? Then you remember the little boy whom our Lord cured of lameness. St. Mark was a disciple of St. Peter and his Gospel is really a record of the facts which he learned from St. Peter.

TODAY: How ready are you to help further an enterprise which you yourself have not initiated? Suppose a member of your class suggests, "Let us get up a program for our English period on this or that author," are you tempted to say to somebody else, "So-and-so does love to order us around," or do you go right to work and say, "Fine! What can I do?"

SLOGAN: The dog in the manger could not eat the hay himself, but neither would he allow the horse to have it.

April 26.   OUR LADY OF GOOD COUNSEL

The devotion of Our Lady of Good Counsel is spreading rapidly through the Church. It originated in Genazzano, a village in the neighborhood of Rome, where an Augustinian church, in which is enshrined a miraculous picture of our Lady, has been for centuries a place of popular pilgrimage.

Let us all rejoice in the Lord, celebrating a festival day in honor of the Blessed Virgin Mary, Mother of Good Counsel, in whose solemnity the angels rejoice and give praise to the Son of God. — *Introit.*

Happy is he whom truth teacheth by itself, not by figures and passing sounds, as it is in itself. — *Imitation: Book I*

IDEAL: You should know the story of this feast. Look for the name Genazzano in the *Catholic Encyclopedia* now and you will find a very fine account.

TODAY: We pray to Our Lady of Good Counsel for advice as to what we should do in important issues. Pray to her today very particularly for the grace of knowing what to do for a life's work. It would be an excellent thing to put your vocation and your future success entirely in the hands of Our Lady of Good Counsel.

SLOGAN: Mother, tell me what I am to do.

April 27.   ST. PETER CANISIUS, Confessor and Doctor of the Church

The feast of this saint was extended to the universal Church in 1926. He was born in Holland and spent his missionary life in Germany. By his eloquent preaching, by the foundation of several colleges, by the missions intrusted to him by the Sovereign Pontiff, he stopped the progress of Protestantism and caused Catholic life to flourish.

O God, who didst strengthen blessed Peter Thy Confessor, for the defense of the Catholic Faith: grant in Thy mercy, that by his example and teaching the erring may be brought to repentance, and the minds of the faithful remain firm in the confession of the truth. — *Collect*

I shall have, moreover, for my consolation and a mirror of life, Thy holy books, and above all these, Thy most holy Body for my special remedy and refuge. — *Imitation: Book IV*

IDEAL: St. Peter Canisius believed that Catholics would live better and be better able to defend their faith if they themselves knew it better. Therefore, he arranged the main truths of our faith in a system of question and answer, from which we have our present-day catechism.

TODAY: Unless you know your faith and continually study it, you will not be able to answer the questions that arise in your own mind, nor those that others put to you.

SLOGAN: The greatest need of the Church today is intelligent laymen who can explain their faith.

April 28. ST. PAUL OF THE CROSS

The eighty-one years of this saint's life were modeled on the Passion of Jesus Christ. When a little boy, a heavy bench fell on his foot. He spoke of the wound as a "rose from heaven." St. Paul founded the Order of the Passionists. He died while the Passion was being read to him.

When his holy one called, the Lord heard him, and gave him peace. — *Matins: First Antiphon*

Then all the servants of the Cross, who in their lifetime, have conformed themselves to Him that was crucified, shall come to Christ their Judge with great confidence. — *Imitation: Book II*

IDEAL: The Passionist Order of priests was founded by this saint who established the Order that he might thus propagate devotion to the Passion of our Lord.

TODAY: Suppose you were sentenced to be executed tomorrow at ten and somebody, a good friend of yours, offered to take your place that you might go free, could you ever forget such kindness? And suppose that friend was God? That is your case exactly; think about it today, and since you cannot really thank Him as He deserves, at least refrain from insulting Him.

SLOGAN: He loved *me* and delivered Himself up for *me*.

April 29.   ST. PETER OF VERONA, Martyr

St. Peter was a Dominican who preached against the heretics of Lombardy and converted many. Once when exhorting a vast crowd in the burning sun, the heretics defied him to secure shade. St. Peter prayed and a cloud overshadowed the audience, thus proving his Creator's protection.

May the Sacraments of which we have partaken defend Thy faithful people, O Lord, and by the intercession of blessed Peter, Thy martyr, insure them safety against all the attacks of their enemies. — *Postcommunion*

Do, Lord, as Thou sayest, and let all wicked thoughts fly from before Thy face. — *Imitation: Book III*

IDEAL: Born of heretical parents, Peter became a Dominican and spent his life working against the heretics. It is said that he never committed a grievous sin. People who claim to know far more than they really do know, will tell you that it is impossible to go through life without grievous sin. Know from the example of this saint and, God grant, from your own life, that it is possible with God's help which we can obtain through prayer.

TODAY: Listen carefully to every bit of instruction given you, study your lessons well, when you are told of some weakness of character you have, be grateful and set about trying to strengthen your character along those lines, that, like Cyrano de Bergerac, you may carry unsullied to God's throne the white plume of your virtue.

SLOGAN: If anyone love Me, he will keep My word, and My Father will love him, and We will come to him and make Our abode with him.

April 30.   ST. CATHERINE OF SIENA

In her childhood, St. Catherine chose Jesus for her Spouse. She subjected her delicate body to severe mortifications; her only support during prolonged fasts was Holy Communion. She received the stigmata from her crucified Lord. It was by her persuasion that Gregory XI left Avignon to return to Rome.

In the virginal fragrance of the virtues of blessed Catherine, whose feast day we are keeping, together with the Saving Victim to be laid upon Thine altar, may our prayers, O Lord, mount on high to Thee. — *Secret*

I am He that in an instant elevateth the humble mind to comprehend more reasons of the eternal truth than if any-one had studied ten years in the schools. — *Imitation: Book III*

IDEAL: She was a member of a very large family, which was probably one of the main reasons for her sanctity. Boys and girls who have many brothers and sisters learn at home to be unselfish, to be kind, to be forebearing, which virtues an only child does not learn so readily.

TODAY: Perhaps you are very courteous and gentle with strangers and friends but cross and pettish with your brothers and sisters at home. Resolve to be on your best manners at home where nothing can be too good for those who love you as only they do.

SLOGAN: Whatever brawls disturb the street, there should be peace at home;
Where brothers dwell and sisters meet, quarrels should never come.

May 1. SS. PHILIP and JAMES, Apostles

St. Philip was one of the first chosen disciples of our Lord. On the way from Judea to Galilee our Lord found Philip and said: "Follow Me." Philip straightway obeyed. On the dispersion of the Apostles among the nations, St. James was left as Bishop of Jerusalem. The Jews so venerated his purity, mortification, and prayer, that they called him "the Just."

Let not your heart be troubled; ye believe in God, believe also in Me. In My Father's house are many mansions. — *Vespers: Antiphon*

Oh, how many and grievous tribulations did the Apostles suffer, and the Martyrs, and Confessors, and Virgins, and all the rest who resolved to follow the steps of Christ. — *Imitation: Book 1*

IDEAL: These two of the Twelve have their feast together as Simon and Jude have theirs in October. This James is not the son of Zebedee, however, whose feast is in July.

TODAY: Instead of wasting your time wishing you had lived at the time of our Lord, go right over to church or stop there on your way home this noon and thank our Lord for living next door, where you are sure to find Him at any time, rather than have you go to Bethsaida and find He had gone with His disciples to Jerusalem.

SLOGAN: Behold I am with you all days.

May 2. ST. ATHANASIUS, Doctor

St. Athanasius was one of the chief defenders of the Church against Arianism. Though firm and adamant in defense of the faith, he was meek and humble, pleasant and winning in converse, beloved by his flock, unwearied in labors, in prayer, in mortifications, and in zeal for souls.

O God, the rewarder of faithful souls, grant that we obtain pardon by the prayers of blessed Athanasius, Thy Confessor and Bishop, whose venerable festival we celebrate. — *Postcommunion*

The saints that are highest in the sight of God are the least in their own eyes; and the more glorious they are, the more humble are they in themselves. — *Imitation: Book II*

IDEAL: Athanasius was continually hounded by the Arians whose schemes God averted each time in favor of the saint. One time the Arians were on board the same ship with Athanasius and about to board another ship in pursuit of him whom they hoped to find on the other ship. Athanasius shouted to them, for they did not know him: "He is very close to you." Thinking he was on the other ship they rushed away leaving the saint perfectly safe and satisfied.

TODAY: If you put your trust in God, and cease worrying, just trust in God and depend upon Him to take care of you, He will not forsake you, provided you endeavor to serve Him meanwhile as well as you can.

SLOGAN: He is at too great a hazard who places not his trust in God.

May 3. THE FINDING OF THE HOLY CROSS

At the beginning of the second century, Hadrian had covered Calvary and the Holy Sepulcher under a terrace on which had been erected a statue of Jupiter and a temple of Venus. St. Helen ordered them razed to the ground; while digging up the soil, they discovered the nails and the cross. The miraculous cure of a woman authenticated the True Cross.

O Cross, brighter than the stars, famed throughout the world, lovely unto men, of all things the most holy, who alone wast worthy to bear the ransom of the world. — *First Vespers: Antiphon*

In the Cross is salvation; in the Cross is life; in the Cross is protection from enemies. — *Imitation: Book II*

IDEAL: You know that the Romans after sacking the city of Jerusalem had built temples and statues to their gods over the holy places. St. Helena spared neither time nor wealth to discover the True Cross of our Saviour.

TODAY: Read up the account of the finding of the holy cross and ask to give a report on it at class today. You will be honoring our Lord, St. Helena, and yourself, and you will be doing your class a great favor.

SLOGAN: We adore Thee, O Christ, and bless Thee, because by Thy Holy Cross Thou hast redeemed the world.

May 4. ST. MONICA

Born in Africa, St. Monica married a pagan, whom she converted by her virtues. Having become a widow she devoted herself to her son, Augustine, whose mind was corrupted by heresy and whose soul was steeped in sin; for about eighteen years she prayed and then saw her sorrow changed into joy.

And when He drew near the gate of the town, behold a dead man was being carried out, the only son of his mother; and she was a widow. — *Gospel: Luke 7*

Learn now to die to the world, that then thou mayest begin to live with Christ. — *Imitation: Book I*

IDEAL: St. Monica illustrates the fruits of persevering prayer. The fact that she prayed and suffered for eighteen long years should prove to us how difficult it is to win back for God a soul that has let itself go freely into sin.

TODAY: If you are praying for some person's conversion, do not lose courage; pray on, practice little acts of mortification for the same intention; know that you are doing a work most pleasing to God.

SLOGAN: He that shall convert one sinner from his evil way, shall save his own soul from death.

May 5. ST. PIUS V

It was through the prayers of this holy pontiff to the Mother of God that the Christian forces were victorious over the Ottoman forces at Lepanto. He was famous for his intrepid defense of the Church's faith and discipline, and for the spotless purity of his own life.

His glory is great in Thy salvation: Honor and great majesty shalt Thou lay upon him. — *Third Nocturn: Psalm 20*

If there be joy in the world, truly the man of pure heart possesseth it. — *Imitation: Book II*

IDEAL: A particularly energetic pope was Pius V. Everything that concerned the Church, especially divine worship, was of interest to him.

TODAY: If you have not a Missal, ask your teacher if some could be ordered for the class and get one. Nowhere else will you find the beauty that is to be found in the Liturgy. While Cecil De Mille was making the film "King of Kings" he witnessed a Holy Mass, and said he had never witnessed anything half so exquisite.

SLOGAN: Rather one day in Thy courts, O Lord, than to dwell among thousands.

May 6. ST. JOHN BEFORE THE LATIN GATE

The Emperor Domitian caused St. John to be brought to Rome and condemned him to be plunged into a caldron of boiling oil. But St. John, by a striking miracle, came forth from the torment more healthy and vigorous than before.

This is the disciple whom Jesus loved, who leaned on the Lord's breast at supper. — *Third Responsory*

Although thou shouldst have been rapt to the third heaven with St. Paul, thou art not thereby secured that thou shalt suffer no adversity: I, said Jesus, will show him how great things he must suffer for My Name. — *Imitation: Book II*

IDEAL: St. John suffered the pains of martyrdom right outside the city of Rome, but he did not die, as you know. Today the Church keeps the feast commemorating his martyrdom.

TODAY: When your baby sister draws what she calls a picture and gives it to your mother saying, "Mother, I drew this picture for you, and you are the only one who may have it," your mother hugs her and loves her — for what? Because she had the *intention* to please her very much. We cannot do anything really worthy of God, but, like little children, we can draw our awkward pictures and give them to Him, our loving desire to please Him shining in our souls all the while.

SLOGAN: Our heart is restless until it rests in Thee.

May 7.   ST. STANISLAUS, Bishop and Martyr

Stanislaus, born in Poland, was made Bishop of Cracow. He became an object of hatred to Boleslas II, whom he reproached for his tyranny and dissolute life. One day, while he was saying Mass, the prince rushed at him and slew him.

O God, in defense of whose honor the glorious Bishop Stanislaus fell before the sword of the wicked; grant we beseech Thee, that to all prayers put up to him, there be vouchsafed in all fullness the wished for answer. — *Collect*

The greatest saints shunned the company of men when they could, and chose rather to live unto God in secret. — *Imitation: Book I*

IDEAL: When his enemies tried to institute court proceedings against this saint unlawfully, he called to witness a man who was dead several years. The dead man came from his grave and bore witness, to the false accusers' confusion.

TODAY: St. Stanislaus was a priest. There is this sentence in Holy Scripture, "Touch not My anointed." God punishes almost immediately and severely even in this life any irreverence to His priests. Resolve today never to say or do the least thing ever so slightly disrespectful to priests.

SLOGAN: Touch not My anointed.

May 8.   THE APPARITION OF ST. MICHAEL THE ARCHANGEL

St. Michael appeared in Italy on the summit of Monte Gargano, near the Adriatic. He requested that a sanctuary should be erected to him where God should be worshiped, in memory of himself and all the angels, and this place became celebrated on account of numerous miracles.

> Thus we praise with veneration
> All the armies of the sky:
> Chiefly him, the warrior Primate
> Of celestial chivalry:
> Michael, who in princely virtue
> Cast Abaddon from on high. — *Vespers: Hymn*

If in the angels Thou hast found depravity, and hast not spared them, what will become of me? — *Imitation: Book III*

IDEAL: There are two feasts of St. Michael. You recall we had one in September. Persons who say that the people "thought" they saw this vision may be distrusted when they make a statement on anything they claim to have seen, for it is certainly as easy to "think" one saw another person laughing at us as to think one saw an archangel.

TODAY: By this time you have probably established so close an intimacy with your angel that you need no further encouragement. That is fine. Keep it up always!

SLOGAN: He hath given His angels charge over thee.

May 9. ST. GREGORY NAZIANZEN

On account of the extraordinary depth of sacred learning which this saint had acquired, he is called "the Divine." He and St. Basil were great friends. He was a graceful poet, a preacher at once eloquent and solid.

He was one of the latest champions of the doctrine that the Son is of one substance with the Father. No one has ever won greater praise for goodness of life, neither was any man more earnest in prayer. — *Matins: Sixth Lesson*

He attributeth nothing of good to any man, but referreth it all to God, from whom, as from a fountain, all things proceed, and in whom, as in their end, all the saints repose in fruition. — *Imitation: Book I*

IDEAL: St. Gregory was a Father of the Church, a great

friend of St. Basil. It is said of them that they knew only two paths, one to church and one to school.

TODAY: These two saints had an influence for good upon each other. So have you an influence upon those with whom you spend much time. What is your influence? Are your friends better or worse for their association with you?

SLOGAN: Birds of a feather flock together.

May 10. ST. ANTONINUS, Bishop

At the age of sixteen he entered the Order of St. Dominic. Having become Archbishop of Florence, St. Antoninus excelled in his pastoral office by the austerity of his life, his charity, and his sacerdotal zeal. His prudence earned for him the title of Antoninus of Counsel.

I have laid help upon one that is mighty, and have exalted one chosen out of My people; for My hand shall help him. — *Fifth Responsory*

Peace, therefore, is not in the heart of the carnal man, nor in the man who is devoted to outward things, but in the fervent and spiritual man. — *Imitation: Book I*

IDEAL: At the age of sixteen, Antoninus entered the Dominican Order, and spent in that congregation a life of great virtue and sanctity.

TODAY: The great majority of the saints served God from their youth. Those who put off their improvement until later may find that there is no later for them.

SLOGAN: Here and now is your opportunity; do now.

May 11. ST. MAMERTUS, Archbishop

St. Mamertus was the first to institute the Rogation Days. Through his prayer a fire that threatened to destroy the city was extinguished. The saint took occasion of this miracle to instruct the people on the necessity and efficacy of prayer.

In the midst of the congregation did the Lord open his mouth. And filled him with the spirit of wisdom and understanding. — *Eighth Responsory*

The kingdom of God is peace and joy in the Holy Ghost: which is not given to the wicked. — *Imitation: Book I*

IDEAL: When the Rogation Days are kept, will you think that this saint is responsible for their institution? Their purpose is largely to ask God's blessing on the crops.

TODAY: You think nothing of sitting down at table and having bread or vegetables, etc. Will you try to imagine a time when there would be no food? There would be none at all were it not for God's goodness to give fertility to the soil. So, when the Rogation Days come around, pray and pray hard for God's blessing on the crops that *you* may not starve.

SLOGAN: That Thou wouldst give the fruits of the earth and preserve them, we beseech Thee to hear us.

Rogation Days — About 470 St. Mamertus, Bishop of Vienne, France, introduced the Rogation Days with public processions and recitation of the Litanies, after several severe calamities had visited the country.

The Rogation Days are now considered as days of special prayer for the averting of calamities and for blessing on the crops of the coming season.

(See Ascension and dependent feasts at close of March.)

May 12. SS. NEREUS, ACHILLES, DOMITILLA, and PANCRAS, Martyrs

Nereus and Achilles were servants in the house of Flavia Domitilla, a noble Roman matron. All three of these gave their life for their faith. Pancras was a boy of fourteen in the reign of Diocletian who gave up his life also, rather than give up his faith.

This is the true brotherhood which overcame the wickedness of the world. — *Gradual*

O sacred state of religious servitude which maketh men equal to angels! — *Imitation: Book III*

IDEAL: For all that these saints have names not exactly

like Robert and Phyllis, they were courageous people who feared God alone and not men. Domitilla was the wife of a Roman magistrate who was a pagan, but it did not deter her one little bit from serving God instead of idols.

TODAY: You think the day of serving idols and worshiping mere men is over. Have you ever been deterred from obeying your own conscience because you were in the presence of some man you wished to impress or at least not offend? Idols!

SLOGAN: I am the Lord, thy God. Thou shalt have no strange gods before Me.

May 13.   ST. ROBERT BELLARMINE, Confessor

St. Robert was born in Italy in 1542. He is one of the early Jesuits, for the Company had been organized not too long before his time. St. Robert was made a cardinal, gave his First Holy Communion to St. Aloysius Gonzaga, and was read by our own Thomas Jefferson.

I preferred her (wisdom) before kingdoms and thrones, and esteemed riches nothing in comparison with her. — *Epistle*

All the hopes and desires of the saints aspired after the good things that are eternal. — *Imitation: Book I*

IDEAL: Robert Bellarmine was a past master in political science. There are many people who do not know that, nor do they know how much they owe him for some of the political science they themselves have learned. But that recognition makes very little difference so long as the facts are there.

TODAY: The more one studies of the lives of the saints the more one finds how very smart they were to concentrate on doing God's will and then to let the rest of the world go by.

SLOGAN: Work for God; then let the rest of the world go by!

May 14. ST. PACHOMIUS, Abbot

Attracted to the Christians by their charity and goodness, Pachomius, a pagan, became a Christian. Eager to live the perfect life, he became a solitary. An angel gave him a rule of life by means of which he led many in the way of perfection.

Blessed is the man that is found without blemish, and hath not gone after gold, neither hath put his trust in riches, nor in treasure. Who is he and we will call him blessed? For wonderful things hath he done in his life. — *Lauds: Chapter*

If thou aim at and seek after nothing else but the will of God and thy neighbor's benefit, then shalt thou enjoy interior liberty. — *Imitation: Book II*

IDEAL: Pachomius, a heathen, was a member of a troop of soldiers who accidentally came upon some men one day who were called Christians. He inquired what the word "Christian" meant and became a monk, and is one of the great saints of the desert.

TODAY: It was no accident that Pachomius should meet these Christians; it was God's direct plan. So, in your life, when pleasant things happen, don't take them for granted; know that God has put those things in your way to make you happy; when difficulties come your way, He sends those, too, to see if you love Him.

SLOGAN: Man must be tried by fire as gold in the furnace.

May 15. ST. JOHN BAPTIST DE LA SALLE, Confessor

Because of his virtue, his gentle nature, and the keenness of his mind, St. John was a general favorite. His love for young people inspired him to found the Congregation of the Brothers of the Christian Schools.

Novena for the feast of Our Lady Help of Christians begins.

And Jesus called a little child to him, set him in their midst, and said, "Amen I say to you, unless you turn and become like little children, you will not enter into the kingdom of heaven." — *Gospel: Matthew 18*

For thus one and the same and unshaken can he stand, directing, through all this variety of events, the single eye of his intention unflinchingly toward Me. — *Imitation: Book III*

IDEAL: Always very popular among the youth of his day for his gentle disposition and his virtue, St. John founded a religious order of teachers, called the Christian Brothers, or the Brothers of the Christian Schools. The order has flourished and exists in large numbers in our country. You probably know several of these splendid teachers yourself.

TODAY: Whether you ever intend to become a religious teacher or not, pray for "laborers in the vineyard." Will you think today, too, of what you would be doing if your teachers, or St. John Baptist, had been as selfish as you are and had thought only of themselves? Will you not think of others and do something for them that they may enjoy the blessing of a Catholic education as you do?

SLOGAN: Do unto others as you would have others do unto you.

May 16. ST. UBALD, Confessor

St. Ubald was born in Gubbio, Italy, later to become famous also through the episode of St. Francis and the wolf of Gubbio. It may well have been some of the fine influence of St. Ubald that brought St. Francis and his ministrations to the town. This saint was himself famous for his great zeal and charity to the poor.

Behold a great priest who in his days pleased God. — *Gradual*

Be not a lover of thyself, but earnestly zealous that My will be done. — *Imitation: Book III*

IDEAL: It makes very little difference to St. Ubald that

you do not know more about him than the little contained in this sketch, nor that we scarcely know how to pronounce his name. Think of what it has meant to him, since 1160 when he died, to be seeing God!

TODAY: Whether yours is a name easy to pronounce or difficult, the one thing that matters is that it be written in the Book of Life, and that it be read by the Judge who will say to you: "Come, blessed of My Father, take possession of the kingdom prepared for you from the foundation of the world. . . ."

SLOGAN: I rejoiced at the things that were said to me: we shall go into the house of the Lord.

May 17. ST. PASCHAL BAYLON

As a child St. Paschal tended sheep on the hills of Aragon. At the age of twenty-four he entered the Franciscans as a simple lay Brother. His love and devotion to the Blessed Sacrament induced him to remain for hours on his knees in prayer. Unlettered as he was, he drew such stores of wisdom and learning from prayer that he was counted by all a master in theology and spiritual science.

O God, who didst imbue blessed Paschal, Thy confessor, with wondrous love of the sacred mysteries of Thy body and blood; teach us, like him, to draw fatness of soul from this divine banquet. — *Collect*

There is not anything that I can present to Him more acceptable than to give up my heart entirely to God, and closely unite it to Him. — *Imitation: Book IV*

IDEAL: Paschal was devoted to the Blessed Sacrament all his life. He has been assigned as patron of the Eucharistic Congresses.

TODAY: Will you think for about five minutes today of what you would do without the Blessed Sacrament? Can you think of no Holy Mass, no Benediction, no Holy Communion? Why, you would lose your mind not to have anybody who really understood to whom you could tell your little worries.

SLOGAN: I could not do without Him: Jesus means more
to me
Than all the nearest, dearest things on earth
could ever be.

May 18. ST. VENANTIUS

At the age of fifteen, St. Venantius was led before Anti-
ochus. He was made to suffer cruel torments, but angels came
and assisted him. His tormentors were touched with repentance by his constancy and many were converted.

Most humbly we entreat Thee, O Lord, that the prayers
of blessed Venantius, Thy martyr, may avail to win for us
Thy forgiveness and favor, whom Thou has fed with the
Sacrament of Life Everlasting. — *Postcommunion*

IDEAL: St. Venantius was beheaded about A.D. 250 for
refusing to give up his faith.

TODAY: The only penalty that threatens you for living up
to your faith is an occasional sneer, or maybe later on a
forfeiture of your position; but, understand that God will not
be outdone in generosity, and if you endure hardship rather
than displease Him, He will see to it that you are compen-
sated in due time.

SLOGAN: God is the reward of them that trust in Him.

May 19. ST. PETER CELESTINE, Pope

Born in 1221, he retired into the desert while still young.
His virtues soon drew disciples to him and he founded the
Celestines. At the age of seventy-two, he was forced to leave
his solitude and assume the responsibilities of the papacy.
Believing himself incapable of filling this high office, he
resigned.

Behold a great priest, who in his days pleased God, and
was found just; and in the time of wrath he was made a
reconciliation. — *Epistle: Book of Wisdom*

Esteem not thyself better than others, lest, perhaps, thou
be accounted worse in the sight of God, who knoweth what
is in man. — *Imitation: Book I*

IDEAL: St. Peter was a Benedictine, who wished to escape the honors of the world. Nevertheless, he was forced from his solitude and elected pope.

TODAY: If you have noticed, those who desire honors and attention so very much usually end by drawing upon themselves contempt. It is as our Lady sang, "The mighty He hath thrust down from their seats and exalted the humble."

SLOGAN: He that humbleth himself shall be exalted.

May 20. ST. BERNARDINE OF SIENA

This saint renounced all his wealth and became a humble son of St. Francis. Traveling through towns and villages, everywhere he preached the name of Jesus and thereby wrought many miracles.

O Lord Jesus, who didst imbue blessed Bernardine, Thy confessor, with wondrous love of Thy name: moved by his merits and prayers, graciously pour forth, we beseech Thee into our hearts, the spirit of love of Thee. — *Collect*

O Light perpetual! transcending all created lights, dart forth that light from above, which may penetrate all the secret recesses of the heart. — *Imitation: Book III*

IDEAL: The burning love of this saint was for the holy name of Jesus. He had it emblazoned on a tablet which he kept exposed in the pulpit whenever he preached.

TODAY: What would you do if you heard some wicked men saying ugly things and using your mother's name? If you were big enough you might attack them, and even if you were not big enough, the love for your mother would arouse your anger so that you would attempt almost anything. Even Catholic boys and — shocking it is to say — sometimes girls use the holy name of Jesus irreverently. There is nothing to be said about it. It is simply beyond understanding.

SLOGAN: At the name of Jesus, every *knee* should bow.

May 21. ST. HOSPITIUS, Recluse

St. Hospitius shut himself up in an old tower near Villafranca. He practiced the severest austerities and lived on bread and water. He had the gift of prophecy and foretold the ravages which the Lombards would make in Gaul. These barbarians, upon discovering the saint, threatened to kill him. God protected him and the soldiers retired.

> Lo, a servant of God who esteemed earthly things but little
> And by word and work laid him up treasure in heaven.
> — *Antiphon*

For when the grace of God cometh to a man, then he is powerful for all things; and when it departeth, then is he poor and weak, and left only as it were to scourgings. — *Imitation: Book II*

IDEAL: St. Hospitius left the world to live alone. When some soldiers invaded his tower they thought him a prisoner who had been bound there; he acknowledged that he was a great sinner, but they could not harm him, because God prevented it.

TODAY: Perhaps you do not mind saying disparaging things about yourself from time to time; but how do you feel about it if somebody else says those very things about you; or even believes what you are saying? You dislike that; that is evidence of a kind of silly pride.

SLOGAN: O wad some power the giftie gie us
> To see oursels as ithers see us. — *Burns*

May 22.   ST. RITA OF CASCIA, Widow

St. Rita (Margarita), after eighteen years of married life, lost, by death, her husband and her two sons. Called afterward to the religious life, she professed the Rule of St. Augustine at Cascia. In a lifelong and terrible malady her patience, cheerfulness, and union by prayer with almighty God never left her. She is the saint of "Impossible Cases."

> I am the flower of the field, and the lily of the valley;
> As the lily among thorns, so is my love among the daughters. — *Epistle: Book of Wisdom*

But they that love Jesus for Jesus' sake, and not for the

sake of some consolation of their own, bless Him no less in tribulation and anguish of heart than in the greatest consolation. — *Imitation: Book II*

IDEAL: The mother of a family, Rita lost by death her husband and her two sons. She then entered an order of Augustinian nuns and lived there in great sanctity. She suffered intensely from a miraculous wound in her forehead. Devotion to St. Rita has been revived in the past century.

TODAY: Pray for courage when sufferings come, and for resignation in difficulties. Try to learn to take things as they come. You must anyway, you might as well be gaining merit by doing so.

SLOGAN: Be ye lords or emperors, the earth keeps turning regardless of our wishes.

May 23. ST. JULIA, Virgin and Martyr

St. Julia was a noble virgin, who was sold into slavery. Her master treated her with the greatest kindness, and Julia, on her part, served the household with the utmost care. Her master took her to Gaul on one of his voyages. She was captured by a pagan and upon refusing to give up her faith, she was tortured and hung on a cross until she expired.

Come, O My chosen one, and I will establish My throne in thee, for the King hath greatly desired thy beauty. — *First Responsory*

Let me love Thee more than myself, and myself only for Thee, and all others in Thee, who truly love Thee, as the law of love commandeth, which shineth forth from Thee. — *Imitation: Book III*

IDEAL: Though of noble origin, Julia was sold as a slave. Resigned to her lot, she proved so faithful that her master trusted and allowed her every liberty in the practice of her faith.

TODAY: You see how philosophic the saints were; if they met with an accident that deprived them of one hand, they were grateful it was not a foot they had lost, etc. If it rains when you had planned a baseball game or a hike, be grateful it is not a tornado.

SLOGAN: For them that love God, all things work together unto good.

May 24. OUR LADY HELP OF CHRISTIANS

Pope Pius V, after the famous battle of Lepanto in which the Christians gained a signal victory over the Turks, ordered that in the Litany of Loreto this Queen of Heaven should be styled, among other titles, "Help of Christians."

> Ofttimes when hemmed around by hostile arms,
> The Christian people lay all sore dismayed,
> Faith's eye hath traced the Virgin gliding down,
> To lend her loving aid. — *Vespers: Hymn*

And the more thou withdrawest from creatures, the sweeter and the more powerful consolations wilt thou find in me. — *Imitation: Book III*

IDEAL: This feast is very similar to the feast of our Lady in September. But this whole month is dedicated to our Lady. Surely, you have thought of that, have you not? This bulletin has never reminded you, fearing to offend you by mentioning anything that should be taken for granted.

TODAY: Do not allow your devotion to our Lady to assume the air of the mere fascination of school children. Let it be something that becomes a part of your life, so that later on in your law office or at your desk or while preparing a meal or getting ready to go out on the stage, you will form the habit of saying a *Hail Mary* and "In your honor, dear Mother"; you will be ever so much more successful if you do that.

SLOGAN: Show thyself my Mother.

May 25. ST. GREGORY VII, Pope

Probably no pope since the time of the Apostles undertook more labors for the Church or fought more courageously for her independence than Pope Gregory VII. While he was saying Mass a dove was seen to come down on him. The Holy Ghost thereby bore witness of the supernatural views that guided him in the government of the Church.

When His holy one called, the Lord heard him, yea, the Lord heard him and gave him peace. — *Antiphon*

Bless. and sanctify my soul with heavenly benediction that it may be made Thy holy habitation and the seat of Thy eternal glory; and let nothing be found in the Temple of Thy divinity that may offend the eyes of Thy Majesty. — *Imitation: Book III*

IDEAL: This Pope lived a life of martyrdom on account of the constant battling with princes who encroached on the rights of the Church. Though he might have won the friendship of these princes by giving in, he remained steadfast in what he knew to be right.

TODAY: You may be called a "dead one" and other names for not doing all that the crowd does, or because you obey the rules your parents set down for you; but, do not mind. Even a dead fish may swim downstream; it takes a very live one to struggle against the current.

SLOGAN: Run not always with the herd.

May 26. ST. PHILIP NERI

St. Philip left everything to serve the divine Master and founded the Congregation of the Oratory. He would spend whole nights in the contemplation of heavenly things. He loved young men: "Amuse yourself," he said to them, "but do not offend God."

My heart grew hot within me and in my meditations a fire shall flame forth. — *Gradual*

Oh, if one had but a spark of real charity truly would he feel that all earthly things are full of vanity. — *Imitation: Book I*

IDEAL: This interesting saint should be well known. You would enjoy reading his life; it is full of interesting anecdotes and of a wonderful interest in neglected little boys, who had no one to take any interest in them or plan fun for them.

TODAY: After you have read St. Philip's life, perhaps you will feel like working out a scheme for fixing up a place where children who have no place to play could come to play with some older person taking care of them.

SLOGAN: Amen, I say to you, as long as you did it for one of these, the least of My brethren, you did it for Me.

May 27.   ST. BEDE, Confessor and Doctor of the Church

Born at Yarrow in Northumberland, St. Bede entered the Benedictine monastery at a very early age. The wisdom and unction of the Holy Ghost are evident in his manifold writings. He was one of the most learned churchmen of the eighth century.

O right excellent teacher, light of the holy Church. St. Bede, blessed lover of the Divine Law, pray for us to the Son of God. — *Antiphon*

If thou wouldst persevere dutifully and advance, look on thyself as a pilgrim and an exile upon the earth. — *Imitation: Book I*

IDEAL: You read of this man in your literature. He was an early English writer; he translated large parts of the New Testament.

TODAY: Are you not more and more fascinated to note that no matter what your hobby is, there is no line of work in which you cannot serve God, save your soul, and become a saint?

SLOGAN: Do thy duty, that is best;
Leave unto the Lord the rest.

May 28.   ST. AUGUSTINE OF CANTERBURY

St. Augustine was sent to England by St. Gregory. Received by the English king, Ethelbert, at Canterbury, the capital of the kingdom, he built a monastery there and later established there his episcopal seat. The example of his life brought the king over to the true faith and St. Augustine baptized over 10,000 Englishmen on Christmas day.

Brethren, we had confidence in our God to speak unto you the Gospel of God in much carefulness. — *Epistle: Thess.*

The sufferings of this time are not worthy to be compared with the future glory which shall be revealed in us. — *Imitation: Book III*

IDEAL: This is the apostle of England. He was sent there with forty monks to convert the island. St. Gregory sent them, though he would have loved to go himself.

TODAY: Thank God today for the gift of faith. Had not some missionaries brought the faith to the ancestors of your parents you would not be a Catholic today. You can hardly imagine what it means not to have the true faith.

SLOGAN: Lord, Thou hast blessed us and filled us beyond all our meriting.

May 29. ST. MARY MAGDALEN OF PAZZI

At the age of ten, St. Mary Magdalen consecrated her virginity to Christ, whom she chose as her Spouse. She took the Carmelite habit and subjected herself to the severest mortifications. Her motto was: "Suffer and not die." She received many divine revelations.

O God, the lover of chastity, who was pleased to kindle in the heart of blessed Mary Magdalen, the virgin, a fierce fire of love for Thee, and to endow her, moreover, with heavenly gifts: we beseech Thee, enable us, who keep this feast day, in her honor, to strive after purity and charity like unto hers. — *Collect*

If, in the beginning of thy religious life, thou dwell in it and keep it well, it will be to thee afterward as a dear friend and most delightful solace. — *Imitation: Book I*

IDEAL: This is not the penitent who washed the feet of Jesus, but a nun who chose the name of Mary Magdalen when she became a nun. She loved her convent so much and was so glad to be there that she frequently would kiss the walls.

TODAY: Do you think it queer for a woman to kiss the

walls of her convent? What do you think of women who shower their affections on a poodle or an Airedale?

SLOGAN: I have chosen to be an abject in the house of my God rather than to dwell among thousands.

May 30. ST. FELIX, Pope and Martyr

This saint commanded Masses to be said over the tombs of martyrs, and it is in remembrance of this prescription that the relics of martyrs are placed in a small cavity of the altar stone. He was martyred under the persecution of Aurelian.

Thou hast loosed my bond, I will offer to Thee the sacrifice of thanksgiving, and will call upon the name of the Lord. — *Vespers: Psalm 115*

Thou art my glory, Thou art the exultation of my heart. — *Imitation: Book III*

IDEAL: St. Felix is the Pope who first ordered the celebration of Mass over the tombs of the martyrs. From that time the custom of having some relics in the altar stone began as well.

TODAY: Find out today from your pastor what relics are in the altar stone of your church; then, look up the life of that saint. Perhaps it is one whom you already know.

SLOGAN: The bodies of the saints are in the hands of God.

May 31. ST. ANGELA MERICI, Virgin

"The disorders of society," St. Angela used to say, "are caused by those in families; there are few Christian mothers, because the education of young girls is neglected." She formed a new society for the education of youth. She placed it under the patronage of St. Ursula.

Novena for the feast of Mother of Divine Grace begins.

May the sacrifice, O Lord, which we offer Thee in remembrance of blessed Angela, both implore for us the pardon of our iniquity, and procure for us the gifts of Thy grace. — *Secret*

But they that follow Thee, by the contempt of worldly things and the mortification of the flesh, are found to be wise indeed; for they are translated from vanity to truth, from the flesh to the spirit. — *Imitation: Book III*

IDEAL: St. Angela founded a religious order of women whom she called Ursulines, thus to conceal her own connection with their establishment; this she did out of humility.

TODAY: Most of us like to get credit for what we do; there is nothing wrong about that either; but, of course, there is more virtue in being retiring and humble.

SLOGAN: Not to us, O Lord, but to Thy name be glory.

PENTECOST

This has been called the birthday of the Church. It is pre-eminently the feast of the Holy Ghost.

Receive ye the Holy Ghost; whose sins ye shall forgive, they are forgiven them. — *Antiphon*

What I have promised, I shall give; what I have said, I shall fulfill, so that a man abide true in my love unto the end. — *Imitation: Book III*

IDEAL: You know that when our Lord promised the Holy Ghost, He called Him the Paraclete, Comforter, Advocate, and Consoler. We are very easily liable to neglect the Holy Ghost, but if you pray to Him in moments of distress and perplexity, you will find that He is in very truth a Comforter.

TODAY: Get into the habit of saying some little prayer to the Holy Ghost for light when you are in doubt what to do, regardless of the nature of the matter in which the doubt arises. If you pray devoutly to the Holy Ghost and make yourself reasonably deserving of His blessing in the meantime you will be much more certain about choosing in the matter of business ventures; certainly, this will hold even more true in case of things spiritual.

SLOGAN: Come Holy Ghost, fill the hearts of Thy faithful, and enkindle in them the fire of Thy divine love.

CORPUS CHRISTI

It was at the special request of our Lord to St. Juliana that this feast was introduced into the calendar to celebrate the institution of the Blessed Sacrament. It is not possible to give due solemnity to the day on Holy Thursday, immersed as the whole Church is at that time in contrition and sorrow over the commemoration of the sufferings of her divine Spouse.

How sweet, O Lord, is thy spirit, who to show thy sweetness to thy children hast given them the sweetest bread from heaven. — *Antiphon*

Who will give me that I may find thee alone and open my whole heart to thee as a friend is wont to speak to a friend? — *Imitation: Book IV*

IDEAL: This feast is Christmas all over again, and the lovely part of it is that it commemorates an event that makes each day of the year Christmas. But it is Christmas for those only who make it so. The fact that our Lord asked — we can scarcely imagine a thing like that — for this special feast, gives us some idea how very much He minds our thoughtlessness of His love. We are, of course, far too mean and small to realize what it means to have God say to us individually, "Son, give Me thy heart."

TODAY: We simply cannot understand such love, for the reason that we have human standards only by which to judge. If you are so fortunate as to live in a place where the Corpus Christi procession is held, do not miss the opportunity to join the cortege of the King.

SLOGAN: Fling out your hearts with your roses to honor Christ the Lord. — *E. C. Donnelly*

SACRED HEART OF JESUS

Our Lord asked for this feast through St. Margaret Mary Alacoque. He meant it to be particularly a feast of reparation. You cannot get His own words out of your mind, "Behold this heart that has so loved men, and yet from so many it receives naught but coldness and neglect."

Who hast willed that Thy only-begotten Son, hanging upon the cross should be transfixed by the lance of a soldier, so that His open heart, the sanctuary of divine largess, might pour out upon us torrents of mercy and grace. — *Preface of the Mass*

Let all men be loved for Jesus' sake, and Jesus for Himself. — *Imitation: Book II*

IDEAL: Disappointment in friends is the most poignant ache the human heart can endure. Realizing that all men, as is so perfectly shown in the *Hound of Heaven*, would turn to every possible creature for satisfaction of the natural craving to love and to be loved; knowing, too, how "restless is the human heart until it rests" in the Heart of God, the Sacred Heart calls through the din made by other loves, "Come to Me, all you that labor."

TODAY: The privilege is ours. But those who have had experience join their voices with that of the divine King of hearts to say, "Oh, taste and see that the Lord is sweet." Never need we fear that He might not prove true, for He *could not* deceive us, being God; never need we fear that He would not understand our particular want, being man.

SLOGAN: I could not do without Him.
Jesus means more to me
Than all the nearest, dearest things
On earth, could ever be.

TRINITY SUNDAY

All the feasts of the ecclesiastical year up to this feast commemorate some historical fact in our redemption; the feast of the Holy Trinity is, however, exclusively a feast of faith. In fact, this day celebrates the profoundest mystery of our holy faith. Until quite recently, Mother Church made scarcely any effort to present to her children the solemnity due this mystery, feeling so utterly incapable of doing anything that would in the least approach adequacy. The feast has, however, been raised to the dignity of a double of the first class. Let us worship the sublime mystery with the submission of our intellect; thank the Father, the Son, and the Holy Ghost for Creation, Redemption, and Sanctification with all the gratitude of our poor heart; and offer to the Three Persons in one God our willingness for service and obedience to His commandments.

June 1. ST. JUSTIN, Martyr

St. Justin was born of heathen parents. He was well educated. While studying, his one object was to find knowledge that satisfied the heart as well as the intellect. One day an old man met him and told him about the teachings of Christ. He bade St. Justin seek light and understanding in prayer. Justin became a Christian and gave his life for his faith.

His delight was in the law of the Lord day and night. — *First Antiphon*

Thou oughtest, then, to recall the heaviest sufferings of others, that thou mayst the easier bear the very little things thou sufferest. — *Imitation: Book III*

IDEAL: Justin had not the opportunity of knowing the true faith early in his life as you have. We who have lived as Catholics all our life scarcely realize what it means to be obliged to grope about for the truth.

TODAY: This begins the month of the Sacred Heart. The devotion to the Sacred Heart is the great devotion of this age, and particularly is it the devotion for young hearts that are so open to love and to whom a disappointment means so much.

SLOGAN: Love Him who, when all others fail you, still will not forsake you.

June 2. SS. MARCELLINUS and PETER, Martyrs; ERASMUS, Bishop and Martyr

St. Peter of this group was cast into prison and succeeded, by his example, to convert his jailer. Marcellinus baptized the jailer and his family, was caught and sentenced to death.

Erasmus is more popularly known as St. Elmo, a special patron of sailors. He, too, was martyred in the fourth century.

The just cried and the Lord heard them and delivered them out of all their troubles. — *Introit of the Feast*

It is good for us now and then to have adversities. — *Imitation: Book I*

IDEAL: The Introit of the feast today tells the whole story. In this second half of the twentieth century, we are witnesses to great effort to destroy God and the notion of God in the hearts of men. What a waste of time! "The Lord delivered them out of all their troubles." The very enemies of the Church are likely responsible for sending more souls to heaven than much effort by missionaries.

TODAY: It is assuring to know that God exists, that He is all-powerful, and that He is long-suffering and that — may He be forever praised! — He is all merciful.

SLOGAN: Pray for the persecutors of the Church that they may be saved.

June 3.   ST. CLOTILDA, Queen

St. Clotilda's wit, beauty, modesty, and piety made her the idol of the court. Clovis, king of the Franks, won her in marriage. Her sweetness of disposition, her tactfulness, and her prayer converted this warlike king. St. Clotilda was in every way a model wife and mother.

Let your light so shine before men that they may see your good works and glorify your Father who is in heaven. — *Third Nocturn: Eighth Lesson*

The perfect victory is to triumph over oneself. — *Imitation: Book III*

IDEAL: This charming queen is the loveliest saint you could wish to know. Clovis, the king, was converted by her clever understanding of how to "manage" her affairs.

TODAY: It was mainly her ability to make allowances for the peculiar nature of different people that won over her husband to a love for the faith that made his beloved

Clotilda so sweet and patient, pious and holy. Genuine piety makes us considerate of others, not selfishly wrapt up in ourselves.

SLOGAN: I strove to become all things to all men that I might win the more to Christ. — *St. Paul*

June 4. ST. FRANCIS CARACCIOLO

St. Francis is noted for his ardent love for Jesus in the Blessed Sacrament. He founded the Order of Clerks Regular, who took turns in perpetual adoration of the Blessed Sacrament. Francis was commonly called the Preacher of Divine Love.

> Gentle was he, wise, pure, and lowly hearted,
> Sober and modest, ever foe to strife,
> While in his frame there flowed as yet unparted
> Currents of life. — *First Vespers: Hymn*

Grace walketh in simplicity, turneth aside all appearance for evil, offereth no deceits, and doth all things purely for God, in whom also it resteth as its last end. — *Imitation: Book III*

IDEAL: Devotion to the Blessed Sacrament is closely coupled with devotion to the Sacred Heart for devotion to the Sacred Heart is devotion to the love of Christ.

TODAY: Using terms that we more readily understand, we may say that the Sacred Heart in the Blessed Sacrament beats with joy when the church door opens and *you* dash in even if for just two seconds to say, "I stopped in to say I love You, Lord, and I am thinking of You all the while. We are having a test in history this afternoon, and I would like to do well. I shall drop in after school to tell You of it."

SLOGAN: Even if a mother should forget her child, yet will not I forget Thee.

June 5. ST. BONIFACE, Bishop and Martyr

St. Boniface was the apostle of Germany. His zeal for the salvation of souls knew no bounds. Bavaria, Thuringia, Friesland, Hesse, and Saxony became Christian through his efforts. Fearing that he might lose the coveted crown of martyrdom, he chose to bring the Gospel to the most savage German tribe where he was martyred.

I am the true vine, ye are the branches. He that abideth in Me, and I in him, the same bringeth forth much fruit. — *Seventh Responsory*

Son, as much as thou canst go out of thyself, so much wilt thou be able to enter into Me. — *Imitation: Book III*

IDEAL: Like St. Patrick, this saint was not of the nation which he converted, for which he spent his life. But Boniface was a Christian and it was Christians he wished to make of those among whom he labored.

TODAY: Thank God for the gift of faith; there is no reason why you were not born of non-Catholic parents or in the wilds of Africa except that God has been especially merciful to you.

SLOGAN: Holy God, we praise Thy name.

June 6.   ST. NORBERT, Bishop and Confessor

Called to a life of perfection by an extraordinary dispensation of God, St. Norbert chose a retreat in a desert spot called Premontre and founded there the order that bears his name. He governed his religious family, which, before his death, numbered one thousand, with prudence and zeal.

Behold a high priest, who in his days pleased God: therefore the Lord assured him by an oath that He would multiply his seed among his people. — *Second Responsory*

For though I burn not with so great desire as Thy specially devout servants, yet, by Thy grace, I have a desire of this same greatly inflamed desire, praying and wishing that I may be made partaker with all such fervent lovers, and be numbered in their holy company. — *Imitation: Book IV*

IDEAL: You certainly know the White Fathers, as they are called, because they wear a white habit. Their real name is Premonstratensians. Look up St. Norbert today and find the account of his institution of this order.

TODAY: You will learn of the accident that turned the tide in St. Norbert's life. Learn to see a purpose in things that seem to be accidental in your life; learn to know that God wills or permits all things for your good. If they do not work out that way, it is because you do not use them correctly.

SLOGAN: To them that love God, all things work together unto good.

June 7. ST. ROBERT OF NEWMINSTER

As abbot, St. Robert guided his monks more by his example than by his words. Once when he was about to accept a dispensation from the rule, he refrained from doing so lest he might scandalize his brethren. Our Lord in person accepted his sacrifice.

> Grant, then, that we, O gracious God,
> May follow in the steps he trod;
> And freed from every stain of sin,
> As he hath won, may also win. — *Lauds: Hymn*

They were given for an example to all religious; and ought more to excite us to advance in good, than the number of the lukewarm induce us to grow remiss. — *Imitation: Book I*

IDEAL: St. Robert became the abbot of a large monastery, where his example served to retain all the monks in good discipline.

TODAY: Your companions dislike being preached at as much as you do, but if they see you doing your duty and attending to your duty as you should they will be inspired to do the same. If you hustle about this evening at home, somebody will ask, "Why the rush?" If you inform them that you are trying to get to Mass each morning during June, and doing a bit of the morning work ahead of time, you will be spreading devotion to the Sacred Heart.

SLOGAN: Actions speak louder than words.

June 8. ST. MEDARD, Bishop

St. Medard was noted for his compassion for the poor. With them he shared all he owned even to his garments. As bishop he originated the custom of crowning as May queen the most deserving girl of the village.

Blessed is everyone that feareth the Lord, that walketh in His ways. — *Vespers: Psalm 127*

I became the most humble and most abject of men, that thou mightest overcome thy pride by My humility. — *Imitation: Book III*

IDEAL: St. Medard was a bishop in France. He himself had known St. Remigius, who had baptized Clovis. You note his connection with our lovely devotion to Mary, as Queen of May.

TODAY: Two devotions should go with you into life: devotion to our Lady and devotion to the Sacred Heart. Cultivate those two devotions during your school life; no one will encourage you each day as you are being encouraged to those things now.

SLOGAN: Devotion to the Mother must necessarily be bound up with devotion to the Son.

June 9. SS. PRIMUS and FELICIAN, Martyrs

Primus and Felician were Romans. Brothers by blood, they became brothers still more when they were called upon to testify to their faith. After having been tortured, they were led to the amphitheater, but the lions who were to devour them crouched at their feet. They were beheaded.

Feast of the Mother of Divine Grace.

This is the true brotherhood which overcame the wickedness of the world; it followed Christ, attaining the noble kingdom of heaven. — *Gradual*

He who would be too secure in the time of peace will often be found too much dejected in the time of war. — *Imitation: Book III*

IDEAL: Felician was nailed to a tree through hands and feet and left thus for three days. Since this did not end his life, he was beheaded.

TODAY: Should this kind of persecution arise what would you do? If you have a chance to cheat in a test what do you do? Suppose you sit behind a student who always knows his work; do you ever copy?

SLOGAN: He that is faithless in little is faithless in that which is great.

June 10. ST. MARGARET, Queen of Scotland

Filled with the fear of God, St. Margaret brought the king, her husband, to a better life and her subjects to more Christian morals. She brought up her eight children with such piety that several became religious. Her charity toward her neighbor was admirable. She was called the mother of orphans.

The kingdom of heaven is like unto a merchantman, seeking goodly pearls, who, when he had found one pearl of great price, gave up all that he had and bought it. — *Antiphon*

Happy they who penetrate into internal things, and endeavor to prepare themselves more and more by daily exercises for the receiving of heavenly secrets. — *Imitation: Book III*

IDEAL: Another charming queen like St. Clotilda, St. Margaret was the mother of eight children, several of whom became very holy. She was loved by her subjects whom she inspired to a good life by her own lovely example. The last six months of her life were spent in intense suffering, which purified from the least stain her beautiful soul.

TODAY: There are members of your class whom you yourself consider quite holy; why not you?

SLOGAN: If wishes were horses, then beggars would ride.

June 11.   ST. BARNABAS, Apostle

A good man and full of the Holy Ghost, St. Barnabas evangelized, during twelve years, with St. Paul, the pagans in the island of Cyprus and in a great number of towns and countries. Separated from St. Paul, he returned to Cyprus where he was stoned to death.

They stand before the Lamb, clothed with white robes, and palms in their hands. They are all filled with light. — *Third Responsory*

He that liveth without Jesus is in wretched poverty; and he who is with Jesus is most rich. — *Imitation: Book II*

IDEAL: Do you remember the account of Barnabas and Paul being thought Jupiter and Mercury by the poor pagans? We have the feast of that St. Barnabas today. Though he labored much with St. Paul, he is not ordinarily mentioned as an Apostle.

TODAY: St. Barnabas is a type of man who does not work for the glory he is to get out of it, but for love of God. It never entered the mind of St. Barnabas when he worked with St. Paul and the latter was getting all the glory, "What do I get out of this?" He knew he was pleasing God and that is all that matters.

SLOGAN: All for the greater honor and glory of God.

June 12.   ST. JOHN OF ST. FACUNDUS, Confessor

St. John was favored by the Holy Ghost with a marvelous gift for peacemaking. He distributed his rich revenues among the poor and devoted his time to works of charity, to prayer, and to the contemplation of divine wisdom.

O God, the author of peace, and lover of charity, who didst adorn blessed John, Thy confessor, with a wonderful grace for reconciling those at variance; grant by his merits and intercession, that, being established in Thy charity, we may not by any temptations be separated from Thee. — *Collect*

Peace, therefore, is not in the heart of the carnal man,
nor in the man who is devoted to outward things, but in
the fervent and spiritual man. — *Imitation: Book I*

IDEAL: St. John had a special gift for making peace among
his neighbors. He became an Augustinian monk later to
prepare himself to meet his Master.

TODAY: We are told so often to prepare for death, that
we scarcely hear it any more. But, there is no second
chance, as we all know.

SLOGAN: Blessed is that servant who, when the Master
calls, is found watching.

June 13.   ST. ANTHONY OF PADUA, Confessor

Full of the Holy Ghost, St. Anthony entered the Franciscan
Order. The wisdom of his doctrine and his eloquence caused
him to be called the Ark of the Testament and the Hammer
of the Heretics. He was favored with visions of the divine
Child.

The Lord loved him, and adorned him: He clothed him
with a robe of glory. — *Gradual*

Many are His visits to the man of interior life, and sweet
the conversation that He holdeth with him; plenteous His
consolation, His peace, and His familiarity. — *Imitation:
Book II*

IDEAL: This dear, dear saint needs no introduction. He
is always at everybody's beck and call, finding things for
them, doing almost impossible things to satisfy them, and
the more wretched the suppliant and the more forsaken, the
quicker he is to hasten to their aid.

TODAY: If you have very little patience to wait for the
things you ask in prayer, make St. Anthony your patron. If
you try to be kind to others meantime, he is like a servant
right at hand for anything you must have at once.

SLOGAN: If great wonders thou desirest,
         Hopeful to St. Anthony pray.

June 14. ST. BASIL THE GREAT

After having completed his studies at Constantinople and Athens with his intimate friend Gregory of Nazianzen, he renounced the world, left his family, and entered a monastery. He was chosen Bishop of Cæsarea. His commanding character, his firmness and energy, his learning and eloquence, his humility and austerity made him a model for bishops.

O God, the rewarder of faithful souls, grant through the prayers of blessed Basil, Thy confessor and bishop, whose venerable feast day we are celebrating, we may receive the pardon of our sins. — *Postcommunion*

Fear God, and thou shalt not be afraid of the terrors of man. — *Imitation: Book III*

IDEAL: This is the friend of St. Gregory. With St. Gregory he, too, has been called a Father of the Church. He labored to root out heresy.

TODAY: Try to imagine your plight if you knew nothing of the beauties of our holy faith. How much you would be missing of the things that make life worth while!

SLOGAN: He that is mighty hath done great things to me.

June 15. SS. VITUS, MODESTUS, and CRESCENTIA, Martyrs

St. Vitus was a young noble Sicilian. Together with Modestus, his tutor, and Crescentia, his nurse, he was plunged into a caldron of molten lead. After having tested them like gold in the furnace, God delivered them from all these sufferings.

Sing ye to the Lord a new canticle: Let His praise be in the church of the saints. — *Gradual*

Because if thou die with Him, thou shalt also live with Him; and if thou art His companion in suffering, thou shalt also be His companion in glory. — *Imitation: Book II*

IDEAL: This is the most interesting group of saints of the whole year. You must read the account of their lives.

TODAY: How much do the troubles and the distress of others affect you? It is rather a dreadful thing to assume the attitude of Cain, "Am I my brother's keeper?"

SLOGAN: There is nothing so kingly as kindness. — *Phoebe Cary*

June 16.   ST. JOHN FRANCIS REGIS

At the age of eighteen, this saint entered the Society of Jesus. Impelled by the fire of missionary zeal, he labored uninterruptedly for the salvation of souls. On one of his journeys he injured his leg which was healed miraculously so that his work continued without interruption.

I will liken him to a wise man who built his house upon a rock. — *Antiphon*

Lift up thy heart to Me in heaven, and the contempt of men on earth shall not grieve thee. — *Imitation: Book III*

IDEAL: John Francis was on fire with the love of God so much so that when one time while on a missionary tour, he broke his leg, he managed to make the rest of the journey of six miles and then went straight to the confessional regardless of pain.

TODAY: When a man finishes a football game in spite of a broken collarbone or a broken nose, we think he is quite a hero, and he is. Why should not the love of God prompt heroic souls to do brave things like that; and are not such men heroes? They are.

SLOGAN: The zeal of Thy house hath eaten me up.

June 17.   ST. AVITUS, Abbot

St. Avitus ruled his monastery with prudence and zeal. By his holy example he induced others to walk the way of perfection.

Well done thou good and faithful servant, thou hast been faithful over a few things, I will make thee ruler over many things; enter thou into the joy of thy Lord. — *First Responsory*

And unless a man be elevated in spirit, and freed from attachment to all creatures, and wholly united to God, whatever he knows, and whatever he has, is of no great importance. — *Imitation: Book III*

IDEAL: Just a simple monk he was, who said his prayers devoutly, loved his fellow men, worked for God, was content with the ordinances of Providence, and now he is a saint in heaven.

TODAY: It all sounds so simple, and, if we love God very intensely, it is easy. You know what St. Augustine says: "Love God and do as you please."

SLOGAN: My Beloved to me and I to my Beloved.

June 18.   ST. EPHREM, Deacon

St. Ephrem is the light and glory of the Syriac Church. By his eloquent preaching and his musical ability he won the hearts of all. In the Syriac Liturgy he is still known as "The Harp of the Holy Ghost."

Fear not, little flock, for it hath pleased your Father to give you a kingdom. Sell what you possess and give alms. Make to yourselves bags that grow not old, a treasure in heaven which faileth not. — *Gospel*

If thou aim at and seek after nothing else but the will of God and thy neighbor's benefit, then shalt thou enjoy interior liberty. — *Imitation: Book III*

IDEAL: St. Ephrem was passionate by nature, but from the time he entered religion no one saw him angry. In his humility he refused the dignity of the priesthood. Humility made him meek and meekness kept him humble.

TODAY: Are we developing our God-given powers to the best of our ability? Whether God has given us one talent or five talents, they are ours only that we may trade with them and purchase heaven. Are we investing our talents wisely or foolishly?

SLOGAN: Look to the end.

June 19. ST. JULIANA FALCONIERI, Virgin

At the age of fifteen St. Juliana became a nun. Her life was an unbroken prayer in that she walked always in the presence of God. She was visited in her last hour by angels in the form of doves, and Jesus Himself crowned her with a garland of flowers.

Come, O My chosen one, and I will establish My throne in thee, for the King hath greatly desired thy beauty. — *First Responsory*

Learn now to despise all things, that then thou mayst freely go to Christ. — *Imitation: Book I*

IDEAL: How wonderful to have this saint of the Blessed Sacrament during the month of the Sacred Heart. Love and youthful enthusiasm are in the air during this month. Watch for the delightful list of fine young men and women who seem to cluster about the object of their love.

TODAY: Think of the Sacred Heart as of the heart of one who knows every longing of the human heart, who has felt himself every pang of the human soul, who knows what it means to be lonely, to feel slighted, to be forgotten, to meet with ingratitude.

SLOGAN: Son (daughter) give Me thy heart.

June 20. ST. SILVERIUS, Pope and Martyr

As a disciple of Christ, this holy pontiff followed Him, bearing the cross. Because of his refusal to compromise in matters of faith, he was banished from Rome. No amount of persecution could force him into submission.

But you, my beloved, building yourselves upon your most holy faith, praying in the Holy Ghost, keep yourselves in the love of God, waiting for the mercy of our Lord Jesus Christ. — *Epistle: St. Jude*

O Jesus, Brightness of eternal glory, Comfort of the pilgrim soul, with Thee is my mouth without voice, and my silence speaketh to Thee. — *Imitation: Book III*

IDEAL: St. Silverius seemed so very congenial that an Arian empress thought to frighten him easily into submission to the heretical bishops. Silverius answered firmly: "There may be many kings, but there is only one Pope."

TODAY: Be good-natured; be always in good humor; be always ready to do anybody a good turn; be agreeable to surrender your opinion for the common good; but, when there is question of right or wrong, stand by your guns, be immovable.

SLOGAN: Truth and right know no compromise.

June 21.   ST. ALOYSIUS GONZAGA, Confessor

At the age of nine, St. Aloysius made a vow of chastity before the altar of the Blessed Virgin. He entered the Society of Jesus where he became a living model of the rule. When a contagious disease broke out in Rome, St. Aloysius offered to take care of the sick. He fell a victim to his charity.

Thou hast made him a little less than the angels: Thou hast crowned him with glory. — *Introit*

If there be joy in the world, truly the man of pure heart possesseth it. — *Imitation: Book II*

IDEAL: The model and patron of youth, Aloysius strove all his life to keep the whiteness of his soul unstained.

TODAY: The very great care Aloysius took to guard the innocence of his soul seems to indicate that one is always in great danger of contamination. If you do not pray directly to St. Aloysius, follow his wise example of calling fervently upon our Lady for protection.

SLOGAN: Blessed are the clean of heart, for they shall see God.

June 22.   ST. PAULINUS, Bishop and Confessor

St. Paulinus was educated with great care; his genius and eloquence, in prose and verse, were the admiration of men of his time. God drew him on the way of suffering and sorrow. He offered himself as a slave to release a poor widow's son.

You know the grace of our Lord Jesus Christ, that, being rich, He became poor for your sakes; that through His poverty you might be rich. — *Epistle: St. Paul*

Put thyself in the lowest place, and the highest shall be given thee; for the highest standeth not without the lowest. — *Imitation: Book II*

IDEAL: This wealthy man had been married but with the consent of his wife, who entered a convent, he left the world, gave his earthly possessions (which were slight, after all, compared with heaven which was purchased by their sacrifice) to the poor, and lived the life of a devout monk. His friends upbraided his foolishness, but their taunts did not affect him; he was satisfied that Jesus loved him.

TODAY: If you wish to do good in the world, people must like you, so if you have traits that others mind very much, correct them; but when you are doing your best and things do not turn out as you would like, be satisfied that you are trying to please God; and nothing else matters.

SLOGAN: Do your duty; that is best;
                Leave unto the Lord the rest.

June 23.   ST. ETHELDREDA, Abbess

Much against her will, this saint was obliged to marry. Upon the death of her first husband, she was forced into a second marriage. After some years she obtained her husband's consent to retire from the world. A miracle testified to the wisdom of her choice, showing that God approved and accepted her former sacrifices.

God hath chosen her, and fore-chosen her. — *Matins: Verse*

Hold fast this short and perfect word; forsake all, and thou shalt find all: relinquish desire, and thou shalt find rest. — *Imitation: Book III*

IDEAL: Though Etheldreda would have preferred the life of a nun, she was obliged to marry a king of the Mercians. After his death, she thought to be allowed to live as she had so long desired, but she was pressed to marry a second time; however, with the consent of her second husband, she was permitted to enter a convent.

TODAY: Resignation to the ordinances of Providence makes it easier to bear the little hardships that come our way.

SLOGAN: Be it done unto me according to Thy word.

June 24.   ST. JOHN THE BAPTIST

The birth of St. John was foretold by an angel of the Lord to his father, Zachary, who was offering incense in the temple. It was the office of St. John to prepare the way for Christ. Christ Himself pronounced the panegyric of the saint in the words: "Verily I say unto you, among those that are born of women there hath not risen a greater than John the Baptist."

> Greatest of Prophets, messenger appointed
>   Paths for thy Lord and Saviour to prepare,
> O for a tongue unsoiled, thy praise and wonders
>   Meet to declare! — *Vespers: Hymn*

If thou wilt not suffer, thou refusest to be crowned; but if thou desirest to be crowned, fight manfully, and endure patiently. — *Imitation: Book III*

IDEAL: This is the great patron of the French. And, what a splendid man he was!

TODAY: Read the Gospel of St. Matthew and notice St. John's straightforward manner of telling people what is what. There is no mincing of matters; St. John believed that if persons were worth while they would appreciate knowing what to do; if they were not worth while, telling them the right thing would not harm.

SLOGAN: Speak the truth, 'tis better far.

June 25.   ST. WILLIAM, Abbot

William was born of noble parents in Piedmont. Having left his family and renounced his riches he built a monastery. His holy life was spent entirely in meditation on divine things and he became famous for his miracles.

Blessed is the man that doth meditate in the law of the Lord: his delight is therein day and night, and whatsoever he doeth shall prosper. — *First Antiphon*

Look upon the lively examples of the holy Fathers, in whom shone real perfection and the religious life, and thou wilt see how little it is, and almost nothing, that we do. — *Imitation: Book I*

IDEAL: St. William wished to live entirely for God in retirement. When his cave was discovered, he fled somewhere else.

TODAY: You need not live in a cave, nor be on your knees all day to be praying always. Make the good intention and so consecrate your whole day to God's service.

SLOGAN: All for the greater honor and glory of God.

June 26. SS. JOHN and PAUL

These two saints were officers in the army under Julian, the apostate. They glorified God by a double victory; they despised the honors of the world, and gained the martyr's crown.

The righteous stand in the presence of the Lord, and are not divided the one from the other; they drank of the Lord's cup and they are called Friends of God. — *Vespers: Antiphon*

Fight like a good soldier; and if sometimes thou fall through frailty, resume greater courage than before, confiding in My more abundant grace. — *Imitation: Book III*

IDEAL: Two fine soldiers who fought for their emperor until that emperor ordered them to offer sacrifice to the gods; then, their only King was Christ and for Him they gave their lives.

TODAY: We cannot get away from the appeal that an upstanding soldier makes to us. And we are soldiers, all, in the army of Christ by the sacrament of confirmation.

SLOGAN: I am a soldier who would joust for my King;
Life is love's tournament.

June 27.   ST. LADISLAUS, King
(Also the Feast of Our Lady of Perpetual Help)

St. Ladislaus was distinguished for his chastity, his meekness, and his piety. His life in the palace was austere; he was frugal and abstemious, but most liberal to the Church and the poor.

The Lord made him honorable, and defended him from his enemies, and kept him safe from those that lay in wait for him, and gave him perpetual glory. — *Responsory*

Keep thy resolution firm, and thy intention upright, toward God. — *Imitation: Book III*

IDEAL: This king ruled an enormous kingdom wisely, but he ruled also the private kingdom of his own soul.

TODAY: What will be the advantage of counting your victories by so many acres added to your domain, if you have not mastered your own soul and saved it for your King?

SLOGAN: He that ruleth his spirit is better than he that taketh cities.

June 28.   ST. IRENAEUS, Bishop and Martyr
(Vigil of SS. Peter and Paul)

This saint was a pupil of St. Polycarp. He had the deepest veneration for his holy teacher. He listened to his instructions with an insatiable ardor, and so deeply did he engrave them on his heart that the impressions remained even unto his old age.

Stand in the multitude of the prudent priests, and from thy heart join thyself to their wisdom, that thou mayest hear every discourse of God. — *Gradual*

With good reason oughtest thou willingly to suffer for Christ, since many suffer great things for the world. — *Imitation: Book II*

IDEAL: St. Irenaeus was a bishop of the early ages who gave his life for Christ. He was a learned man and had written several treatises in defense of the Church.

TODAY: As the beautiful month of June runs to its end, we learn more and more of what others have done to return the love of Christ. Have you as much love; as much courage?

SLOGAN: No love but Thine can fill my heart, and I would burn with love of Thee.

June 29. THE HOLY APOSTLES PETER AND PAUL

Today the whole Church rejoices for "God has consecrated this day by the martyrdom of the Apostles Peter and Paul." In both the grand basilicas erected at Rome over the tombs of these two princes, who by the cross and sword have obtained their seat in the eternal senate, this double sacrifice was celebrated. Later, on account of the distance which separates the two churches, the festival was divided, St. Peter being more especially honored on June 29, and St. Paul on June 30.

Triduum for the Feast of the Visitation begins.

> Fathers of mighty Rome, whose word
> Shall pass the doom of life or death,
> By humble cross and bleeding sword.
> Well have they won their laurel wreath.
> — *Vespers: Hymn*

Humble contrition for sins is an acceptable sacrifice to Thee, Lord, of far sweeter odor in Thy sight than the burning of frankincense. — *Imitation: Book III*

IDEAL: Though the two princes were martyred on the same day, this day is especially dedicated to St. Peter. Dear, impetuous, excitable St. Peter, on fire with love for his Master; who can help but to love him?

TODAY: Read any one of the Gospel stories, preferably St. Mark's, and watch St. Peter all the way through. If you are open to impression at all, you will be fired to throw every ounce of energy into working for Christ; every fiber of your being will vibrate with love for him; every pulsation of your heart will throb for Christ.

SLOGAN: I would my heart were a burning fire to burn itself out for Thee.

June 30.   COMMEMORATION OF ST. PAUL

"The Tiber, on entering Rome," writes an ancient poet, "salutes the Basilica of St. Peter and, on leaving it, that of St. Paul. The heavenly doorkeeper has built his sacred abode at the gates of the eternal city which is an image of heaven. On the opposite side, the ramparts are protected by Paul's portico: Rome is between the two." With Peter, the new Moses, leader of the new Israel, is associated Paul, the new Aaron, more eloquent than the first, chosen from his mother's womb to announce to the Gentiles the riches of the grace of Christ.

O Holy Apostle Paul, preacher of the truth, and teacher of the Gentiles, pray for us to God who hath chosen thee. — *Antiphon*

But true glory and holy exultation is to glory in Thee, and not in oneself. — *Imitation: Book III*

IDEAL: What shall we say of St. Paul? Read his epistles. There is not a thing St. Paul does not know; there is not a thing he cannot do. And he acquired all those skills purposely that he might use them as a means for winning souls for Christ.

TODAY: Take your New Testament today and read any one of the epistles of St. Paul. You'll scarcely be able to stop; they are so fascinating. If you want a type of lover of Christ, St. Paul's is the best example.

SLOGAN: By the grace of God, I am what I am, and His grace has not been void in me. — *St. Paul*

July 1. MOST PRECIOUS BLOOD OF OUR LORD

The whole month of July is devoted to the Most Precious Blood, but this first day of the month reminds us every year that at this date, in 1849, the Revolution which had driven the pope from Rome was happily ended. To perpetuate the memory of this triumph and to show that it was due to the Saviour's merits, Pius IX, at the time a refugee at Gaeta, instituted the feast of the Precious Blood. The liturgy of today reminds us of all the circumstances in which our Lord's precious blood was shed.

Brethren, Christ being come, a high priest of the good things to come, by a greater and more perfect tabernacle not made with hands, that is, not of this creation, neither by the blood of goats or of lambs, but by His own Blood, entered once into the holy of holies, having obtained eternal redemption. — *Vespers*

He that eateth My Flesh and drinketh My Blood abideth in Me and I in him. — *Imitation: Book IV*

IDEAL: In June, all our devotions were centered on the Sacred Heart. It is the Sacred Heart that makes this adorable blood circulate through the body of our Lord.

TODAY: Dearest Jesus, suffer not my tongue which has been and is so often blessed with Thy Precious Body and Blood, to speak well of myself or ill of others, so that no uncharitable word may be recorded in the "Book of Life" on the Day of Judgment. Accept all the victories I gain over my tongue as a preparation for my next Holy Communion.

SLOGAN: Save me by Thy Precious Blood.

July 2. THE VISITATION OF THE BLESSED VIRGIN MARY

The Angel Gabriel had announced to Mary that God

143

would soon give a son to Elizabeth. The Blessed Virgin at once went to Hebron, where her cousin resided. That is the mystery of the Visitation, which is celebrated on the day following the octave of the Nativity of St. John the Baptist.

My soul doth magnify the Lord; and my spirit hath rejoiced in God my Saviour. — *Gospel*

What shall I give Thee for all these thousand favors? Would that I could serve Thee all the days of my life. — *Imitation: Book III*

IDEAL: It was on this day that the Blessed Virgin expressed the exultation of her heart in that beautiful canticle, the *Magnificat*. It was on this day, too, that Elizabeth first used the words which we repeat so often, "Blessed art thou among women and blessed is the fruit of thy womb."

TODAY: If you are not familiar with the *Magnificat,* don't fail to become acquainted with this literary masterpiece. Say the *Hail Mary* with special fervor today.

SLOGAN: Holy Mary, Mother of God, pray for us sinners *now* and at the hour of our death.

July 3.   ST. LEO II, Pope and Confessor

St. Leo was a great musician. When he became pope he devoted his musical talent to perfecting the melodies of the psalms and hymns of the Church. By his example and his preaching he led others to the practice of virtue.

I will clothe her priests with salvation: and her saints shall rejoice with exceeding great joy. There will I bring forth a horn to David: I have prepared a lamp for my anointed. — *Gradual*

See how far yet thou art from true charity and humility; which knoweth not how to feel anger or indignation against anyone but oneself. — *Imitation: Book II*

IDEAL: Amid all the cares and business of the papacy this saint found time to help the needy and the poor. Those in distress found in him a father and a friend.

TODAY: To read about virtue is one thing; actually to practice virtue is quite another thing. Can you remain sweet tempered and considerate if others bother you when you are very, very busy? Try it.

SLOGAN: Blessed are the meek.

July 4. ST. BERTHA, Widow and Abbess

This saint was a remarkable woman. Descended from a line of kings, she was the mother of two saints, SS. Gertrude and Deotila. After her husband's death she became a nun, devoted her wealth to the erection of churches and convents, and spent her last years in entire seclusion in a convent cell.

Who shall find a valiant woman? Far and from the uttermost coasts is the price of her. The heart of her husband trusteth in her, and he shall have no need of spoils. — *Epistle*

Oh, how great thanks am I bound to render unto Thee, for Thou hast vouchsafed to show me and all the faithful a right and a good way to Thine everlasting kingdom. — *Imitation: Book III*

IDEAL: St. Bertha shows us how much good can be accomplished by those who are ever on the alert to further the greater glory of God. As mother in her home and as nun in her convent she had one aim in view — to do something for God.

TODAY: At least five times today stop for just a second and ask yourself: Why am I doing this?

SLOGAN: All for the greater honor and glory of God.

July 5. ST. ANTONY-MARY ZACCARIA, Confessor

Antony-Mary was born of a noble family in Cremona. Two characteristics made him a leader among his school fellows — keenness of intellect and integrity of life. The degree of doctor of medicine was conferred on him by the University of Padua. He founded the Order of Clerks Regular.

Let no man despise thy youth: but be thou an example of the faithful, in word, in conversation, in charity, in faith, in chastity.

Till I come, attend unto reading, to exhortation, and to doctrine. — *Epistle*

It is a great thing to be even the least in heaven, where all are great; because all shall be called, and shall be, the children of God. — *Imitation: Book III*

IDEAL: St. Paul was the model and ideal of St. Antony-Mary. Like St. Paul, he strove to measure up to the full stature of Christ. He was, like the great Apostle, filled with Christ's supereminent knowledge.

TODAY: We grow like those whom we love and admire. If you want to know whether you are aiming high or low, notice the type of man or woman whom you would like to resemble. That is your answer.

SLOGAN: Aim high.

July 6. ST. GOAR, Priest

St. Goar was a holy priest who brought many to Christ by his preaching and by his example. Wishing to serve God entirely unknown to the world he shut himself in a cell. His reputation for sanctity drew crowds who came to seek inspiration and advice.

The mouth of the just shall meditate wisdom, and his tongue shall speak judgment: The law of his God is in his heart. — *Introit*

If thou wilt be My disciple, deny thyself. If thou wilt possess a blessed life, despise this present life. — *Imitation: Book III*

IDEAL: St. Goar attracted many to Christ as an active missionary. Many more came to him after he had retired to his solitary cell. We often do more for our neighbor by silent, prayerful good example than by argument and force.

TODAY: Don't argue, or contradict anyone today. Instead of attempting to bring people to your way of thinking by eloquence, try prayer.

SLOGAN: The voice of the Lord is not in the whirlwind.

July 7.   SS. CYRIL and METHODIUS, Bishops and Confessors

These two saints were brothers. To them belongs the glory of having converted the Slavs. They invented writing for their language and translated Scripture in the idiom of which they are considered the authors.

God is wonderful in His saints: The God of Israel is He who will give power and strength to His people: Blessed be God. — *Offertory*

The glory of the good is in their own consciences, and not in the mouth of men. The joy of the just is from God and in God, and their rejoicing is in the truth. — *Imitation: Book III*

IDEAL: These two saints promised under oath to persevere in the Roman Catholic Faith. Their own deep faith and personal love for Christ made it easy for them to convert others. Consider the gift of faith one of your most priceless possessions.

TODAY: Not only today but every day make a fervent act of faith. Thank God with all your heart for making you a Catholic, and live like one.

SLOGAN: If your faith were but as a grain of mustard seed, you shall say to this mountain: Remove from hence hither and it shall remove.

July 8.   ST. ELIZABETH, Queen and Widow

A daughter of Peter III, king of Aragon, she inherited the name and virtue of her great aunt, St. Elizabeth of Hungary. She bore with great patience the grief caused by a jealous and faithless husband. Her meekness and forbearance made her a power in settling quarrels and disputes.

She hath opened her mouth to wisdom and the law of clemency is on her tongue. Her children rose up and called her blessed: her husband praised her. — *Epistle*

Great tranquillity of heart hath he who careth neither for praise nor blame. — *Imitation: Book III*

IDEAL: St. Elizabeth heard Mass every day and prepared by severe austerities for her frequent Communions. But her devotions were so arranged that they did not interfere with the duties of her state.

TODAY: Even one Mass has infinite value. The privilege of being present with Christ and His Blessed Mother on Calvary is yours for the effort of getting up in time and going to church. One of your sweetest consolations at the hour of death will be the Masses you assisted at fervently.

SLOGAN: Lord, increase my faith.

July 9.   SS. THOMAS MORE and JOHN FISHER

These two men lived in the reign of Henry VIII of England and gave their lives for their convictions during his reign. St. Thomas was a humorist in the truest Christian sense, his fellow countryman Chesterton having described him as "the man who died laughing."

Our soul has been delivered as a sparrow out of the snare of the fowlers. — *Psalm 123*

The good man's glory is the testimony of a good conscience. — *Imitation: Book II*

IDEAL: How St. Thomas More must have relished the quotation from the Psalm 123: "Our soul has been delivered as a sparrow from the snare of the fowlers." Henry VIII thought himself quite tricky to get rid thus of the man who bothered his own "tender" conscience so much, but Thomas More, like Stephen, might well have "seen the Heavens open and Jesus Christ at the right hand of His Father."

TODAY: It takes huge courage to say "No" when one must to a person who has endeared himself to one through a thousand friendly overtures, but the man who hesitates is lost in a case like that. It is worth your while to pray to St. Thomas and to St. John for such courage as they had and showed.

SLOGAN: He who hesitates is lost.

July 10.   THE SEVEN BROTHERS, Martyrs, and ST. FELICITAS, Their Mother

By prayer, fasting, and works of charity, this mother merited the gift of martyrdom for her seven sons and the gift of faith for many idolators. Valiant woman that she was, she encouraged her sons who were martyred before her eyes and then suffered death.

The snare is broken and we are delivered, as a sparrow, out of the snare of the fowlers. Our help is in the name of the Lord who made heaven and earth. — *Gradual*

Learn now to die to the world, that then thou mayest begin to live with Christ. Learn now to despise all things, that then thou mayst freely go to Christ. — *Imitation: Book 1*

IDEAL: This feast commemorates the birthday into heaven of a whole family. Wouldn't you love to be sure that you and your whole family were going to heaven! Are you doing anything to make sure this will happen? This family did more than just wish this would happen; they made sacrifices that hurt.

TODAY: God may never ask you to prove your love for Him by martyrdom, but He does ask you to make little sacrifices every day and every hour of the day. Are you a hero or a coward?

SLOGAN: The kingdom of heaven suffereth violence and the violent bear it away.

July 11.   ST. PIUS I, Pope and Martyr

This saintly Pope prescribed that the feast of the Resurrection should be kept only on a Sunday which then became the center and king of all the Sundays. He did much to beautify the churches of Rome.

The Lord made to him a covenant of peace, and made him a prince; that the dignity of priesthood should be to him forever. — *Introit*

Put thy whole trust in God, and let Him be thy fear and thy love. He will answer for thee, and will graciously do for thee as shall be best. — *Imitation: Book II*

IDEAL: Like the Good Shepherd this Pope gave his life for his flock. He made every effort to have Sunday kept as the Lord's Day.

TODAY: Do you look upon Sunday as a day for a good time or as a day to be given the Lord? There is nothing wrong about having a good time provided you have given God what He asks of you by way of Sunday observance.

SLOGAN: Remember thou keep holy the Sabbath Day.

July 12. ST. JOHN GUALBERT, Abbot

One Good Friday, St. John Gualbert, escorted by his army attendants, met alone and unattended the murderer of his brother. He was about to pierce him with his lance when the murderer threw himself at his feet and begged for mercy in the name of the Crucified. John recalled our Lord's forgiveness of His enemies and let the murderer go free.

But I say to you, love your enemies, do good to those that hate you, and pray for those who persecute and calumniate you: that you may be the children of your Father in heaven. — *Gospel*

Christ had enemies and detractors, and wouldst thou have all to be thy friends and benefactors? Whence shall thy patience be crowned, if thou meet with no adversity? — *Imitation: Book II*

IDEAL: Surely it was not an easy matter for St. John Gualbert to forgive when revenge was to be had so easily. Such virtue is not attained without a struggle. This victory over himself was rewarded by a vocation to the religious life.

TODAY: Perhaps God is waiting for some act of self-denial on your part to give you a great grace. Don't miss the opportunity by your selfishness and egoism. Be heroic in little things and the big ones will take care of themselves.

SLOGAN: Fidelity in small things is genuine heroism.

July 13. ST. ANACLETUS, Pope and Martyr

St. Anacletus decreed that all bishops should be consecrated by three other bishops and that clerics should be ordained publicly. He made other laws in regard to the discipline of the Church. He is one of the large number of holy pontiffs who suffered martyrdom.

Thou has set on his head, O Lord, a crown of precious stones. — *Communion*

Little is it thou sufferest, in comparison of those who have suffered so much; who have been so strongly tempted, so grievously afflicted, so many ways tried and exercised. — *Imitation: Book III*

IDEAL: This saint was utterly fearless where the honor of God was concerned. He maintained the discipline of the Church and faced a Roman emperor with the bravery of a soldier of Christ. Dying, his only regret was that he had only one life to give for his God.

TODAY: Surely you admire fearlessness and courage. Are you fearless in professing yourself a Catholic and upholding correct principles, no matter who may be against you? Of such stuff are saints made.

SLOGAN: Dare to do right, dare to be true.

July 14. ST. BONAVENTURE, Bishop, Confessor, and Doctor

O bona ventura! — good luck, exclaimed St. Francis after he had miraculously cured St. Bonaventure of a mortal disease. This saint was remarkable for three things: his learning, his humility, and his practical common sense. He was a personal friend of St. Thomas Aquinas.

O God, the rewarder of faithful souls, grant through the prayers of Blessed Bonaventure, Thy confessor and bishop, whose venerable feast day we are celebrating, that we may receive the pardon of our sins. — *Postcommunion*

Lord, most willingly do I commit all things to Thee; for but little can my own device avail. Would that I might not be too much set upon future events, but unhesitatingly offer myself to Thy good pleasure. — *Imitation: Book III*

IDEAL: When St. Bonaventure heard that the Pope was about to make him a cardinal, he quietly made his escape from Italy. On his way he stopped to rest at a Franciscan convent near Florence. Here the papal messengers found him washing dishes. The saint told them to hang his cardinal's hat on a bush until he had finished the dishes.

TODAY: No cardinal's hat or similar distinction may be offered you today, but there will be opportunities of denying yourself the pleasure of surpassing others or appearing bright and clever. Are you strong enough to make these sacrifices?

SLOGAN: Not to me but to God be glory.

July 15. ST. HENRY, Emperor and Confessor

St. Henry, surnamed the Pious, was king of Bavaria. In a vision he saw his guardian, St. Wolfgang, pointing to the words, "After six." This moved him to prepare for death. After six years he was made king. His six years of preparation for death had fitted him admirably for kingship. He was a model ruler, an intrepid soldier, and at all times a most devout Catholic.

Blessed is the man that endureth temptation: for when he hath been proved, he shall receive the crown of life. — *Gradual*

Snatch me away, and rescue me from all unstable comfort of creatures; for no created thing can fully quiet and satisfy my desire. Join me to Thyself with an inseparable bond of love; for Thou alone art sufficient for the soul that loveth Thee, and without Thee all other things are frivolous. — *Imitation: Book III*

IDEAL: One day when St. Henry was praying in a church at Rome, He saw our Lord Himself saying Mass, assisted by St. Laurence and St. Vincent. After the Gospel, our Lord sent an angel to give St. Henry the Missal to kiss. The angel touched St. Henry slightly on the thigh and said, "Accept this sign of God's love." Ever after that St. Henry limped.

TODAY: Afflictions and sorrows are proofs of God's love for us. Look upon everything that happens to you today as coming directly from the hand of God. Joys and sorrows will then be meaningful.

SLOGAN: Whom the Lord loveth He chastiseth.

July 16. OUR LADY OF MOUNT CARMEL

On July 16, 1251, our Blessed Lady appeared to St. Simon Stock and placed in his hands the habit she wished him to wear. The Pope blessed this habit and attached to it many privileges not only for the Carmelites but also for all those who should join the confraternity of Our Lady of Mount Carmel.

O pleasant and delightful service of God, which maketh a man truly free and holy. O sacred state of religious servitude, which maketh men equal to angels, pleasing to God, terrible to the devils, and commendable to all the faithful. — *Imitation: Book III*

IDEAL: By wearing the scapular, which is a diminutive form of the Carmelite scapular worn by the religious of Mount Carmel, we participate in all the merits of the Carmelites and may hope to obtain through the Blessed Virgin a prompt delivery from purgatory and special protection in this life.

TODAY: The scapular is a visible sign that we are servants of the Blessed Virgin. You have often heard stories of how our Lady protects those who wear her scapular devoutly. If you have lost yours, get a scapular today and wear it. You know that a scapular medal may be substituted for the scapular but the medal must be blessed while the scapular need not.

SLOGAN: Don't put off until tomorrow what you can do today.

July 17. ST. ALEXIUS, Confessor

On his wedding night, St. Alexius left his home in Rome secretly, fled to the Far East, and lived on alms collected at the gate of Our Lady's Church. After seventeen years he returned home but no one recognized him. He was treated like a tramp and given a place under a stairway for a bed. After his death a paper found in his hand revealed his identity.

Godliness with contentment is great gain. For we brought nothing into this world, and certainly we can carry nothing out. — *Gospel*

It is a great honor, a great glory, to serve Thee, and to despise all things for Thee. — *Imitation: Book III*

IDEAL: The life of St. Alexius reads like a strange story. He is rather to be admired than to be imitated. When he returned home, he was treated with the greatest contempt by those who were his slaves, but contempt and suffering were his joy.

TODAY: St. Alexius was probably as sensitively human as we are, but he had schooled himself to follow divine inspiration no matter what the cost to poor human nature. Forget yourself just for one day and do as many kind acts for others as you can. The experiment will be a revelation to you.

SLOGAN: To benefit all, to harm none.

July 18. ST. CAMILLUS DE LELLIS, Confessor

St. Camillus was not always a saint. He was, in turn, a soldier, a spendthrift, a patient at a hospital in Rome, a superintendent of a hospital, and the founder of a religious order. Next to God, St. Camillus ascribed his return to God to St. Philip.

Greater love than this no man hath, that a man lay down his life for his friend. — *Introit*

He that clingeth to the creature shall fall with its falling.
He that embraceth Jesus shall be firmly rooted forever.
— *Imitation: Book II*

IDEAL: St. Camillus atoned for the folly of his youth by self-sacrificing devotion to the sick. With a woman's tenderness he attended to the wants of his patients and no demand of theirs was ever ignored.

TODAY: Friendship carries with it great responsibility. The friendship between St. Philip and Camillus made a saint of the latter. Are your friends being led to God or away from Him by your example? Don't say that you have no influence. You may not be conscious of your power but it is there.

SLOGAN: Be a friend worth while.

July 19. ST. VINCENT DE PAUL, Confessor

St. Vincent was the apostle of the poor and the destitute. But he was not only the savior of the poor but of the rich, for he taught them to do works of mercy. The work so nobly begun by St. Vincent de Paul is still carried on by the order he founded.

The harvest indeed is great but the laborers are few: pray therefore the Lord of the harvest, to send laborers into His harvest. — *Gospel*

But all the saints of God, and all devoted friends of Christ, looked not to what pleased the flesh, nor to what flourished for the time of this life; but all their hopes aspired after the good things that are eternal. — *Imitation: Book I*

IDEAL: One night when St. Vincent was going through the streets of Paris looking for the children left there to die, he was attacked by robbers who thought he carried a treasure. When St. Vincent opened his cloak to show them what he carried, they fell at his feet.

TODAY: Are you carrying burdens for others or do you make others carry yours? Be attentive today to the demands you make on the patience and endurance of others, particularly those of your own family. See how quick you are to blame others and excuse yourself.

SLOGAN: Blessed are the merciful for they shall obtain mercy.

July 20. ST. JEROME AEMILIAN, Confessor

In early life St. Jerome Aemilian was a soldier. While bravely defending his post he was made a prisoner. In his dungeon he called upon the Mother of God for help and promised to lead a better life. Our Lady appeared to him and set him free. He kept his promise, devoted himself to deserted orphan children and to the unfortunate. He became the founder of a congregation of Clerks Regular.

He hath given to the poor; his justice remaineth forever. — *Gradual*

Love is circumspect, humble, upright; not soft, not light, nor intent on vain things; is sober, chaste, steadfast, quiet, and keepeth a guard over all the senses. — *Imitation: Book III*

IDEAL: In distress, St. Jerome made a promise. Not content with fulfilling the mere letter of the promise, he did much more than he had promised. Have you ever prayed very hard for something you wanted very much, and then, when you got it, promptly forgot to say, "Thank You, God"?

TODAY: Be grateful to God even for small favors. We don't like to be considered rude by our fellow men, but are we always polite to God?

SLOGAN: A grateful soul pleaseth the Lord.

July 21. ST. PRAXEDES, Virgin

This saint, a daughter of the Roman senator, Pudens, consecrated her virginity to God and gave her wealth to the poor and to the Church. Shocked by the terrible things she saw under the Emperor Antonius, she begged God to deliver her from this life. Her prayer was answered.

Graciously hear us, O God of our salvation, and grant

that we who keep with joy the festival of Blessed Praxedes, Thy virgin, may by our feeling of loving devotion, advance in our knowledge of Thee. — *Collect*

Rejoice, ye humble, and be glad, ye poor, for yours is the Kingdom of God — if, at least, you walk in truth. — *Imitation: Book III*

IDEAL: St. Praxedes and St. Prudentiana were sisters. Though they might have enjoyed all those things which were offered the wealthy Roman, they preferred to be poor for Christ's sake and live holy and mortified lives. St. Praxedes sighed for death since it meant deliverance of earthly misery and union with God.

TODAY: Suppose you were to die today. Are you ready?

SLOGAN: Death will come as a thief in the night.

July 22. ST. MARY MAGDALEN, Penitent

Mary Magdalen was a sinner. From the depths of her degradation she raised her eyes to Jesus with sorrow, hope, and love. From Jesus' own lips she heard the words of forgiveness. She became His faithful follower and stood at the foot of the cross, the representative of the many who have been forgiven much.

I have done judgment and justice, O Lord, let not the proud calumniate me; I was directed to all Thy commandments; I have hated all wicked ways. — *Communion*

There is one thing that keepeth many back from spiritual progress, and from fervor of amendment; namely, a dread of the difficulty or of the labor that is necessary in the struggle. — *Imitation: Book I*

IDEAL: St. Mary Magdalen made her mistakes but much was forgiven her because she loved much. What a lesson and what a comfort her example is for us.

TODAY: Our falls should be an occasion for greater merit for us. They prove to us how weak we are. Let us be humble as Mary Magdalen was; make an act of perfect love of God and much will also be forgiven us.

SLOGAN: The cry of the humble pierces the clouds.

July 23.   ST. APOLLINARIS, Bishop and Martyr

St. Apollinaris was a disciple of St. Peter and was appointed by him to be bishop of Ravenna. Though this saint is styled a martyr, he did not actually lay down his life for his faith. He suffered untold torments for Christ and thus merited the glory of a martyr.

I have found David My servant; with My holy oil I have anointed him: for My hand shall help him, and My arm shall strengthen him. The enemy shall have no advantage over him: nor the son of iniquity have power to hurt him. — *Gradual*

The better thou disposest thyself for suffering, the more wisely dost thou act, and the more dost thou merit; and thou wilt bear it the more easily if both in mind and in body thou art diligently prepared thereto. — *Imitation: Book III*

IDEAL: St. Apollinaris was cruelly beaten several times and cast into prison. Torments, however, seemed but to increase his zeal for the spread of the kingdom of Christ. He knew no fear but the fear of the Lord.

TODAY: Do difficulties and obstacles frighten you? Are you easily discouraged? Place your trust in the Lord today and *do* manfully.

SLOGAN: You have not yet resisted unto blood.

July 24.   ST. CHRISTINA, Virgin and Martyr

St. Christina was the daughter of a rich and powerful nobleman. After Christina became a Christian she took the golden idols of her father, broke them into small pieces, and distributed them among the poor. Her infuriated father inflicted torture after torture upon her, but God preserved her miraculously. She was finally put to death by her father's successor.

Let the proud be ashamed, because they have done unjustly toward me: but I will be employed in Thy commandments, in Thy justifications, that I may not be confounded. — *Communion*

For with God not anything, how trifling soever, suffered for God's sake, shall go unrewarded. — *Imitation: Book III*

IDEAL: St. Christina was whipped with rods, torn with iron hooks, fastened to the rack, thrown into the sea, but God showed in her how He protects His own. No harm came to her.

TODAY: Why worry? Trust Divine Providence. Nothing can happen to you but by God's will and permission. If you are living the right kind of life, all will be well in the end no matter how dark things may seem at times.

SLOGAN: Even the hairs of your head are counted.

July 25. ST. JAMES, Apostle

St. James was one of the three familiar companions of our Lord. He was one of the three who witnessed the Transfiguration, the raising of the daughter of Jairus, and the Agony in the Garden. He was one of the eleven Apostles who died martyrs' deaths.

Their sound hath gone forth into all the earth; and their words unto the ends of the world. — *Offertory*

Without labor there is no coming to rest, nor without fighting do we arrive at victory. — *Imitation: Book III*

IDEAL: St. James was the "Son of Thunder." It was he who demanded fire from heaven to consume the inhospitable Samaritans. Impetuous, outspoken, and fearless, he loved the Lord with a consuming love.

TODAY: Everybody hates a hypocrite. Don't say what you don't mean. This evening, check over the things you have said today and see how many of them have been the truth and nothing but the truth.

SLOGAN: Always speak the truth.

July 26. ST. ANNE, MOTHER OF THE BLESSED VIRGIN MARY

St. Anne and her husband, St. Joachim, were both of the royal house of David. Their prayer for a child to brighten their home remained unanswered until they were quite advanced in years. Then Mary was born. But St. Anne had vowed her daughter to God. This vow she fulfilled when she offered the Blessed Virgin in the Temple.

Let us all rejoice in the Lord, celebrating a festival in honor of Blessed Anne; on whose solemnity the angels rejoice, and give praise to the Son of God. — *Introit*

Be Thou therefore blessed, O Lord, who hath showed His goodness to Thy servant, according to the multitude of Thy mercies. — *Imitation: Book III*

IDEAL: God made St. Anne wait a long time before He answered her prayer for a child. But how wonderful was the answer when it came. Every good prayer we say is answered. It may not be in our way but God's way is infinitely better.

TODAY: One of our occupations in heaven may be to thank God for the prayers He did not answer our way. Grandmothers are proverbially known to be friends of children. Things that mothers will deny their children are given them secretly by their grandmothers. Did you ever pray to St. Anne?

SLOGAN: St. Anne, grandmother of Jesus, pray for us.

July 27. ST. PANTALEON, Martyr

St. Pantaleon, born a Christian, fell in with pagan companions and apostasized. A zealous Christian brought him back to the Church. The penitent Pantaleon desired to wipe out the guilt of his fall by martyrdom. This favor was granted him under the Emperor Diocletian.

And all that will live godly in Christ Jesus shall suffer persecution. — *Epistle*

That thou mayst, therefore, escape the future eternal punishment, endeavor patiently to endure present evils for God's sake. — *Imitation: Book III*

IDEAL: Evil companionship was fatal to Pantaleon. From a devout Christian he became as pagan as those with whom he associated. A Christian friend was the means of bringing him back to the Church.

TODAY: Don't deceive yourself into believing that you are not influenced by the company you keep. If you are in the wrong kind of crowd, break with them today. Tomorrow may be too late.

SLOGAN: Tell me with whom you associate and I will tell you who you are.

July 28. SS. NAZARIUS and CELSUS, Martyrs;
VICTOR I, Pope and Martyr;
INNOCENT I, Pope and Confessor

The Church honors today several saints who lived at different times and in different countries. Their faith in and love for Christ made them all brothers.

God rendered to the just the wages of their labors, and conducted them in a wonderful way; and He was to them for a covert by day, and for the light of stars by night. — *Epistle*

Blessed is the man whom Thou, O Lord, shalt instruct, and shalt teach him Thy law; that Thou mayst give him rest from the evil days, and that he may not be desolate upon the earth. — *Imitation: Book III*

IDEAL: These saints suffered a short time for Christ here, but their reward is eternal. Their pain was short lived; their glory, everlasting.

TODAY: Did you ever stop to think just what it was that made work so much easier when you were getting ready to go on a picnic or a hike or a trip that you knew you were going to enjoy? You are on a trip now to a most wonderful country. Remember the end and the fatigue of the journey will not trouble you.

SLOGAN: The suffering is temporary; the reward, eternal.

July 29. ST. MARTHA, Virgin

The Gospel tells us that Jesus loved Martha and Mary and Lazarus. That alone is sufficient commendation for canonization. It was Martha's joyful privilege to serve our Lord whenever He accepted the hospitality offered Him in the home at Bethany.

Martha, Martha, thou art anxious and troubled about many things; and yet only one thing is needful. — *Gospel*

O Lord, God, my holy Lover, when Thou shalt come into my heart, all that is within me shall be filled with joy. — *Imitation: Book III*

IDEAL: Martha considered it a great privilege to prepare with her own hands Christ's meals. You may be sure that the best was not good enough in Martha's estimation when there was question of doing something for Jesus' comfort.

TODAY: You can give Christ the same personal service that Martha did. Christ Himself tells you how: "Whatever you do to the least of My brethren for My sake, you do unto Me." Then, too, Christ is still with us. Have you ever done anything to help beautify the church or the altar?

SLOGAN: Only one thing is necessary.

July 30. SS. ABDON and SENNEN, Martyrs

These saints were Persians by birth. When it was learned that they were Christians they were arrested, sent to Rome, scourged with cords weighted with lead, and finally beheaded.

In all things let us exhibit ourselves as the ministers of God, in much patience, in tribulation, in necessities, in distresses, in stripes, in prisons, in seditions, in labors, in watchings, in fastings, in chastity, in long-suffering, in sweetness, in the Holy Ghost. — *Epistle*

To him that shall overcome, saith the Lord, I will give to eat of the tree of life. — *Imitation: Book II*

IDEAL: Not much more is known about these saints than that they were martyred for professing faith in Christ. But we know that the privilege of martyrdom must be earned.

TODAY: The world need not know all about the good you are doing. Your reward will be all the greater if only God knows. He will be your reward exceeding great.

SLOGAN: Let not your right hand know what the left is doing.

July 31.   ST. IGNATIUS OF LOYOLA, Confessor

St. Ignatius was born in northern Spain. His ardent and martial nature caused him to choose a military career. Wounded at the siege of Pampeluna, he was confined to the hospital for a long time. In the absence of books of chivalry for which he had a passion, he was given the *Life of Christ and His Saints*. This was but the beginning of his life of sanctity and service for God and His Church.

I am come to send fire upon the earth, and what will I but that it be kindled. — *Communion*

Happy are they who penetrate into internal things, and endeavor to prepare themselves more and more by daily exercise for the receiving of heavenly secrets. — *Imitation: Book III*

IDEAL: After his conversion St. Ignatius laid his sword at the feet of the Blessed Virgin and his generous soul, once so eager for earthly glory, now longed only for the greater glory of the King whom he henceforth served so well.

TODAY: Don't do anything today except for the glory of God.

SLOGAN: All for the greater glory of God.

Aug. 1. ST. PETER'S CHAINS

This feast commemorates the chains with which St. Peter was bound while in prison at Jerusalem and at Rome. God in His heaven must smile at times — though surely He is used to it by now — over the attempts of some men to control others and bring them to their own mode of thought. St. Peter's chains are one evidence that it cannot be done.

Now I know for certain that the Lord has sent His angel and rescued me. — *Introit of the Mass*

Son, I am the Lord who giveth strength in the day of tribulation. — *Imitation: Book III*

IDEAL: Chains could not hold St. Peter, not even physically, when it pleased God to release him. Things like that or anything else are no problem whatever for God. God's will is done, no matter what obstacles are presented. "His state is kingly," Milton said; and it is; and there are "thousands who at His bidding post o'er land and sea without rest."

TODAY: Put your entire trust in God that He will make even "with temptation issue that you may not be tempted beyond what you can endure." Of course, even God will not force your will. He will not go beyond your co-operation.

SLOGAN: Thy will be done on earth as it is in heaven.

Aug. 2. ST. ALPHONSUS MARY DE LIGUORI, Bishop and Confessor

This Neopolitan nobleman became a doctor of law at the early age of sixteen. A mistake, by which he lost an important case, showed him the vanity of earthly fame, and determined him to work only for the glory of God. He became a priest

164

and founded the Order of the Most Holy Redeemer. His religious books evidence his ardent love of the Saviour and His Blessed Mother.

The Spirit of the Lord is upon me, wherefore He hath anointed me, to preach the Gospel to the poor He hath sent me, to heal the contrite of heart. — *Introit*

Look upon the lively examples of the holy Fathers, in whom shown real perfection and the religious life, and thou wilt see how little it is and almost nothing that we do. — *Imitation: Book I*

IDEAL: St. Alphonsus made a vow never to waste time. Many of his books were written in the odd half hours snatched from his work as a missionary, a religious superior, and bishop, or in the midst of bodily and mental suffering.

TODAY: Don't waste a minute of time today. Even such times as "just waiting" can be utilized by making little aspirations of love.

SLOGAN: They also serve who only stand and wait.

Aug. 3. THE FINDING OF THE BODY OF ST. STEPHEN

This is the feast of the St. Stephen whose birthday into heaven is solemnized on the day after Christmas. Today's feast commemorates the miraculous finding by a priest of the relics of St. Stephen.

In those days Stephen, full of grace and fortitude, did great wonders and signs among the people. — *Epistle*

Fight like a good soldier; and if sometimes thou fall through human frailty, resume greater courage than before, confiding in My more abundant grace. — *Imitation: Book III*

IDEAL: The relics of St. Stephen were discovered miraculously. Many were cured by devoutly venerating these holy relics. One lesson St. Stephen teaches us is courage; the other is forgiveness of enemies.

TODAY: The injunction: "Forgive your enemies," sounds easy but is often very hard to do. Ask St. Stephen today to teach you how to keep your life sweet and wholesome by having only kind thoughts make their home in your mind.

SLOGAN: Do good to your enemies.

Aug. 4.   ST. DOMINIC, Confessor

St. Dominic truly belonged to the Lord, as his name suggests. He is the founder of the Dominican Order. His days were spent in bringing others to know Christ; most of his nights were spent in prayer. God's blessing rested upon all he did.

O almighty God, vouchsafe, we beseech Thee, to us who are under the patronage of Blessed Dominic, Thy confessor, the lightening of the load of sin which bears us down. — *Postcommunion*

Saints and friends of Christ, they served our Lord in hunger and thirst, in cold and nakedness, in labor and weariness, in watchings and fastings, in prayers and holy meditations, in frequent persecutions and reproaches. — *Imitation: Book I*

IDEAL: It was to St. Dominic that the Blessed Virgin taught the use of the rosary. Armed with this weapon against the powers of evil, St. Dominic conquered sin and heresy and converted many.

TODAY: The rosary is made up of the most beautiful prayers we have. The *Our Father*, that perfect prayer taught by our Lord Himself, the Angel Gabriel's message to the Blessed Virgin, and all the other prayers of the rosary are truly a crown of heavenly roses to be offered to our Lady. Say your rosary today making every prayer a rose by the love and devotion with which you say it.

SLOGAN: Do well whatever thou dost.

Aug. 5.   THE DEDICATION OF THE CHURCH OF OUR LADY OF THE SNOW

By a miraculous fall of snow the Mother of God indicated to a wealthy patrician named John that she wished this church to be built.

Hail, holy Mother, who didst bring forth the King, who rules heaven and earth forever. — *Introit*

Let Thy name be praised, not mine; let Thy work be magnified, not mine; let Thy holy name be blessed, but let nothing be attributed to me of the praises of men. — *Imitation: Book III*

IDEAL: The holy manger of Bethlehem is in the Church of Our Lady of the Snow. It resembles an ordinary manger, is kept in a case of silver, and in it lies an image of a child, also of silver. On Christmas Day the holy manger is taken out of the case and exposed.

TODAY: Our Lord let it snow in the summertime to please His Blessed Mother. He hasn't the heart to refuse His Mother anything. Ask our Lady today for some favor, rather a spiritual than a temporal one.

SLOGAN: Behold thy Mother.

Aug. 6.   THE TRANSFIGURATION OF OUR LORD

Our Lord took SS. Peter, James, and John with Him to Mount Tabor. While Jesus prayed, His face became like the sun and his garments became white as snow. Moses and Elias came to talk with Him.

We look for the Saviour, our Lord Jesus Christ, who will reform the body of our lowness, made like to the body of His glory. — *Chapter*

Oftentimes call to mind the proverb: The eye is not satisfied with seeing: nor is the ear filled with hearing. — *Imitation: Book I*

IDEAL: After the Transfiguration, our Lord asked His disciples not to tell anyone about the vision they had seen until He should be risen from the dead.

TODAY: Do you sound a trumpet before you when you are about to do something good or when you have been particularly successful? Imitate our Lord today. Practice the hidden virtues rather than those that call attention. There is less danger of losing the merit for the good you do.

SLOGAN: And thy Father who seeth in secret will repay thee.

Aug. 7.   ST. CAJETAN, Confessor

St. Cajetan was the first to introduce the Forty Hours' Devotion as an antidote to the heresy of Calvin. He had a most tender devotion to our Blessed Lady. On Christmas Eve she placed in his arms the Infant Jesus. At his death our Lady came to take his soul to heaven.

Consider how the lilies of the field grow; they neither toil nor spin; yet I say to you, that not even Solomon in all his glory was arrayed like one of these. — *Gospel*

Thy abode must be in heaven, and thou shouldst look upon all earthly things as it were in passing. — *Imitation: Book II*

IDEAL: When St. Cajetan lay dying our Blessed Lady appeared to him. In profound veneration he said: "Lady, bless me!" Mary replied, "Cajetan, receive the blessing of my Son, and know that I am here to reward the sincerity of your love, and to lead you to paradise."

TODAY: Love and devotion to our Lady is a sign of predestination. Are you faithful to the devotion of the "Three Hail Mary's"?

SLOGAN: Holy Mary, Mother of God, pray for us.

Aug. 8.   SS. CYRIACUS, LARGUS, and SMARAGDUS, Martyrs

St. Cyriacus was a holy deacon at Rome who, with SS. Largus and Smaragdus and twenty others, suffered martyrdom for their faith.

Fear the Lord, all ye His saints; for there is no want to them that fear Him: the rich have wanted and have suffered hunger, but they that seek the Lord shall not be deprived of any good. — *Introit*

They shall gain great freedom of mind, who for Thy name enter upon the narrow way, and relinquish all worldly care. — *Imitation: Book III*

IDEAL: Companionship tells on character. These saints mutually encouraged one another to be steadfast in the time of trial and rather to die than to deny Christ.

TODAY: Make Jesus your best friend. By frequent Communions and visits to Him in the Blessed Sacrament, you will develop a strong personal love for Him that will show in your conduct and tell others of the companionship you are keeping.

SLOGAN: Thou, too, wast with Jesus of Nazareth.

Aug. 9. ST. JOHN MARY VIANNEY, Confessor

In imitation of his divine Master this holy priest preached the Gospel of the kingdom of Christ and cured every sickness and infirmity. His word shone like a torch and his words cured souls as well as bodies. Crowds flocked to the holy priest.

He hath sent me to preach the Gospel to the poor, to heal the contrite of heart. I became all things to all men, that I might save all. — *Gradual*

My son, hear My words, words most sweet, excelling all the learning of philosophers, and of the wise men of this world. My words are spirit and life, and not to be estimated according to human perception. — *Imitation: Book III*

IDEAL: The Curé D'Ars was far from brilliant, but he shows how much good those can do who place no obstacle in the way of God's grace.

TODAY: Get the book called *The Secret of the Curé D'Ars* by Henri Ghéon. You will find it delightful reading and inspirational too.

SLOGAN: God loveth a cheerful giver.

Aug. 10.   ST. LAURENCE, Martyr

St. Laurence was the chief among the seven deacons of the Roman Church. One of his duties was to administer the possessions of the Church, whose revenues he distributed among the poor. Called upon to deliver these riches to the emperor, he asked for three days' time. After three days he had assembled many of the poor of Rome. These he presented to the emperor as the real treasures of the Church.

The levite Laurence wrought a good work, who by the Sign of the Cross restored sight to the blind, and gave the treasures of the Church unto the poor. — *Antiphon*

Put thy whole trust in God, and let Him be thy fear and thy love. He will answer for thee, and will graciously do for thee as shall be best. — *Imitation: Book II*

IDEAL: St. Laurence was martyred by being roasted over a slow fire. His jovial spirit remained with him in his pains. To his tormentors he said: "I am roasted enough on one side; you may turn me over."

TODAY: Can you smile and remain cheerful in the midst of physical pain? It may take more heroism to be gracious when one's head is "splitting" than to fast on bread and water.

SLOGAN: The cross is a ladder to heaven.

Aug. 11.   SS. TIBURTIUS and SUSANNA, Martyrs

St. Tiburtius, a son of the prefect of Rome, was condemned to many tortures and finally beheaded. St. Susanna, having made a vow of virginity, refused to marry. Accused of being a Christian, she suffered a cruel martyrdom.

By faith the saints conquered kingdoms, wrought justice, obtained promises, stopped the mouths of lions, quenched the violence of fire, escaped the edge of the sword, recovered strength from weakness, became valiant in war, put to flight the armies of foreigners: women received their dead raised to life again. — *Epistle*

He, therefore, that despiseth one of the least of My saints, honoreth not the greatest; for I have made both little and great. — *Imitation: Book III*

IDEAL: St. Tiburtius was first thrown into a flaming furnace. The flames did not even singe the hair of his head. He was then beheaded.

TODAY: Nothing can happen to us except by the permission of God. We are in His hands. See the will of God in all that comes your way today, even in such things as the weather.

SLOGAN: God's in His heaven: all's well with the world.

Aug. 12. ST. CLARE, Virgin

St. Clare is the founder of the Poor Clares, for whom St. Francis drew up a rule. They walk barefoot, observe perpetual abstinence, and make poverty the basis of their lives. She died as the Passion was being read, and our Lady and the angels conducted her soul to glory.

After her shall virgins be brought to the King; her neighbors shall be brought to Thee with gladness. — *Gradual*

Oh, the wonderful and hidden grace of the Sacrament, which only the faithful of Christ know, but which unbelievers, and such as are slaves to sin, cannot experience. — *Imitation: Book IV*

IDEAL: The extraordinary devotion of St. Clare to the Blessed Sacrament was rewarded by a miracle. On the day when the Saracens, who besieged Assisi, tried to enter the convent, she held up the ciborium and put them to flight.

TODAY: When St. Clare called upon our Lord in the Blessed Sacrament to help her against the Saracens, He replied: "My protection will never fail you." He will never fail us either if we have St. Clare's confidence in Him. Make a special visit to our Lord today and say with all your heart: "Sacred Heart of Jesus, I trust in Thee."

SLOGAN: In Thee, O Lord, have I trusted and I shall not be confounded.

Aug. 13.   SS. HIPPOLYTUS and CASSIAN, Martyrs

St. Hippolytus was one of St. Laurence's guards while the latter was in prison. He was converted by the saint and followed him to martyrdom. St. Cassian, a schoolmaster, was delivered, with his hands tied behind his back, to his pagan pupils, who pierced him with their stilettos.

Grant, we beseech Thee, O almighty God, that this venerable solemnity of Thy holy martyrs Hippolytus and Cassian may increase our devotion and promote our salvation. — *Collect*

Wait a little and thou shalt see a speedy end of suffering. The hour cometh when all trouble and labor shall be no more. — *Imitation: Book III*

IDEAL: St. Cassian was put to death by those who should have been his defenders. There were surely some among them who stabbed only because others were doing it.

TODAY: Are you easily led to do wrong because others are doing it? Be careful today not to use the stiletto of your tongue on anyone, particularly not on the absent.

SLOGAN: The tongue is a two-edged sword that grows keener by constant use.

Aug. 14.   ST. EUSEBIUS, Confessor

St. Eusebius was imprisoned for seven months in his room by order of the emperor. He sanctified this time by constant prayer.

Come to Me, all you who labor and are burdened and I will give you rest. Take My yoke upon you, and learn from Me for I am meek and humble of heart. — *Gospel*

Oh, how great and honorable is the office of the priests, whom it is given to consecrate with sacred words the Lord of Majesty, to bless Him with their lips, to hold Him with their hands, to receive Him with their mouths, and to administer Him to others. — *Imitation: Book IV*

IDEAL: St. Eusebius was confined to the same room for seven months. Instead of complaining and making life miserable for himself and for others, he made the most of the time to commune with God in prayer and to prepare for death.

TODAY: Be optimistic today and don't complain. Bring some form of cheer to someone today.

SLOGAN: Every cloud has a silver lining; turn the dark clouds inside out.

Aug. 15.   ASSUMPTION OF THE BLESSED VIRGIN MARY

On this festival the Church commemorates the happy departure from this life of the Blessed Virgin Mary, and her translation into the kingdom of her Son, in which she received from Him a crown of immortal glory, and a throne above all the other saints and heavenly spirits. This fact was declared a dogma in 1950 by Pius XII.

The Virgin Mary is taken up into the bridal chamber of heaven, where the King of kings sitteth on His starry throne. — *Antiphon*

Thou wouldst wish to be already in the liberty of the children of God. Now doth the eternal dwelling, and the heavenly country full of festivity, delight thee. — *Imitation: Book III*

IDEAL: After years of patient waiting our Lady was reunited with her divine Son on this day. Who can describe that first embrace of Mother and Son in heaven! And the glory of the heavenly Jerusalem when our Lord led His Blessed Mother to the throne He had prepared for her!

TODAY: Congratulate your heavenly Mother today and ask her to take care of you until you arrive at the throne prepared for you from all eternity.

SLOGAN: All beautiful and sweet art thou, O Daughter of Sion.

Aug. 16.   ST. JOACHIM, Father of the Blessed Virgin

St. Joachim was our Lord's grandfather. We need know no more about him to know how great a saint the dear old man was.

O Joachim, spouse of holy Anne, father of the kindly Virgin, help thy servants to save their souls. — *Gradual*

Nothing, therefore, ought to give so great a joy to one that loveth Thee and knoweth Thy benefits as the accomplishment of Thy will in himself, and the good pleasure of Thy eternal appointments. — *Imitation: Book III*

IDEAL: How near to our Lord and His Blessed Mother St. Joachim must be in heaven, and what a sense of possession he must feel toward our Lord.

TODAY: If Jesus is our elder brother, then St. Joachim is our grandfather too. Commend to St. Joachim the one thing necessary, the salvation of your soul.

SLOGAN: But one thing is necessary.

Aug. 17.   ST. HYACINTH, Confessor

St. Hyacinth was the glorious apostle of Russia and Poland. His wonderful success in converting the pagan people of these countries he ascribed to the Mother of God for whom he had a tender devotion.

The Lord loved and adorned him: He clothed him with a robe of glory. — *Gradual*

In everything attend to thyself, what thou art doing, and what thou art saying; direct thy whole attention to this, that thou mayst please Me alone, and neither desire nor seek anything out of Me. — *Imitation: Book III*

IDEAL: When St. Hyacinth was at Kiev, the Tartars sacked the town. He was just finishing Mass when he heard of the danger. Without stopping to unvest he took the ciborium and was leaving the church. As he passed a statue of the Blessed Virgin a voice said: "Hyacinth, why dost thou leave me behind?" The statue was of heavy alabaster but when Hyacinth took it in his arms it was as light as a reed.

TODAY: If someone in authority asked you to do a thing which to you seemed beyond your strength, would you proceed to do as you were told or would you make excuses? Willing obedience makes light reeds of heavy statues.

SLOGAN: The obedient man shall speak of victories.

Aug. 18.   ST. AGAPITUS, Martyr

St. Agapitus was only fifteen years old when he was put to death by a stroke of the sword. No promise of reward could induce him to deny Christ.

Happy be Thy Church, O God, putting her trust in the prayers of the holy martyr Agapitus: he in glory pleading in her behalf may she devoutly do Thee service, and ever abide in safety and in peace. — *Collect*

For when the grace of God cometh to a man, then is he powerful in all things; and when it departeth, then is he poor and weak and left only as it were to scourgings. — *Imitation: Book II*

IDEAL: In a few short years St. Agapitus earned heaven with the glory of martyrdom. It isn't chronological age that counts with God, but degree of maturity in the service of God.

TODAY: Sanctify every minute of your life by the good intention. The good intention is the philosopher's stone that turns all our actions to gold wherewith to buy the kingdom of God.

SLOGAN: Not many but much.

Aug. 19.   ST. JOHN EUDES, Confessor

St. Eudes did much to promote devotion to the Sacred Hearts of Jesus and Mary. He founded the religious of Jesus and Mary, known as the Eudists and also the Congregation of Our Lady of Charity.

O God, who didst wonderfully inflame Blessed John the Confessor to promote the public worship of the Sacred Hearts of Jesus and Mary, and through him didst will to found new religious families in the Church; grant, we beseech Thee, that we who venerate his merits may also be taught by the example of his virtues. — *Collect*

Better is it to lie hid and take diligent care of thyself, than neglecting thyself, to work miracles. — *Imitation: Book I*

IDEAL: St. John Eudes was beatified in 1909 and canonized in 1925. Gifted with a strong personality, he used his power to attract others to the practice of virtue.

TODAY: Every saint is a strong personality. Sometimes the power of their personality is evident only after death. If you wish to develop your gift of personality, become a saint.

SLOGAN: And five of them were foolish and five of them were wise.

Aug. 20.   ST. BERNARD, Abbot and Doctor

The principal title of glory of St. Bernard is that he celebrated with ineffable tenderness and ardent piety, in his prayers and books and sermons, the varied greatness of Mary. He is called Doctor Mellifluus, the honey-mouthed doctor.

O illustrious doctor, thou light of Holy Church, blessed Bernard, thou lover of Divine Law, intercede with the Son of God for us. — *Antiphon*

Let Thy Name be praised, not mine; let Thy work be magnified, not mine; let Thy Holy Name be blessed, but let nothing be attributed to me of the praises of men. — *Imitation: Book III*

IDEAL: Every day of his religious life St. Bernard offered a challenge to himself with the words: "Bernard, why hast thou come hither?" He was honest with himself in giving the answer and courageous in regulating his conduct with all the answer implied.

TODAY: We know St. Bernard best by his *Memorare*. If you don't know the *Memorare* memorize it today and repeat it frequently. You will soon come to know what unction there is in that beautiful prayer.

SLOGAN: Why hast thou come hither?

Aug. 21.   ST. JANE FRANCES FREMIOT DE CHANTAL

The mother of six children, a widow, foundress of a religious order with the help of St. Francis de Sales, a saint; this, briefly put, is the story of St. Jane Frances.

She hath put out her hand to strong things, and her fingers have taken hold of the spindle. She hath opened her hand to the needy and stretched out her hands to the poor. — *Epistle*

Hold fast this short and perfect word: Forsake all and thou shalt find all; relinquish desire and thou shalt find rest. Consider this well, and when thou hast put it in practice, thou shalt understand all things. — *Imitation: Book III*

IDEAL: With a red-hot iron St. Jane Frances wrote the name of Jesus upon her breast that she might ever remember to whom she belonged.

TODAY: You belong to Christ. By what mark would one know that you do? You need not do as St. Jane Frances did but your conduct ought to show that you are a follower of the meek and gentle Saviour. Bow your head when you pronounce the Holy Name or when you hear it pronounced.

SLOGAN: Behold how they love one another.

Aug. 22.   IMMACULATE HEART OF MARY

This beautiful feast has been formally established in response to our Lady's implied request at Fatima. The feast was established in 1945 by Pius XII who, in 1942, had consecrated the whole world to her Immaculate Heart.

Let us draw near with confidence to the throne of grace,

that we may obtain mercy and find grace to help in time of need. — *Introit*

Above all things and in all things, do thou, my soul, rest always in the Lord, for He is the eternal rest of the Saints. — *Imitation: Book III*

IDEAL: If you accept the authenticity of the apparitions at Fatima, you have a devotion to the Immaculate Heart automatically. "If you pray," she said, "Russia will be converted and there will be peace." The thing that matters is: do you care whether Russia is converted or not, and do you want peace?

TODAY: The effort to double for Mary, as encouraged in the Montfort devotion, does many things for us. If we are conscious of trying to do things as we think our Lady would do them, it will help no end to improve the rough spots in our disposition also.

SLOGAN: Dear Jesus, I am Thine and all I have is Thine through the Immaculate Heart of Mary.

Aug. 23.   ST. PHILIP BENIZI, Confessor

Obedient to his father's wish, St. Philip studied and practiced medicine. But our Lady bade him enter her Order of Servites. He offered himself as a lay Brother but his ability was soon recognized, he was ordained a priest, became master of novices and general of his order. By flight only did he escape being elevated to the papal throne.

The just shall flourish like the palm tree: he shall grow up like the cedar of Libanus. — *Introit*

Put thyself always in the lowest place and the highest shall be given thee. — *Imitation: Book III*

IDEAL: The more St. Philip tried to flee from honors the more they seemed to pursue him.

TODAY: Seek the last place today. To do that effectively and meritoriously you must think little of yourself. Our actions are our thoughts put into execution.

SLOGAN: And the last shall be first.

Aug. 24.   ST. BARTHOLOMEW, Apostle

St. Bartholomew was called to be an Apostle by our Lord Himself. He carried the Gospel to Asia. He is said, by some authorities, to have been seized in Armenia and put to death by being flayed alive.

You, who have followed Me, shall sit on seats, judging the twelve tribes of Israel. — *Communion*

Learn to suffer in little things now, that then thou mayst be delivered from grievous sufferings. — *Imitation: Book I*

IDEAL: St. Bartholomew was flayed alive. Long years of patient endurance in the school of suffering and sacrifice had prepared him to bear this inhuman torture without flinching.

TODAY: To bear pain uncomplainingly is a mark of a strong character. Don't seek childish comfort from others by recounting all your aches and pains. Be glad to suffer in silence some little thing for love of the crucified Saviour.

SLOGAN: To suffer or to die.

Aug. 25.   ST. LOUIS, King and Confessor

Though king of France and a valiant Crusader, St. Louis led the life of a religious. He knew no fear but the fear of offending God. With his arms crossed and lying on a bed of ashes he gave his soul back to his Maker.

O God, who hast made Thy blessed confessor Louis to be a wonder of earth and a glory of heaven; do Thou, we beseech Thee, set him up as the defender of Thy Church. — *Postcommunion*

If thou hadst a good conscience, thou wouldst not much fear death. It were better to shun sin than to fly death. — *Imitation: Book I*

IDEAL: St. Louis introduced in his chapel the devout practice of genuflecting at the words in the Credo: *Homo factus est.* This custom was shortly after adopted by the whole Church.

TODAY: Do you always make the genuflection at the *Incarnatus est* remembering what you are doing? Our Lord once said to St. Gertrude: "When a man genuflects at these words and gives thanks for My Holy Incarnation, I, in turn, bend toward him and offer to My Eternal Father all the merits of My Sacred Humanity to increase his eternal happiness."

SLOGAN: Think!

Aug. 26.   ST. ZEPHYRINUS, Pope and Martyr

St. Zephyrinus is styled a martyr though he probably was not put to death. His pontificate was marked by storms and persecution so violent that he did, indeed, deserve the martyr's crown.

But when the Son of Man shall come in His majesty, and all the angels with Him, then He will sit on the throne of His glory. — *Gospel*

For His sake, and in Him, let enemies as well as friends be dear to thee; and for all these thou must pray to Him, that all may know and love Him. — *Imitation: Book II*

IDEAL: One of the great sorrows of St. Zephyrinus was the apostasy of Tertullian who had shown himself a stanch defender of the Church. Pride led to the downfall of Tertullian.

TODAY: Not he who begins well but he who ends well is crowned. The example of Tertullian ought to make us fear for our own end.

SLOGAN: Pride goeth before the fall.

Aug. 27.   ST. JOSEPH CALASANCTIUS, Confessor

St. Joseph Calasanctius showed his love for children by founding in their behalf the Order of the Clerks Regular of the Christian Schools. No sacrifice was too great for him when there was question of doing something for children.

Come, children, hearken to me. I will teach you the fear of the Lord. — *Introit*

The saints that are the highest in the sight of God are the least in their own eyes; and the more glorious they are, the more humble they are in themselves. — *Imitation: Book II*

IDEAL: After St. Joseph had spent his life for others he was accused to the Holy Office by some of his own subjects. At the age of eighty-six he was led through the streets to prison. With perfect resignation and trust in God that all would be well with him and his order he said: "My work was done solely for the love of God."

TODAY: Suppose you had been in St. Joseph Calasanctius' place, what would you have done? Be courageous enough to admit a truthful answer to yourself. You will know how far advanced you are in the school of the Crucified.

SLOGAN: To seek revenge is a sign of weakness.

Aug. 28. ST. AUGUSTINE, Bishop, Confessor, and Doctor

An ambitious schoolboy of brilliant talents and violent passions, he early lost both his faith and his innocence. The tears and prayers of his mother brought him to his senses and he became the GREAT St. Augustine.

The mouth of the just shall mediate wisdom, and his tongue shall speak judgment. — *Gradual*

But many are deaf and hardened to My voice. The greater number listen more willingly to the world than to God; and are readier to follow the desires of the flesh than the good pleasure of God. — *Imitation: Book III*

IDEAL: For years St. Monica prayed for the conversion of her son, Augustine. God seemed deaf to her prayers but He was only waiting to give her a most abundant reward in bestowing the grace not only of conversion but of sanctity upon her son.

TODAY: Don't be discouraged if God does not answer your prayers immediately. He may be waiting to give you very much more than you ask.

SLOGAN: Knock and it shall be opened to you.

Aug. 29.   THE BEHEADING OF ST. JOHN THE BAPTIST

For fearlessly rebuking Herod, St. John was thrown into prison. Herodias, the illegitimate wife of Herod, used an unexpected opportunity to obtain through her daughter Salome the beheading of the saint who thwarted her criminal passion.

The just shall spring as the lily, and flourish forever before the Lord. — *Gradual*

What I have promised I will make good; if only a man continue to the end, faithful in my love. — *Imitation: Book III*

IDEAL: Telling the truth cost St. John his life. Flattery would have saved him. But he chose rather to tell the truth than to live ignominiously.

TODAY: Are you given to flattery? Some people call it diplomacy but such diplomats have short-lived prosperity. If you have not the courage to tell people the truth about themselves, at least have the grace to keep silence.

SLOGAN: Speak the truth.

Aug. 30.   ST. ROSE OF LIMA, Virgin

The name of Rose was given to this saint because one day her face appeared marvelously transfigured and with all the beauty of a rose. Her penances and her prayers fill us with admiration.

With thy comeliness and thy beauty set out, proceed prosperously and reign. — *Gradual*

For our merit and the advancement of our state consists not in having many sweetnesses and consolations; but rather in bearing great afflictions and tribulations. — *Imitation: Book II*

IDEAL: This South American saint was especially devoted to our Lord in the Blessed Sacrament, which seemed almost her only food. All her penances and sufferings were offered for the conversion of sinners.

TODAY: The prayer you say for another may merit for him the necessary grace to save his soul. Prayer for others is the sweetest charity and is not dependent on either time or circumstance.

SLOGAN: Remember the soul of thy brother in prayer.

Aug. 31. ST. RAYMOND NONNATUS, Confessor

St. Raymond was a member of the Order of Our Lady of Mercy. He was sent to Africa to ransom Christians and gave himself as a hostage to deliver those who were in danger of losing their faith because they had fallen into the hands of the Mohammedans.

The Lord loved him and adorned him. He clothed him with a robe of glory. — *Gradual*

He that loveth must willingly embrace all that is hard and bitter for the sake of the beloved, and never suffer himself to be turned away from Him by any contrary circumstances whatsoever. — *Imitation: Book III*

IDEAL: The Mohammedans closed the mouth of St. Raymond with a padlock which cruelly pierced his lips. He was then thrown into a narrow cell.

TODAY: It might be much better for us at times to have our mouths padlocked than to be allowed to speak. Watch your speech today that nothing contrary to truth or charity escape you.

SLOGAN: Mend thy speech.

Sept. 1. ST. GILES, Abbot

St. Giles was a holy hermit who founded a monastery.

He glorified him in the sight of kings, and gave him commandments in the sight of His people, and showed him His glory. — *Epistle: Ecclesiasticus 45*

It is no small matter to lose or gain the kingdom of God. — *Imitation, Book III*

IDEAL: St. Giles tended his garden and said his prayers and loved his neighbors — and became a saint. Write your English, study your science, etc., as well as you can. Try to realize that those things are a duty.

TODAY: Let each bit of work you do today, at home or in school, be done so perfectly that it may be shown to your credit in heaven.

SLOGAN: Whether you eat or drink or whatever you do, let it be done in the name of Christ Jesus. — *St. Paul*

Sept. 2. ST. STEPHEN, King and Confessor

A descendant of those proud and terrible invaders, the Huns, Stephen was chosen by God to win over his subjects to Christ and His vicar.

Blessed is the man that endureth temptation: for when he hath been proved, he shall receive the crown of life. — *Gradual: St. James 1*

And so the desires of some are on fire after heavenly things, and yet they are not free from temptation of carnal affection. — *Imitation: Book II*

IDEAL: This king of Hungary put his kingdom under the

184

protection of our Lady. He was a most successful king, never lost a war, but never neglected a duty either.

TODAY: You need not be a king to fight successful wars, nor use a sword to slay your enemies. Control your selfish impulses and learn to interpret "Safety First" in terms of the other fellow's interest, too.

SLOGAN: Love thyself last. — *Shakespeare*

Sept. 3. ST. SERAPHIA, Virgin and Martyr

This saint sold all her possessions, distributed the proceeds to the poor, and became a servant.

After her shall virgins be brought to the king: her neighbors shall be brought to thee with gladness. — *Gradual: Psalm 44*

But what art Thou to those that love Thee? What to those that serve Thee with their whole heart? — *Imitation: Book III*

IDEAL: One need not be physically powerful nor do great deeds that call for attention from the multitude to be truly great. Real success and true greatness come of doing one's duty well. Today's saint did that; she was a woman, weak and apparently insignificant, unknown to the people who lived on the next street.

TODAY: Be especially attentive to the wishes of your parents and teachers today, so much that you forget you have any wishes.

SLOGAN: I became all things to all men that I might win the more to Christ. — *St. Paul*

Sept. 4. ST. ROSE OF VITERBO, Virgin

Even as a child this saint was directed by divine grace in a wonderful manner. To defend the Church's rights was her burning wish. This wish found triumphant fulfillment when Innocent IV was brought back to Rome.

Grace is poured abroad in the lips: therefore hath God blessed thee forever and ever. — *Offertory: Psalm 44*

Beyond all hope hast Thou shown mercy to Thy servant; and beyond all desert hast Thou manifested Thy grace and friendship. — *Imitation: Book III*

IDEAL: St. Rose was extraordinary. As a young child, she preached to hundreds of people the message of penance and love of God. A good virtuous life on your part preaches a surer sermon than any words.

TODAY: Be so quiet and gentle about your work today that your fellow students in the classroom may be inspired to do likewise.

SLOGAN: God is not in the whirlwind. — *Holy Scripture*

Sept. 5.   ST. LAURENCE JUSTINIAN

Refusing the offer of a brilliant marriage, he fled secretly from his home at Venice and entered a religious order. He induced a friend, who had come to persuade him to return home, to remain and enter the monastery.

Behold a great priest who in his days pleased God. There was not found the like to him, who kept the law of the Most High. — *Gradual: Ecclesiasticus 44*

The greatest saints shunned the company of men when they could, and chose rather to live unto God in secret. — *Imitation: Book I*

IDEAL: A rich nobleman, St. Laurence was wise enough to recognize the greater riches of God's love. He put by his paltry chests of gold and silver to plunge into the very treasure house of wealth by becoming a religious and making all the glory of heaven more surely his.

TODAY: For five consecutive minutes sometime today, think this over: Nothing goes with me to the Judgment Seat of God, to insure heaven, but a good life.

SLOGAN: What shall it profit a man if he gain the whole world, but suffer the loss of his soul?

Sept. 6. ST. ELEUTHERIUS, Abbot

St. Eleutherius was favored by God with the gift of miracles. He exorcised a child possessed by the devil. He also raised a dead man to life.

The just shall flourish like the palm tree: he shall grow up like the cedar of Libanus. — *Gradual: Psalm 91*

Whilst thou hast time, amass for thyself immortal riches. Think of nothing but thy salvation; care only for the things of God. — *Imitation: Book I*

IDEAL: This saint raised a dead man to life and worked many miracles; nevertheless when once he committed a slight fault of vainglory, he did public penance for it. It requires greater courage than we think (until we have done it) to acknowledge a fault at all; it requires more courage to acknowledge that fault among people who think very highly of us.

TODAY: Try to catch yourself during leisure moments and note what your thoughts are. It will help you get to know what kind of person you are.

SLOGAN: As a man thinketh, so he is. — *Psalms*

Sept. 7. ST. CLAUDE, Confessor

St. Claude was a prince of the royal family of France. To insure his salvation he entered a monastery and became a saint.

Blessed are those servants whom the master, on his return, shall find watching. — *Gospel: Luke 12*

Thy welfare, therefore, lies not in obtaining and multiplying any external things, but rather in condemning them, and utterly rooting them out of thy heart; which I would not have thee to understand only with regard to money and riches, but also with regard to the ambition of honor, and the desire of empty praise; all which things pass away with the world. — *Imitation: Book III*

IDEAL: By special providence, Claude was spared when robbing princes killed his two brothers. He fled to the desert and became a very holy monk, wishing no one to know of his royal descent.

TODAY: Have you ever stopped long enough to think that it was a special mercy that you were born of Catholic parents, that you may attend a Catholic school? Take time to realize your privilege and show by your conduct that you are grateful for your faith.

SLOGAN: He led him about, and taught him: and he kept him as the apple of his eye. — *Deuteronomy*

Sept. 8.   THE NATIVITY OF THE BLESSED VIRGIN

The birth of the Blessed Virgin Mary announced joy and the near approach of salvation to the lost world.

Let us celebrate with joy the nativity of the blessed Mary, that she may intercede for us to the Lord Jesus Christ. — *First Vespers*

Grant me, O Lord, celestial wisdom, that I may learn above all things to seek Thee and to find Thee; above all things to relish Thee and to love Thee, and to understand all other things as they are, according to the order of Thy wisdom. — *Imitation: Book III*

IDEAL: Can you imagine heaven today? Mother of God, Queen of the Angels, Queen of All Saints! Who ever had apparently such reason to be proud, and who was ever as humble?

TODAY: Need anyone tell you what to do on your mother's birthday? Do as your heart dictates; let your love be the measure of your sacrifice.

SLOGAN: He that shall find me shall find rest. — *Canticle of Canticles*

Sept. 9.   ST. PETER CLAVER

St. Peter Claver was a Spanish Jesuit. After his ordination he was sent to the West Indies where he devoted himself to missionary work among the slaves. He called himself "the slave of slaves." For more than forty years he served them in the capacity of apostle, father, physician, and friend. Forty thousand Negroes received baptism through his zeal.

His seed shall be mighty upon the earth: the generation of the righteous shall be blessed. — *Gradual*

When thou shalt arrive thus far, that tribulation shall be sweet to thee, and thou shalt relish it for the love of Christ, then think that it is well with thee, for thou hast found a paradise upon earth. — *Imitation: Book II*

IDEAL: He labored in the West Indies, became a saint working with people who were savages, who scarcely could understand that he was living for them.

TODAY: Train yourself to do good to others for God's sake and be prepared to be met with ingratitude. If you can stand up under a lack of appreciation when you mean to be very kind, you have one good mark of sanctity.

SLOGAN: All for the greater honor and glory of God. — *St. Peter Claver's motto*

Sept. 10.   ST. NICHOLAS OF TOLENTINO

A model of innocence and purity, St. Nicholas was induced to become a monk by a sermon on contempt of the world.

Sell what you have, and give alms. Make for yourselves bags that do not grow old, a treasure unfailing in heaven where neither thief draws near, nor moth destroys. — *Gospel: Luke 12*

What return shall I make to Thee for this favor? for it is not granted to all to forsake all things, to renounce the world, and to assume the monastic life. — *Imitation: Book III*

IDEAL: Listening very attentively to a sermon and carrying out the suggestions of that sermon made Nicholas a saint.

TODAY: Make yourself realize that this little injunction you are reading has been put here for *you*. If you were the only student in this school, there would be no one else to read it. There is a design of Providence in everything you will hear or read today. If you miss an opportunity *today,* and fail to respond to one inspiration *today,* you will miss just that much for eternity. This moment, this day, you will never live again.

SLOGAN: This moment is all. — *Anon.*

Sept. 11.   SS. PROTUS and HYACINTH, Martyrs

These two men were brothers arrested at the same time, tried for their faith, scourged to provoke compliance with the demands that they sacrifice to the gods; finally they died of their wounds in the year A.D. 260.

May the glorious confession of Protus and Hyacinth, Thy blessed martyrs, strengthen us, O Lord. — *Collect*

There I will give thee glory for the contumely thou hast suffered. — *Imitation: Book III*

IDEAL: Possibly the one thought which most strengthened the martyrs during their sufferings, after God's special grace, is that, after all, one can lose only so much blood and one can endure just so much torture and then one dies; and all of it cannot last too long, but eternity lasts forever. They have been in heaven for a good long time.

TODAY: It may require greater heroism to endure patiently the small martyrdoms which come ceaselessly in a busy day; but the same heaven awaits us as the martyrs hoped for; in fact, they are in it, waiting for us as we pray in the collect of the feast.

SLOGAN: Soul of Christ, SANCTIFY me!

Sept. 12.   THE MOST HOLY NAME OF MARY
(Triduum for the Feast of the
Sorrowful Mother)

Just as a few days after Christmas we celebrate the Holy Name of Jesus, so after the Nativity of Mary, we glorify her holy name.

And the Virgin's name was Mary. — *Gospel: Luke 1*

Oh, how great is the abundance of Thy sweetness, O Lord, which Thou hast hidden for those that fear Thee. But what art Thou to those that love Thee? What to those that serve Thee with their whole heart? — *Imitation: Book III*

IDEAL: Our Lady's name means Star of the Sea. You, perhaps, love to call yourself a child of Mary. A child always resembles his mother, if not in his features, then in his gait, in the way he does different things, and, since he thinks his mother is perfect, he tries to be as much like her as possible.

TODAY: When you rise to pray, or sit down to study, or go out to play; when you return home and help with little jobs about home; when you talk to people, try to do those things as you think our Lady would; or, imagine her looking at you while you do them.

SLOGAN: Woman, behold thy Son. *Our Saviour* (on the cross).

Sept. 13.   ST. EULOGIUS, Patriarch of Alexandria

This saint was a brilliant scholar, an authority in literature and Holy Scripture.

Blessed is the man that is found without blemish and that hath not gone after gold, or put his trust in money nor in treasures. — *Epistle: Ecclesiasticus 31*

If thou wilt derive profit, read with humility, with simplicity, and with faith; and never wish to have the name of learning. — *Imitation: Book I*

IDEAL: A brilliant student and learned man in literature and in Holy Scripture, Eulogius turned every bit of his talent to God's service.

TODAY: Be careful not to complain about anything today. Build up a little philosophy like this: If the weather seems warm, imagine how dreadful it would be if you lived in the torrid zone; if you have a toothache, how much worse, if you had an earache besides.

SLOGAN: Lord, give me patience even at this time. — *Imitation*

Sept. 14.   THE EXALTATION OF THE HOLY CROSS

On September 14, A.D. 335, took place the dedication of Constantine's basilica, an inclosure which contained both Calvary and the Holy Sepulcher. "At this date," says Etheria, "the cross was discovered."

And I, if I be lifted up from the earth, will draw all things to Myself. — *Gospel: St. John 12*

Jesus hath now many lovers of His heavenly kingdom, but few bearers of His cross. He hath many that are desirous of consolation, but few of tribulation. — *Imitation: Book II*

IDEAL: The cross on which our Saviour died was discovered by St. Helena, you recall. A basilica was built in which to place the relic, and it was carried there with great pomp on the shoulders of the Emperor Heraclius.

TODAY: How would you feel if you should meet our Saviour with His cross, and He should say: "I want *you* to carry this for Me just this one day"? That is exactly what He does when He allows you to suffer little difficulties during the day. Has He miscalculated your courage, perhaps, or your love for Him? Instead of "grouching" today, hang out a smile and say *inside*, "Thy will be done!"

SLOGAN: Be it done unto me according to Thy word. — *Our Lady*

(See Ember Days)

Sept. 15.   THE SEVEN SORROWS OF THE BLESSED VIRGIN

Mary stood at the foot of the cross where Jesus was hanging, and, as Simeon had prophesied, a sword of sorrow pierced her soul.

There stood by the cross of Jesus, His mother, and His mother's sister Mary of Cleophas, and Salome and Mary Magdalen. — *Introit: John 19*

In the Cross is infusion of heavenly sweetness; in the Cross is strength of mind; in the Cross is joy of spirit. — *Imitation of Christ: Book II*

IDEAL: Were you ever very sick so that your mother worried about you and sat up with you nights and did everything she could think of to make you comfortable? Did you ever watch a mother follow the coffin of one of her children to the grave? Wasn't it painful even for you to see her sorrow? Jesus was our Lady's Son. *You* had a share in His death, and, hence, *you* helped to make our Lady's sorrows.

TODAY: Be especially kind to someone (outside of school) who will probably not appreciate your kindness or who may even say sharp things to you in return. Do not complain even to one person about hurt feelings today, regardless of who hurts them.

SLOGAN: Forgive us our trespasses as we forgive those who trespass against us. — *Our Father*

Sept. 16.   ST. CYPRIAN, Bishop and Martyr

This saint was a convert. He was a genius. St. Jerome says that his works are more brilliant than the sun. His name is listed in the Canon of the Mass.

And though in the sight of men they suffered torments, their hope is full of immortality. Afflicted in a few things, in many they shall be awarded: because God hath tried them, and found them worthy of Himself. — *Epistle: Wisdom 3*

This is not man's power, but the grace of Christ; which doth and can effect such great things in frail flesh, and that what it naturally abhors and flies, even this, through fervor of spirit, it now embraces and loves. — *Imitation: Book II*

IDEAL: Born of pagan parents, he received the wondrous gift of faith. He was so brilliant that he and his works became known to the whole of the Christian and the pagan world of learning of his time and long after. It did not make him foolishly vain, however.

TODAY: Take a sane view of things. People who have accomplishments never need to "show off" because those accomplishments are great enough to be noticed without effort on the part of the possessor. Only the person who "makes believe" must show off to get any attention whatsoever. See how many times today you can catch yourself "putting on airs."

SLOGAN: What fools ye mortals be! — *Shakespeare*

Sept. 17. THE IMPRESSION OF THE STIGMATA ON THE BODY OF ST. FRANCIS

In order that St. Francis might become an example to us, all of his love for Christ Crucified, five wounds, resembling those of Jesus on the cross, appeared on his hands, feet, and side.

But God forbid that I should glory, save in the cross of our Lord Jesus Christ: by whom the world is crucified to me, and I to the world. — *Introit: Galatians 6*

Set thyself then, like a good and faithful servant of Christ, to bear manfully the Cross of the Lord, for the love of Him who was crucified for thee. — *Imitation: Book II*

IDEAL: St. Francis had been one of the gayest young men of his time. Not any of you probably will ever learn to dance as gracefully, nor to fence as dexterously as Francis of Assisi. But, when he resolved to follow Christ, he followed Christ and became, as it is claimed, the closest copy of the Saviour the world has ever known.

TODAY: Forbid yourself thinking that "some people have all the luck." Students, like *you*, from homes like *yours*, with a temper like *yours*, and troubles likes *yours*, have become great saints. You can become one as well. All that is necessary is this: you must *want* to be a saint. But — if you were at the foot of a tall stairway and wanted to get to the top, you would not get there by merely wishing it, would you, unless someone carried you up? Well, no one will carry you to sanctity. You must walk up.

SLOGAN: Would you be a saint? Will it! — *St. Benedict's advice to his sister*

Sept. 18. ST. JOSEPH CUPERTINO, Confessor

St. Joseph was a Franciscan who had the gift of levitation. When he saw a picture of our Lady in the dome of the church, he was lifted from the ground to the cupola, and hence has been called the special patron of fliers. What is far more important, however, is that he is known for his great humility, patience, and penance. He died in 1660, time of the Stuarts in England, remember?

Mercifully grant that we may be lifted up above all earthly desires through the merits and example of Thy seraphic confessor. — *Collect*

First, keep thyself in peace and then thou wilt be able to bring others to peace. — *Imitation: Book I*

IDEAL: St. Joseph's flying up into the cupola of the church must have created quite a sensation, but that was something done principally by God who suspended the law of gravity temporarily for His saint. You can gain far more merit by your effort, assisted by grace, of course, to keep from flying off the handle when you have been particularly irritated.

TODAY: Nobody can know how it feels to be suddenly lifted into the air by some propulsion outside oneself; but most of us know the feeling of keeping our feet on the ground when we are very near taking off into the upper regions of a hot temper.

SLOGAN: He that ruleth his spirit is greater than he that taketh cities.

Sept. 19. ST. JANUARIUS and HIS COMPANIONS

From the nineteenth to the twenty-sixth of September, the blood of St. Januarius preserved in a phial liquefies when brought near his body. He and his companions were martyred.

But I say to you, My friends: Do not be afraid of those

who kill the body, and after that have nothing more that they can do. — *Gospel: Luke 12*

Give me courage to resist, patience to endure, and constancy to persevere. — *Imitation: Book III*

IDEAL: There is power in a "gang." Usually all the members do the same things in the same way. Januarius was the leader of such a gang. They were all upstanding young men who believed in Christ and were proud of their faith and of their ideal, Christ. St. Januarius was so wonderful and so good that his whole group followed him anywhere and when he was put to death for his faith, his companions were so inspired by his example that they stood torture and death bravely just as their leader had done.

TODAY: Watch the students in your class today to see what things they do better than you and then try to copy them. Do the right things they do better than you. If you notice anybody doing what he should not, profit by his example and don't do worse.

SLOGAN: Make it like unto the pattern I have shown you on the mount. — *God's direction to Moses*

Sept. 20. ST. EUSTACE and HIS COMPANIONS, Martyrs

St. Eustace was a general in the army of the Emperor Trajan. Returning victorious from an expedition, he refused to thank the gods for this triumph. He and his wife and children were exposed to the lions. St. Eustace is one of the fourteen auxiliary saints.

Our soul hath been delivered as a sparrow out of the snare of the fowlers. — *Gradual: Psalm 123*

They hated their lives in this world, that they might keep them unto life eternal. — *Imitation: Book I*

IDEAL: A general in the Roman army, he fought battles for his emperor and risked his life for his empire, but when he was commanded to pour a grain of incense on the coals to honor the gods, he refused. He was martyred; also his wife and children.

TODAY: When someone says to you: "Come on, let's do so-and-so," what do you do? Find out today if you are a tag-along or if, like St. Eustace, you obey when you should, and refuse to obey when you should refuse, regardless of consequences. If you find you are a tag-along, set about acquiring a head of your own.

SLOGAN: Be not as the dumb driven cattle; be a hero in the strife. — *Longfellow*

Sept. 21. ST. MATTHEW, Apostle and Evangelist

St. Matthew wrote one of the four Gospels. He is represented by the young man, because he commences his Gospel by the line of ancestors from whom Jesus descended as man. His name is in the Canon of the Mass.

Now as Jesus passed on from there, He saw a man named Matthew sitting in the tax-collector's place, and said to him, "Follow Me." And he arose and followed Him. — *Gospel: Matthew 9*

Oh, how many and grievous tribulations did the Apostles suffer, and the Martyrs, and Confessors, and Virgins, and all the rest who resolved to follow the steps of Christ. — *Imitation: Book I*

IDEAL: St. Matthew was Levi, a rich taxgatherer. Our Saviour passed his booth one day, looked in at the little window, and said two words, "Follow Me!" That was all. Levi gathered up his money, went to his officials, turned in the money, resigned his position, and followed Christ. You notice he wasted no time wondering, "If I could only be real sure that I have a vocation," etc. He heard the call and went.

TODAY: Perhaps you have noticed that when people set about finding a suitable mate for life, they do not seem to wonder a great deal whether they are "called" for that life or not. Have you ever felt you would like to serve God more directly in the religious life? One in every 3000 is said to have the call. Laborers are needed in the vineyard. Pray today *definitely* for light to know your own vocation, and pray for the missionaries in foreign fields. Add one *Hail Mary* for your teachers.

SLOGAN: Pray, therefore, the Lord of the harvest that He send laborers into His vineyard. — *Our Lord to the Apostles*

Sept. 22.   ST. THOMAS OF VILLANOVA, Bishop and Confessor

St. Thomas came of a very wealthy family. Because he had a great deal of good sense, he used his wealth in works of charity especially for poor girls. He belonged to the same Order as Martin Luther and lived at the same time in the sixteenth century. St. Thomas died, a member of the Augustinians, in 1559.

The Lord made to him a covenant of peace, and made him a prince. — *Introit*

From a pure heart proceedeth the fruit of a good life. — *Imitation: Book III*

IDEAL: An old proverb comes to mind as one reads the first line of the Introit for today's feast, "and made him a prince." It is this: "You cannot get blood out of a turnip," for the simple reason that there is no blood there. Likely God could not make a prince of St. Thomas either if there were not the qualities of a prince in him.

TODAY: When our Lord told the parable of the talents, He made it very clear that if we have been given five talents, we must bring in ten; if two, four; if one, two; always doubling what we have received. Well? Any questions? Christ told the parable and He is God and will be the Judge when all of His servants come back with their earnings.

SLOGAN: To whom much has been given, of him much shall be required.

Sept. 23.   ST. LINUS, Pope and Martyr

St. Linus was the second pope, having been elected immediately after St. Peter, and you might know that he, too, died a martyr's death. "They have persecuted Me, they will persecute you," our Lord has said; and they most certainly did, and still do. But St. Linus has been in heaven with St. Peter and the Master since the year A.D. 79.

If thou lovest Me, Peter, feed My lambs. — *Introit*

Fear God, and thou shalt not fear the terrors of men. — *Imitation: Book III*

IDEAL: Since it was so very much taken for granted that becoming a Christian meant certain death by martyrdom, that was particularly so in the case of the Pope. But our Lord promised that the gates of hell would never prevail against His Church. That is a comfort.

TODAY: When there is such unabashed persecution of the Church and of Catholics in our day — and it may become worse — we need to do all we can by way of prayer and study to steady our faith and try to confirm that of others, as our Lord asked St. Peter to do.

SLOGAN: And thou, being once converted, confirm thy brethren.

Sept. 24.   OUR LADY OF RANSOM

The Blessed Virgin appeared on the same night to St. Peter Nolasco, to St. Raymond Pennafort, and to James, king of Aragon, requesting them to found a religious order for the ransom of Christian captives from the Saracens who then held a great part of Spain.

It is truly meet and just, right and availing unto salvation, that we should at all times and in all places give thanks unto Thee, O Holy Lord, Father Almighty, everlasting God; and on the feast of the Blessed Mary, ever a virgin, should praise and bless and proclaim Thee. — *Preface*

If thy love be pure, simple, and well-ordered, thou shalt not be in captivity to anything. — *Imitation: Book III*

IDEAL: During the time that so many Christians were usual. She asked three men, great friends of hers on earth, to establish a religious order for the redemption of captives. Do being seized by the Turks, our Lady came to the rescue, as you get some notion from this fact of how very interested in all of us our Lady is?

TODAY: Say some very definite prayers today; *first,* to thank God you are a Catholic; *second,* for the conversion of sinners; *third,* for the poor souls. Tonight, tell our Lady you did these things to show your willingness to help her in a work she wants done so badly.

SLOGAN: He who causeth a sinner to be converted from the error of his way, shall save his soul from death, and shall cover a multitude of sins. — *Our Saviour*

Sept. 25.   ST. FINBARR, Bishop

This saint built a school at Lough Eire which formed the nucleus of the city of Cork. He was bishop of Cork seventeen years and distinguished himself by his love for the poor.

O Priest and Bishop, thou worker of all virtue, good shepherd of thy people, pray unto the Lord for us. — *Antiphon at the Magnificat*

For Thou, O God, hast chosen the poor and the humble, and those that are despised by this world, for Thy familiar friends and domestics. — *Imitation: Book III*

IDEAL: This saint did nothing extraordinary. He was a bishop who went about administering confirmation, encouraging the building of schools, and doing a great many things for which he never received any credit. For instance, few people know that it was he who established the beginnings of the city of Cork. But that makes little difference. He did establish the city; God knew it and, after all, God is the only One who makes a real recompense to anybody.

TODAY: Don't lose time worrying that the world does not appreciate you. The world is not big enough to appreciate genuine worth, anyway, which may be the reason for your being neglected. Anyway, you are working for heaven and for God, and you would not want some subaltern to pay you with slugs when the Master Himself has told you to wait until He gives you all of heaven for a few years of service.

SLOGAN: And only the Master shall praise us, and only the Master shall blame. And no one shall work for glory, and no one shall work for fame, but just for the joy of the working. — *Kipling*

Sept. 26. ST. ISAAC JOGUES and the NORTH AMERICAN MARTYRS

Let us count them out: Isaac Jogues, John de Brébeuf, Charles Garnier, Anthony Daniel, Gabriel Lallemant, Noel Chabanel, John de Lalande, and René Goupil. And what men they were! Within a period of seven years, they gave their lives, every one, for Christ, among the Indians of our country.

As the sufferings of Christ abound in us, so also through Christ does our comfort abound. — *Gradual*

Forsake all and thou shalt find all. — *Imitation: Book III*

IDEAL: When these men pronounced the words of their great founder: "Accept my whole will, my liberty, my memory. Whatever I have or possess, Thou hast given me. I return it all to Thee," they meant precisely what they said. We say, too, "Thy will be done on earth as it is in heaven," and proceed at once to assert our own against His. That is worse than Indian-giving.

TODAY: Take just five minutes out today to think seriously of what you are saying when you say: "Thy will be done!" And resolve to mean it each time you say it.

SLOGAN: Thy will be done on earth as it is in heaven.

Sept. 27. SS. COSMAS and DAMIAN, Martyrs

These two saints were brothers, Arabian physicians, who healed souls as well as bodies. They were most cruelly tortured to death for their faith.

This is the true brotherhood which overcame the wickedness of the world: it followed Christ, and possesses the peerless kingdom of heaven. — *Gradual*

For in whatsoever way I may arrange for my peace, my life cannot be without war and sorrow. — *Imitation: Book III*

IDEAL: Two physicians these two brothers were, who used their skill in healing bodies to win sick souls back to the service of their Creator. We might end the little rhyme: "Doctors, lawyers, merchants, chiefs" this way: "can become saints by the same method: doing their duty well."

TODAY: Think seriously about the kind of work you would like to do after you leave school. While you are thinking about it, keep in the front of your mind the desire to do as much good as possible.

SLOGAN: He serveth best who loveth best.

Sept. 28.   ST. WENCESLAUS, Duke and Martyr

This saint was duke of Bohemia. With his own hands he sowed the wheat and pressed the grapes which were used for the Holy Sacrifice of the Mass. While praying in church he was killed by a band of conspirators.

Novena for the feast of the Holy Rosary begins.

In Thy strength, O Lord, the just man shall joy. — *Introit: Psalm 20*

O pleasant and delightful service of God, which maketh a man truly free and holy. — *Imitation: Book III*

IDEAL: He loved the Blessed Sacrament so much that he himself raised the wheat and the grapes for the bread and wine to be used at Mass. Would you be shocked if someone showed you a soiled piece of linen and told you it was to be used next day for the lining of a tabernacle? The lining of the tabernacle never really touches our Lord in the Blessed Sacrament, but your tongue does.

TODAY: If ever in your life you are tempted to say an improper word or to speak unkindly of one of Christ's friends (and all men are that), remember that you must ask our Saviour to rest on that very tongue in Holy Communion. Keep your tongue holy for that very reason.

SLOGAN: Body of Christ, save me. — *Anima Christi*

Sept. 29. ST. MICHAEL

The Archangel Michael is invoked in the Confiteor. The Church summons him to the side of her children in the agony of death, and chooses him as their escort from purgatory to heaven.

Holy Archangel Michael, defend us in the battle; that we may not perish in the dreadful judgment. — *Gradual*

Fight like a good soldier; and if sometimes thou fall through frailty, resume with greater courage than before, confiding in My more abundant grace. But take very great care against vain complacency and pride. — *Imitation: Book III*

IDEAL: St. Michael knows by victorious experience how to fight and to conquer the devil and his hosts. We pray to him each day after Mass, if you notice, for victory over the devil.

TODAY: Cultivate a devotion to St. Michael and to the angels in general. We are inclined to take the angels and their ministrations very much for granted. They are powerful intercessors with God; you will find them very prompt in their attention to your prayers if you call upon them often.

SLOGAN: He hath given his angels charge over you to keep you in all your ways. — *Psalm 90*

Sept. 30. ST. JEROME, Priest, Confessor, and Doctor

This saint spent many years of his life in Bethlehem. He translated the Bible from Hebrew to Latin. Because of his learning and sanctity he has been called a Doctor of the Church.

O God, who for the expounding of Holy Scripture, didst raise up in Thy Church the great and holy doctor, Jerome: grant, we beseech Thee, that, helped by Thy grace we may put in practice what he has taught us both by word and by work. — *Collect*

If thou didst know the whole Bible outwardly, and the sayings of all the philosophers, what would it all profit thee without charity and the grace of God? — *Imitation: Book I*

IDEAL: A brilliant Latin student, St. Jerome turned all his ability to the translation of Holy Scripture. Not any accomplishment you will have, need ever stand in your way to sanctity. Indeed, if you use your talent as God intends, everything will be an aid to increasing God's pleasure in your soul.

TODAY: Look back over the month. It is over now. What you have gained by way of self-mastery is yours forever. What you have lost, you must regain. Resolve today to spend October, a day at a time, as nearly as you can in conformity with the suggestions you will read.

SLOGAN: Let the dead past bury its dead. — *Longfellow*

Oct. 1.   ST. REMIGIUS, Bishop

St. Remigius became archbishop at the age of twenty-two. His pity and charity were boundless. By converting Clovis, king of the Franks, he made that whole nation Christian.

Well done, good and faithful servant, because thou hast been faithful over a few things, I will set thee over many; enter into the joy of thy Master. — *Gospel: Matthew 25*

And if thou couldst make a choice, thou oughtest to prefer to suffer adversities for Christ, than to be delighted with much consolation; because thou wouldst more resemble Christ, and be more likened to all the saints. — *Imitation: Book II*

IDEAL: This saint brought King Clovis into the Church, as you know from your history. He lived as far back as A.D. 533 and has been greatly responsible for the Christianizing of all of France.

TODAY: Have you ever noticed how very little and insignificant the things are that we "preen our feathers" over? We wonder the world does not stand at attention at our passing in parade. Fourteen hundred years ago, one very holy man converted a nation, and we — ? ? ? Think about it today; you will have accomplished something if tonight you can mean what you say when you tell yourself, "I am not very important after all."

SLOGAN: Behold the handmaid of the Lord! — *Queen of Heaven*

Oct. 2.   THE HOLY GUARDIAN ANGELS

It is generally thought that countries, states, cities, families, churches each have their protecting angel. We all have a guardian angel whose eyes are ever upon us.

Thus saith the Lord God. Behold, I will send My Angel, who shall go before thee, and keep thee in thy journey, and bring thee unto the place that I have prepared. — *Epistle: Exodus 23*

For it is God that overseeth us, and we should exceedingly stand in awe of Him, and walk in His sight wherever we may be, as the Angels do in purity. — *Imitation: Book II*

IDEAL: This whole month is dedicated to the devotion to our guardian angel. Also, October has been assigned to honor especially Our Lady of the Rosary. The rosary, you know, is made up of prayers that have been composed almost entirely by God Himself. If John D. told you personally, "Whenever you want anything, just come to me and say 'thus and so,'" what would you do? Our Saviour told us, "When you pray, say 'Our Father, who art in heaven,' etc."

TODAY: Men like St. Alphonsus and St. Bernard have said that no client of Mary has ever been lost. Resolve today upon some *definite* thing you will do each day in honor of our Lady and make it a life's habit. Also, look up a picture of the guardian angel guiding two little children over a bridge, the picture you loved so much when your mother first told you of your angel at your side. Make yourself realize that you have such an angel still, whether you be waxen four or lofty seventeen.

SLOGAN: Pray for us, sinners, *now* and at the *hour* of our death.

Oct. 3. ST. THÉRÈSE OF THE CHILD JESUS
(The Little Flower)

"I do not intend to remain inactive in heaven," this saint said on her deathbed. "I wish to go on working for the Church and for souls. After my death I will let fall a shower of roses."

I confess to Thee, O Father, Lord of heaven and earth, because Thou hast hid these things from the wise and prudent and hast revealed them to little ones. — *Gradual: Psalm 70*

Whosoever, therefore, with simplicity of heart shall raise up his intention to God, and disengage himself from all inordinate love or dislike of any created being, he shall be the most apt to receive grace, worthy of the gift of devotion. For the Lord bestoweth His benediction there where He findeth vessels empty. — *Imitation: Book IV*

IDEAL: This little saint is a type of saint who became great by doing little things perfectly. That is all you need do: your duty well.

TODAY: Try to say your prayers with as little distraction as possible; write each task as neatly as you can, have no spelling mistakes, no crossings over, nor accidental blots. If you happen to make a mistake, keep cool and do not allow anything to make you impatient.

SLOGAN: Patience hath a perfect work. — *St. Paul*

Oct. 4. ST. FRANCIS OF ASSISI, Confessor

"The more the sublime enthusiast," says Montalembert, "humbled himself and depreciated himself to make himself worthy by humility and men's contempt to be the vessel of divine love, the more, by a wonderful effect of God's grace, men rushed to follow him."

Lo! Francis, he who was poor and lowly enters, a rich man, into heaven: with their hymns the Angels give him welcome. — *Gradual*

Set thyself, then, like a good and faithful servant of Christ, to bear manfully the Cross of thy Lord, for the love of Him who was crucified for thee. — *Imitation: Book II*

IDEAL: We had one feast of this saint on the seventeenth of September, the Impression of the Five Wounds on his body. Today, we keep the feast of St. Francis as founder of the Franciscan Order. He called his friars "Jokers of the Lord" and believed that if one was pleasing to God, he could always be happy. St. Francis called all things in nature brother or sister. All creatures made him think of God and seemed to exhort him to praise the Lord as they did.

TODAY: If you are a live wire, bring a copy of St. Francis' *Hymn to the Sun* to class and ask your teacher to read it. If you believe in "letting George do it," you will miss one of those opportunities you were told the other day would never come your way again.

SLOGAN: Sun and moon, bless the Lord! — *Ps. Benedicite*

Oct. 5. ST. PLACID and HIS COMPANIONS

This saint, when only four years old, was committed to the care of St. Benedict who loved to take Placid with him when God gave him miracles to work. St. Placid became a monk, built a monastery, and was put to death by barbarians.

The white-robed army of martyrs praises Thee, O Lord. — *Gradual*

He that seeketh anything else but simply God, and the salvation of his soul, will find nothing but trouble and sorrow. And he who doth not strive to be the least and subject to all, cannot long remain in peace. — *Imitation: Book I*

IDEAL: St. Placid began living in a monastery when he was still a very young child. Being good does not seem to have taken the joy out of his life any more than it does out of your life, as you notice on days when you make special effort.

TODAY: Have you ever said to yourself, "Some time I am going to get into the habit of going to Mass each morning," etc. Do that right now, *today*. You will never again be as young as you are today.

SLOGAN: As the twig is bent, the tree's inclined. — *Pope*

Oct. 6. ST. BRUNO, Confessor

St. Bruno was gifted both by nature and by grace. He renounced positions of honor and preferment to live a life of retirement and penance in a wild solitude called the Chartreuse, where he founded the Carthusian Order.

Very humbly, we implore, O Lord, the succor of the prayers of St. Bruno, Thy confessor: by our evil deeds we have deeply offended Thy Majesty; may his merits and intercession win for us Thy forgiveness. — *Collect*

Look upon the lively examples of the Holy Fathers, in whom shone real perfection and the religious life, and thou wilt see how little it is, and almost nothing, that we do. Alas, what is our life, if it be compared with theirs! — *Imitation: Book I*

IDEAL: Some people are intended to be leaders, others followers. The success of the scheme depends upon each person playing his proper role. The successful tragedian would probably make a mess of things if he attempted controlling the lights. St. Bruno was intended to live the life of a leader. Those men who fell into their role as his followers have become saints.

TODAY: Study your own case today. Can you take direction from others, even of your own age and position? When you assume leadership in any enterprise, can you get response from others without "bossing" them? If you want a test for possible leadership in yourself, find out if it is very easy for you to obey.

SLOGAN: Neither can he successfully command who has not learned willingly to obey. — *Imitation*

Oct. 7. THE MOST HOLY ROSARY OF THE BLESSED VIRGIN MARY

To the Queen of the Holy Rosary, Daughter of the Father, Mother of the Son, and Spouse of the Holy Ghost, the Church asks us to offer a triple chaplet, or three crowns of roses which she calls the rosary.

Make us, O Lord, we beseech Thee, to prepare ourselves as is meet, for the offering up to Thee of this sacrifice: and in the mysteries of the most holy Rosary, so devoutly to go over the life, passion, and glory of Thine only-begotten Son, as to be made worthy of His promise. — *Secret*

Where thy treasure is, there also is thy heart. If I love heaven, I love to think on heavenly things. — *Imitation: Book III*

IDEAL: You remember our Lord taught the Apostles how to pray the *Our Father*. Our Lady taught St. Dominic how to pray the rosary and asked him to exhort the whole Church to practice this devotion. Need any more be said as to how very much our Lady must love to hear *you* praying the rosary? You understand, of course, that the wealth of indulgences attached to the recital of the rosary can be obtained only on fulfillment of the conditions: state of grace and meditation on the mysteries during the recitation.

TODAY: Can you manage to recite the rosary today? It takes fifteen minutes or less. Can you manage that much tomorrow? Do you think you could say it every day? Perhaps you might establish so intimate a relation with our Lady that you would feel uncomfortable on any day you slighted her. Say the rosary each day for one week and see if you can stop it after that time. Establish the family rosary in your home.

SLOGAN: Remember it has never been known that anyone who fled to thy protection was left unaided. — *St. Bernard*

Oct. 8.   ST. BRIDGET OF SWEDEN, Widow

Bridget was born of the Swedish royal family. She was married and brought up her eight children in a holy way. One of them became St. Catherine of Sweden.

Who shall find a valiant woman? Far and from the uttermost coasts is the price of her. The heart of her husband trusteth her, and he shall have no need of spoils. She will render him good and not evil, all the days of her life. — *Epistle: Book of Wisdom 31*

Prepare thyself to suffer many adversities, and divers evils, in this miserable life; for so it will be with thee, wherever thou art, and so indeed wilt thou find it, wheresoever thou hide thyself. — *Imitation: Book II*

IDEAL: The mother of a large family, St. Bridget became a great saint by doing her duties well. Her duties were principally those of a faithful wife and good mother. She did this so successfully that her eight children are honored as saints. She herself became a nun after her husband died and her children had all been provided for.

TODAY: As the year goes on you will find that among the saints are mothers of large families, farmers, monks, merchants, soldiers, students, boys and girls in the fourth grade, seventh grade, and high school. Do each duty today as if you were a finished saint and did not want to spoil your record; then, keep that up tomorrow and do not ruin things the day after. You may die the day after tomorrow and you will be very glad for two days of saintliness.

SLOGAN: As the tree falleth, so shall it lie. — *Our Saviour*

Oct. 9.   ST. JOHN LEONARD, Confessor

St. John was a contemporary of St. Philip Neri and of St. Joseph Calasanctius, both of whom worked diligently to improve conditions in their immediate environment. So often, the Communists take all the credit for interesting themselves in the poor. Here are three men who devoted their whole life to helping restore men to a consciousness of their own dignity as human beings.

I have become a minister of Christ by virtue of the office which God has given me. — *Offertory*

I will hear what the Lord will speak to me. — *Imitation: Book III*

IDEAL: St. John Leonard was canonized only recently though he died in 1609. He had been a pharmacist's assistant before he left all to become a priest himself and then to found the Clerks Regular of the Mother of God. It is gratifying to know that so many of the persons who are wrapping up large and small packages and punching the keys of the cash register are keeping their mind occupied meantime with God and their own love for Him.

TODAY: The saints never decided upon becoming saints;

they decided upon doing God's will each moment; saint-hood followed.

SLOGAN: If you love Me, keep My commandments.

Oct. 10.   ST. FRANCIS BORGIA, Confessor

After providing for the settlement of his children, St. Francis entered the Society of Jesus where, despising all honors, he made a vow out of humility to refuse all dignities.

O Lord Jesus Christ, who art both the reward and the pattern of true humility; we beseech Thee that, even as Thou madest Blessed Francis follow gloriously in Thy foot-steps by spurning earthly honors, so Thou wouldst suffer us also to become his companions alike in following Thee and in his glory. — *Collect*

It is vanity, therefore, to seek perishable riches and to trust in them. Vanity, also it is, to court honors and to lift up one-self on high. — *Imitation: Book I*

IDEAL: Francis Borgia was a grandee of Spain. The sight of the transformation in the beautiful countenance of Queen Isabella by death brought home to him the vanity of earthly things and he resolved to leave the world and become a religious.

TODAY: If you say to yourself, "I think I shall go out to the country to see the lovely leaves that are so wonderful this fall," you will never go at all if you wait until the first week in December to see them. Why? Because your oppor-tunity is gone. The leaves simply don't wait. This account of St. Francis Borgia is meant to inspire you to set about being a saint. *Be one today!*

SLOGAN: Today I begin. — *Motto of St. Ignatius*

Oct. 11.   MATERNITY OF THE BLESSED VIRGIN MARY

This lovely feast was instituted by Pius XI in 1931 to com-memorate the Council of Ephesus of 431; it has been raised to a feast of the second class. The Council of Ephesus refuted the heresy which denied that our Lady is truly the Mother of God.

O sing unto the Lord a new song for He has done marvelous things. — *Psalm of the Introit*

What they (the saints) believed, I believe. — *Imitation: Book IV*

IDEAL: How surely our dear Lord does "remain with His church even to the consummation of the world," and how manifest is His divinity in the church! In a world grown so cold and so turned from heavenly things to the earth, comes this beautiful concentration on our Blessed Mother through a lovely new feast honoring her maternity.

TODAY: This is the Mother whom Christ our Saviour gave to us in His last moments on the cross. This is the Mother who came to us at Lourdes, at Fatima, as she had come at La Salette, to warn us and encourage us on our way home to her and to her Son. Each time she has asked us to pray and to "cease offending my divine Son." Let us ourselves heed her request and pray for all the world.

SLOGAN: Son, behold thy mother!

Oct. 12. ST. WILFRED, Bishop

"A quick walker, expert at all good works, with never a sour face." As a bishop he had to combat the passions of wicked kings and the errors of holy men; yet the battle he fought was won.

Behold a great priest, who in his day pleased God. There was not found the like to him, who kept the law of the Most High. — *Gradual: Ecclesiasticus 44*

They were aliens to the world, but they were very near and familiar friends of God. — *Imitation: Book I*

IDEAL: You would have liked St. Wilfred had you lived at his time and known him. He was energetic and, once he saw what was to be done, he lost no time getting the work done and done well. You know the little saying about an idle mind being the devil's workshop. When you dally about,

the tempter soon finds a way to give you something to do
at once. "Steal a march" on him by being always so busy
doing what you should that he may never catch you idle.

TODAY: It is Columbus' Day besides. How far would
Columbus have gone with his dreams if he stopped at "Now,
I believe if someone sailed west, he would come up on the
eastern side." He would have died at the pier. Do you
admire St. Wilfred and Christopher Columbus? Be like them!
DO THINGS!

SLOGAN: Know you're right; then, go ahead. — *Anon.*

Oct. 13.   ST. EDWARD, King and Confessor

It is said of St. Edward that all who approached him endeavored to regulate their lives according to his. He was
called the father of the poor and of orphans.

Blessed is the man that is found without blemish and that
hath not gone after gold, nor put his trust in money nor
in treasures. — *Epistle: Ecclesiasticus 31*

The noble love of Jesus impelleth us to do great things
and exciteth us always to desire that which is the more
perfect. — *Imitation: Book III*

IDEAL: This was Edward III, the predecessor of William
the Conqueror. We do not ordinarily think of kings and
great magistrates as being great saints at the same time,
because we think they must necessarily be so busy, they have
no time to serve God. How queer! What is serving God?
It is doing our duty as well as we can, and doing that duty
to please God, or because we love God and naturally want
to do all things as He would like us to do them.

TODAY: This idea of "doing one's duty" is getting monot-
onous. Try to think of it this way: imagine our Lord meeting
you right here and now and saying: "I have several little
tasks I want done today. This particular list of little tasks
I should like *you* to do, if you will." Have you the heart to
do any of them slovenly, or to omit one or the other entirely?
He will know the record this evening.

Oct. 14. ST. CALLISTUS, Pope and Martyr

This Pope instituted the Ember Day fasts. He reigned during the troublesome days of persecution. Instead of living at the Vatican, he lived among the poor. He was martyred on October 14.

Every high priest taken from among men is ordained for men in the things that appertain to God, that they may offer up gifts and sacrifices for sins. — *Epistle: Hebrews 5*

Be ready on thy part to bear tribulations, and account them the greatest consolations: for the sufferings of this life are not worthy to be compared with the glory to come, although thou alone couldst suffer them all. — *Imitation: Book I*

IDEAL: Though this man had been raised to the highest position a man can hold, he remained very simple in heart, thus meeting the requirement our Saviour set up when He said: "Unless you become as little children, you shall not enter into the kingdom of heaven."

TODAY: Look for the poem "The Boy and the Angel" by Robert Browning and read it today. The notes will probably help you understand it. Otherwise you can understand it by thinking about it while you read. Let it be an inspiration to you to do your best, no matter what your task.

SLOGAN: Life is a bundle of little things. — *Holmes*

Oct. 15. ST. TERESA, Virgin

St. Teresa is the only woman whose writings are considered of equal value with those of a Doctor of the Church. She converted thousands by her prayers. The Infant Jesus appeared to her and called Himself Jesus of Teresa.

Graciously hear us, O God our Saviour; that as we rejoice in the festival of Thy blessed virgin Teresa, so we may be fed with the food of her heavenly teaching and grow in loving devotion towards Thee. — *Collect*

Drink of the chalice of the Lord lovingly, if thou desirest to have part with Him. — *Imitation: Book II*

IDEAL: St. Teresa of Spain is the kind of saint you must know very well. There are so many lovely things in her life. Bring a *Life of St. Teresa* to your teacher and ask to have it read in class, or look up the life yourself and ask to tell it to the class. She is one of the most interesting persons in heaven, and you must know all about her.

TODAY: The outstanding feature about St. Teresa is her intense love for our Lord. When you think very much of anybody, you feel you can't do enough for him. St. Teresa felt that way toward our Lord. She wanted never to die, but to live on and suffer real pain of every kind rather her love for Christ. Don't express even one complaint today, but watch for opportunities to do things you find rather hard to do and offer them as proofs of your love for our Saviour. Perhaps you are not very brave.

SLOGAN: But the greatest of these is charity (love). — *St. Paul*

Oct. 16. ST. HEDWIG, Widow

This saint was the wife of Henry, duke of Poland, the mother of six children. She assisted at Mass every day, served the poor at table in person, and took care of the sick.

She hath looked well to the paths of her house, and hath not eaten her bread idle. Her children rose up and called her blessed: her husband praised her. — *Epistle: Book of Wisdom 31*

They shall gain great freedom of mind, who for Thy name enter upon the narrow way and relinquish all worldly care. — *Imitation: Book III*

IDEAL: You notice this saint was a very busy housekeeper. She managed somehow to attend to her work, look after her six children, and still have time to attend Mass each morning and to wait on the poor and sick.

TODAY: It is said one never knows how much one can do until one must. If you want badly enough to attend Mass each morning or to receive the sacraments often you will find a way to do so. Do you want to?

SLOGAN: Where there's a will, there's a way.

Oct. 17. ST. MARGARET MARY, Virgin

In 1675 our dear Lord chose this Visitation nun to spread to the world the devotion to His Sacred Heart, and, with Father Claude Columbière, S.J., to have the feast of the Sacred Heart established.

I to my Beloved and His turning is to me. — *Gradual*

Behold, the heaven of heavens cannot contain Thee and Thou sayest: Come ye all to Me. — *Imitation: Book IV*

IDEAL: One is torn between deep gratitude at so great a love and heart-rending regret at His mild reproach when one reads the words our Lord spoke to St. Margaret Mary: "Behold this Heart which has so loved men and is so little loved in return." Just what would any one of us do, if we should hear our Lord speak to us in those same words some morning after Holy Communion?

TODAY: If you listen to your own heart today, surely you will feel the promptings of grace inviting you, too, to make some reparation, possibly for your own neglect of His love, and certainly for that of all the world. How many there are who do not love Him; how many who do not even know Him!

SLOGAN: Behold this Heart which has so loved men and is so little loved in return!

Oct. 18. ST. LUKE, The Evangelist

St. Luke, by profession a physician, was a companion of St. Paul on his missionary travels. He is symbolically represented as an ox because he begins his Gospel with the account of the priesthood of Zacharias and because the ox was usually the victim in the sacrifices of the old law.

Grant, we beseech Thee, O almighty God, that the great gift we have received from Thy holy altar, may through the prayers of the Blessed Luke, Thine Evangelist, sanctify our souls and be our reliance. — *Postcommunion*

If only thy heart were right, then every created thing would be to thee a mirror of life and a book of holy teaching. — *Imitation: Book II*

IDEAL: Physician and painter that he was, you notice the little details he gives in the Gospel story. For instance, he is the one who tells that our Lord slept on a pillow that night in the boat. As you read his Gospel, you find he seems to paint the pictures for us, to help us live with our Lord as we read the story.

TODAY: Try to imagine what it would mean to you if you knew nothing of the loveliest story in the world, the story of Christ's life on earth. Then, say a prayer of thanksgiving, first for your faith, and then for the sanctity and skill of St. Luke in writing his version of the story of Jesus among men.

SLOGAN: These things are written that, believing, you may have life. — *St. John*

Oct. 19.   ST. PETER OF ALCANTARA, Confessor

St. Peter was a Franciscan. His penances were extraordinary. After his death he appeared to St. Teresa and said: "O blessed penitence which has earned for me such great glory."

Brethren, the things that were gain to me, the same I have counted loss for Christ. — *Epistle: Phil. 3*

Hold fast this short and perfect word: "Forsake all, and thou shalt find all; relinquish desire, and thou shalt find rest." — *Imitation: Book III*

IDEAL: Whenever a saint is said to have been a confessor, that means that he lived a holy life, but did not die a martyr. It does not always mean that he was a confessor as we usually think of that term. Today's saint was both, a holy man who did not die a martyr and a confessor as we understand that term. He was the confessor of the lovely St. Teresa you know so well from four days back.

TODAY: St. Peter was responsible for the sanctity of St. Teresa to the extent that he helped her on toward a greater love for God. By touching your cap when you pass a church, or by making a careful sign of the cross or genuflecting very devoutly, you may inspire someone to do the same; you become responsible for the act of virtue that person subsequently makes when he copies you.

SLOGAN: That men may see your good works and glorify your Father in heaven. — *Our Lord*

Oct. 20.   ST. JOHN CANTIUS, Confessor

St. John was a graduate of the University of Cracow where he received all the academical degrees. He taught several years at this university. Generously he shared his meals and the contents of his wardrobe with the poor. He is especially invoked in cases of consumption.

The compassion of man is toward his neighbor; but the mercy of God is upon all flesh. — *Introit: Ecclesiasticus 18*

The more thou knowest, and the better, so much heavier will thy judgment therefore be, unless thy life be also holy. — *Imitation: Book I*

IDEAL: A university man, who taught at the university during the day, he went about among the poor at night and tried to aid them in every way.

TODAY: Very small minds easily get "stuck up" when they think they have a little more education than those among whom they live. That is because it takes so very little to fill such minds to running over. If you want to do any real good in the world, you must first make people like you; but nobody likes a person who assumes superiority. Watch your thinking today and find if ever you think, "Dear me, I'm glad I am not like so-and-so."

SLOGAN: He that exalteth himself shall be humbled. — *Our Lord*

Oct. 21.   ST. HILARION, Abbot
(St. Ursula is commemorated.)

At the age of fifteen this saint broke all home ties and went to live in the desert with St. Anthony. The aim of his life was to do good to others and to remain unknown.

Beloved of God and of men, whose memory is in benediction. — *Epistle: Ecclesiasticus 14*

It is a great honor, a great glory, to serve Thee, and to despise all things for Thee. For they who willingly subject themselves to Thy most holy service shall have great grace. — *Imitation: Book III*

IDEAL: Only fifteen, and he left home to become a hermit. Ordinarily, we don't mind doing great things once in a while, but we do want to get the credit for it, and we see to it that the world knows *we* have done this and that.

TODAY: Just how many chances can you "sneak" today to do nice things for other people, for your parents first of all, without letting them know who did it?

SLOGAN: When thou dost an almsdeed, stand not in the market place. — *Our Lord*

Oct. 22.   ST. SALOME, Mother of SS. James and John

This is the wife of Zebedee. She is the mother who went with her two sons one day to ask for the right and left places at His throne in the kingdom. It may not be the least recommendation for those two sons that they were so much loved and esteemed by their own mother. Salome was one of the women also who went "early in morning with spices" to embalm the body of Christ, while her two stalwart sons were hiding away behind bolted doors.

Blessed are the undefiled in the way who walk in the way of the Lord. — *Introit*

All desire to rejoice with Him, but few are willing to endure anything for His sake. — *Imitation: Book II*

IDEAL: You may smile at the temerity of this mother who went boldly to our Lord and asked for the first places for her sons, but she was not afraid either to "go into suffering and death" if need be, when there was question of ministering to Him. In fact, she likely thought of no danger, but merely of doing what she thought should be done.

TODAY: While there is often great talk about women being moved by their hearts and not guided by their heads, you notice that our Lord knew whom He could depend upon when He wanted things done.

SLOGAN: Can you drink the chalice that I must drink? We can!

Oct. 23. ST. THEODORET, Martyr

Rather than make a compromise in matters of religion, St. Theodoret suffered a cruel martyrdom. He threatened his judge with the judgment of God. A little later the judge died.

> For thou hast prevented him with blessings of
> sweetness
> Thou hast set on his head a crown of precious
> stone. — *Introit: Psalm 20*

No man is fit to comprehend heavenly things who hath not resigned himself to suffer adversities for Christ. — *Imitation: Book II*

IDEAL: St. Theodoret died for his faith. You may never be called upon to die for your faith, but you are expected each day to live for it.

TODAY: If your neighbors did not know you were a Catholic, is there anything about your life that would lead them to surmise as much? Be very careful about your conduct on the street and among people. A Catholic is always under very severe scrutiny. You can be a missionary without going into foreign parts.

SLOGAN: Thy kingdom come. — *Our Father*

Oct. 24.   ST. RAPHAEL THE ARCHANGEL

St. Raphael, whose name means "God heals," was sent by God to cure Tobias. He is one of the seven spirits who always stand before the Lord and offer Him the incense of their adoration and that of men.

May the Angel Raphael, physician of our salvation, help us from the heights of heaven, heal all diseases and guide our faltering steps toward the true life. — *Hymn at Lauds*

Lo! heaven and earth, which Thou hast created for the service of man, stand prepared, and daily perform whatsoever Thou hast commanded. And this is but little; for Thou hast also created and appointed angels for the service of man. — *Imitation: Book III*

IDEAL: About this time in September we had St. Michael. Raphael is the angel who accompanied Tobias on his journey. He is a patron of travelers, and as we are all travelers through life, it is well to call on St. Raphael, especially when we are about to make important decisions.

TODAY: Say a prayer today to St. Raphael for the grace to know your vocation in life and also a prayer for the grace of perseverance in God's grace.

SLOGAN: He hath given his angels charge over thee.

(See Feast of Christ the King after October 31.)

Oct. 25.   SS. CRISPIN and CRISPINIAN, Martyrs

These two brothers were missionaries in France. During the day they preached and at night they worked at making shoes. The example of their holy lives converted many to the faith.

In the sight of the unwise they seemed to die; and their departure was taken for misery; and their going away from us for utter destruction: but they are in peace. — *Epistle: Wisdom 3*

Out of Me both little and great, poor and rich, as out of a

living fountain, draw living water; and they who freely and willingly serve Me shall receive grace for grace. — *Imitation: Book III*

IDEAL: These two men were shoemakers, if you please. During the day they worked for souls and at night they mended soles. Because they were so industrious and pious, they converted many to the faith.

TODAY: Does not the example of all this galaxy of saints set you on fire to be a saint in your particular occupation? You can be a saint running an oil station or a millinery shop. Just love God and your neighbor. If you truly love God and your neighbor, you will keep all the commandments.

SLOGAN: On these two commandments depend the whole law and the prophets. — *Our Lord*

Oct. 26. ST. EVARISTUS, Pope and Martyr

St. Evaristus was a Greek by birth. He was the first pope to create cardinals. He suffered martyrdom under Trajan.

Blessed is the man that endureth temptation: for, when he hath been proved, he shall receive the crown of life. — *Epistle: James 1*

Now the way of man is not always in his own power, but it belongeth to God to give and console when He willeth, as much as He willeth, and whom He will, just as it shall please Him and no more. — *Imitation: Book III*

IDEAL: Head of the Church, he gave his life for his faith. Our Lord had said, "They have persecuted Me, they will persecute you." These men felt honored when they could suffer something for their faith. Do you?

TODAY: When things go a bit roughly with you, try to think that you deserve much worse, and remember that others have suffered far more than you would be brave enough to bear.

SLOGAN: To suffer or to die. — *St. Teresa's motto*

Oct. 27.   ST. FRUMENTIUS, Bishop
(Vigil of SS. Simon and Jude)

A pirate crew captured the ship on which St. Frumentius was sailing to Ethiopia. All the passengers were put to death but the saint and his brother. They were saved because of their wit.

Watch, therefore for you know not at what hour our Lord is to come. — *Gospel: Matthew 24*

I am He who teacheth men knowledge, and who giveth a more clear understanding to little ones than can be taught by man. — *Imitation: Book III*

IDEAL: St. Frumentius saved his life from the pirates when he was captured by them, by being funny and witty. You remember about St. Francis calling his men Jokers of the Lord. St. Paul says that "the Lord loveth a cheerful giver" and St. Francis de Sales, "You can catch more flies with a spoonful of honey than with a barrel of vinegar."

TODAY: Be just as cheerful as you can all day. If it rains when you wanted to go hunting, smile anyway, and be glad it is fine for those who want to fish.

SLOGAN: Whatever way the wind doth blow,
Some heart is glad to have it so.

Oct. 28.   SS. SIMON and JUDE, Apostles

St. Simon was called Zelotes. With untiring zeal he brought many souls to Christ. St. Jude is popularly invoked as the saint of "impossible cases."

Their sound went forth into all the earth; and their words to the ends of the world. — *Offertory: Psalm 18*

For he that loveth God with his whole heart, feareth neither death, nor punishment, nor judgment, nor hell; for perfect love giveth secure access to God. — *Imitation: Book I*

IDEAL: You do not know much about these two men, nor does anybody, and yet they were our Lord's Apostles. The world need not know much of you, if only our Lord thinks well of you.

TODAY: Try to imagine a case in which you are misjudged of something. Store up courage now to bear that patiently should it ever happen (and it will), and take comfort in the fact that our Lord knows better.

SLOGAN: And only the Master shall praise us
And only the Master shall blame. — *Kipling*

Oct. 29. ST. NARCISSUS, Bishop

To help people out of a difficulty, this saint once changed water into oil. God protected this saint by visibly punishing those who wished to harm him.

I have found David My servant, with My holy oil I have anointed him: for My hand shall help him, and my arm shall strengthen him. — *Offertory: Psalm 88*

There is no man in the world without some trouble or affliction, be he king or pope. — *Imitation: Book I*

IDEAL: Like the miracle our Lord worked to help people out of an embarrassment, this saint changed water into oil for people who needed it. Of course, that kind of miracle is going on each day in nature about us.

TODAY: Do you ever stop to say, "Thank you, Lord, for the lovely weather, or for my kind parents, or for the beautiful stars"? You complain often enough when the weather is not as you would have it. Make up for some of that lack of balance today.

SLOGAN: For, all things great or small,
The good God made them all.

Oct. 30. ST. MARCELLUS, The Centurion and Martyr

A distinguished captain in the army of Trajan, this fearless soldier of Christ refused to sully his honor. Unflinchingly he suffered death for his faith.

He kept him safe from his enemies, and defended him from seducers, and gave him a strong conflict, that he might overcome and know that wisdom is mightier than all. — *Epistle: Wisdom 10*

Give all for all; seek nothing; call for nothing back; stand purely and with a full confidence before Me, and thou shalt possess Me. — *Imitation: Book III*

IDEAL: Another Roman soldier, who knew how to handle a sword for his emperor when that was the thing to do and how to bend his neck to the sword when that was the right thing.

TODAY: Always, we must come back to the same chorus of the old song: Be a saint by doing what you should when you should. Do it today!

SLOGAN: Do the duty that lies nearest thee.

Oct. 31.   VIGIL OF ALL SAINTS. FEAST OF ST. QUINTIN, Martyr

Finding St. Quintin proof against promises and threats, the persecutors tortured him barbarously. Amid his sufferings, he prayed for others.

If any man will come after Me, let him deny himself and take up his cross and follow Me. — *Communion: Matt. 16*

Drink the chalice of the Lord lovingly. — *Imitation: Book II*

IDEAL: The lovely month of October is over. Have you had the heart ever to omit the rosary? How do you feel about it now? And your guardian angel? When he compares notes with the other angels of this school, is he embarrassed to death or does he go right to the head of the rank with the best protégé of all?

TODAY: Of course, this is Hallowe'en, and you want to have some fun. Do have it and "loads" of it, but have the kind that your angel will join and that our Lady and our Lord may look on in satisfaction.

SLOGAN: I shall never pass this way again.

THE LAST SUNDAY OF OCTOBER, CHRIST THE KING

Feast of the Kingship of Our Lord Jesus Christ. This feast was instituted at the end of the Holy Year of Jubilee, 1925, by His Holiness Pius XI. This feast sets the crowning glory upon the mysteries of the life of Christ already commemorated during the year.

> Ruler of all from heaven's high throne,
> O Christ, our King ere time began,
> We kneel before Thee, Lord to own
> Thy empire o'er the heart of man.

> — *Second Vespers of the Feast: Hymn*

For the sake of Jesus, we have taken up the Cross; for Jesus' sake let us persevere in it. He will be our helper, who is our Captain and Forerunner. Behold our King marcheth before us, who will fight for us. — *Imitation: Book III*

IDEAL: Just before the Grand Review which our King, the King of kings, is to have on the first of November, He Himself holds a reception. Always He is the meek and humble Christ, going about among men in the hidden guise of the Eucharist. Even today He makes no sound. What glory shall come to Him, must come through the spontaneous offering of His loyal subjects. And shall we not glorify Him?

TODAY: Will you not glow with pride today to be a follower of Christ? Let there be an exultation in your prayers today. Let them be prayers of thanks and praise. Let your prayers be offerings of your heart, of your whole being to Him. It is little to offer. None but your loving King would want you (knowing you as only He does), but He does. Do not permit Him to say, "Son, give Me thy heart." Offer it to Him. This one day, be all His. Have no time for anyone, for anything else in the world, but for your King. You are on private duty today for heaven's King, for *your* King; you cannot be requisitioned by even a subaltern officer, much less by any mere private.

SLOGAN: My King and my God!

Nov. 1.   THE FEAST OF ALL SAINTS

In addition to the saints whom the Church honors day by day, there are hundreds whose names are not recorded. Among them are undoubtedly members of your own family. It is to honor *all* the saints in heaven that this feast has been established.

This day we keep, with one great cry of joy, a feast in memory of all God's holy children; His children whose presence is a gladness to heaven; His children, whose prayers are a blessing to earth; His children, whose victories are the crown of the Holy Church. — *Second Nocturn: Fourth Lesson, St. Bede*

It is a great honor, a great glory, to serve Thee, and to despise all things for Thee. — *Imitation: Book III*

IDEAL: In a few years, this will be our special day of celebration in heaven, if we have lived a holy life, day for day, that is.

TODAY: Do not waste your time wishing you were a saint. That gets you nowhere. *Will* to be one. How? That sharp answer you were just going to give to so-and-so, don't say it. The unkind remark you were about to make, say something kind, or say nothing. That complaint about your aches and pains, or about the weather, swallow it; be glad you have something to suffer to prove your love for God. And so on, through this day, do the lovely things you have been doing all these days in conformity with the suggestions in these pages. If you succeed in doing most of those things today, you will probably find it possible to do the same tomorrow. By and by, it will become a habit to do things right, and you'll be a saint before you know it.

SLOGAN: He that perseveres to the end, he shall be crowned.

228

Nov. 2.   ALL SOULS' DAY

On this day the Church makes intercession for all those who suffer the pains of purgatory. The souls in purgatory are helped by the suffrages of the faithful, especially by Holy Mass.

> Full of tears and full of dread,
> Is the day that wakes the dead;
> Calling all with solemn blast,
> From the ashes of the past;
> Lord of mercy, Jesus blest,
> Grant the faithful light and rest. Amen.
>
> — *Sequence: Dies Irae, Thomas de Celano*

IDEAL: Have you ever been very homesick? Have you ever longed to see someone you knew you could simply never see again? Can you imagine a longing like that intensified to such a degree that death would be a relief? That is the longing of the souls in purgatory for the vision of God. Our soul has been made for God, and naturally wants to fly to Him when released from the body.

TODAY: You have it in your power to satisfy that intense longing of the poor souls. Our Lord's longing for these souls is infinitely greater than their longing for Him. Will you not do what you can so easily do to satisfy His craving and theirs incidentally? Attend Mass for that intention each day. Say the Way of the Cross whenever opportunity presents. You will not forget, will you, that your turn is coming perhaps next week, or tomorrow?

SLOGAN: Have pity on me, have pity on me, at least you my friends, for the hand of the Lord hath smitten me. — *Job*

Nov. 3.   ST. HUBERT, Bishop

This saint is the patron of hunters. In his honor bread is blessed in some churches. The Church asks God to preserve those who eat of this bread from the bite of mad dogs, and the plague, and other diseases.

My truth and My mercy shall be with him: and in My name shall his horn be exalted. — *Offertory: Psalm 88*

Behold I know all men, and see all things that are done under the sun; and I know how it is with everyone — what he thinks, what he would have, and at what his intention aims. — *Imitation: Book III*

IDEAL: Not so long ago, we had two saints who were shoemakers. This saint was a remarkable hunter. In fact, he is the patron of hunters. It is said, though, that he was too fond of the chase, and God brought him to his senses by a vision at which Hubert left forever the sport he so loved and gave himself entirely to the service of God and hunting souls.

TODAY: Perhaps you simply must have some ice cream or a cookie or two after school each day or you think you will die. You cannot love those things more than St. Hubert loved hunting. Give them up for today. For this one day, give up as many things as possible that you might class under luxuries. The self-control which is developed by giving up luxuries for the love of God makes you strong and soldierlike.

SLOGAN: Give and it shall be given you, pressed down and heaped up and running over.

Nov. 4. ST. CHARLES BORROMEO

Created a cardinal when only twenty-three years old, St. Charles was one of the most prominent figures in affairs of the Church. Though a prince of the Church, he devoted much of his time to the poor and sick. The city of Milan will never forget his charity during the great plague.

O thou priest and bishop, thou worker of mighty works, thou good shepherd over God's people, pray for us unto the Lord. — *Antiphon*

If thou aim at and seek after nothing else but the will of God and the neighbor's benefit, then shalt thou enjoy interior liberty. — *Imitation: Book II*

IDEAL: While St. Charles was bishop, the great plague

visited Milan. He led the procession in a garb of penance and prayed God to stop the plague. His prayer was heard.

TODAY: You have certainly thought, if not said, "I've prayed and prayed and I don't get anywhere." Have you? How much effort have you made in the meantime to overcome some of your little "meannesses" or to do little penances to merit God's attention? Try that on one thing you want very badly and see how well it works.

SLOGAN: Lord that I may see!

Nov. 5. FEAST OF THE HOLY RELICS

After having solemnized on All Saints' Day the feast of the holy souls who have entered heaven, the Church honors on this day the holy relics of their bodies which will remain on earth until the glorious resurrection, a pledge of which we venerate in their ashes.

Many are the afflictions of the just, and out of all these the Lord hath delivered them: the Lord keepeth all their bones; not one of them shall be broken. — *Introit: Psalm 33*

Saints and friends of Christ, they served our Lord in hunger and thirst, in cold and nakedness, labor and weariness, in watchings and fastings, in prayers and holy meditations, in frequent persecutions and reproaches. — *Imitation: Book 1*

IDEAL: Our bodies are temples of the Holy Ghost. That accounts for the solemnity of Christian burial, and consecration of the ground in which those bodies are buried. That explains, too, why we venerate in a special manner the relics of the saints.

TODAY: You know, of course, that relics of some saint are sealed in the altar stone of every Catholic church. Go over to church today and say just a little greeting to the saint whose relics are in the church. It was with that body that saint walked this earth as you do today. Ask for some direction as to how to reach the goal as well as the respective saint did.

SLOGAN: Know ye not ye are temples of the Holy Ghost?

Nov. 6.   ST. LEONARD

The holy example of St. Remigius led this saint to leave the court of France and become a missionary. He spent much of his time in inducing prisoners to accept their imprisonment in the spirit of penance.

Do not be afraid, little flock, for it has pleased your Father to give you the kingdom. Sell what you have and give alms. — *Gospel: Luke 12*

Spiritual consolations, indeed, exceed all the delights of the world and pleasures of the flesh. — *Imitation: Book II*

IDEAL: A splendid example of a man who believed in making the best of things. He saw the fine example of another man who was making a saint of himself, and set out to do the same. That is seizing an opportunity; that is what you are being asked to do every week or so.

TODAY: Do you like the weather today, or the length of the lessons you are getting, or the kind of work you are asked to do at home, or the high cost of living? Unless you can really change those things, make the best of them, and don't complain. If you mind being caught in the rain without an umbrella, probably everybody who gets drenched feels the same, so — make the best of it.

SLOGAN: It is better to be able to like what you have than to have what you like.

Nov. 7.   ST. WILLIBRORD

The blessing of God rested almost visibly on the apostolic work of this saint. His pleasantness of manner won the hearts of all. He worked many miracles and had the gift of prophecy.

Behold an high priest who, in his days, pleased God and was found righteous. — *Lauds: First Antiphon*

The lover flieth, runneth, and rejoiceth, he is free, and cannot be restrained. He giveth all for all, and hath all in all; because he resteth in one sovereign good above all, from whom all good floweth and proceedeth. — *Imitation: Book III*

IDEAL: St. Willibrord was the kind of saint you were asked to become yesterday. Nothing could disturb his peace of mind. In all things that happened he could find some means for practicing virtue. He was the kind of saint who would rejoice with the ducks on the day it rained when he wanted to go to a picnic.

TODAY: You have probably read or heard the poem that ends at each stanza with "It all depends upon the state of mind." That was a slogan of the saints. They feared nothing, nor fretted about anything except a possible offense of God. Think about it; nothing else in the world is really a misfortune except that. Bring *Everyman* to class and ask your teacher to read it to you; it will prove that statement made in the last sentence.

SLOGAN: What exchange shall a man give for his soul?

Nov. 8.   THE OCTAVE DAY OF ALL SAINTS

In the Liturgy of the Church the feast of All Saints is celebrated for eight days. These eight days are called an octave.

Dearly beloved brethren, we should keep well in our mind and thoughts that we are living here meanwhile as strangers and pilgrims. — *Second Nocturn: Lesson, St. Cyprian*

Jesus hath now many lovers of His heavenly kingdom, but few bearers of His cross. — *Imitation: Book II*

IDEAL: In heaven, of course, there are no nights to break up the days; but, when a great feast like that of All Saints occurs, the Church keeps the feast for eight days — on earth, that is. And a few years hence, if you have lived well — done your duty, day for day — you will be included among those whose feast we keep.

TODAY: Do you know anything of Dante's *Paradiso?* No one can ever imagine heaven, because no one can ever imagine a being so generous and wonderful as God; but, take a little time off today to try to imagine yourself in heaven and then suddenly be asked to forfeit your place because you were unwilling to make a little sacrifice to do a little duty you do not like. And then . . . ?

SLOGAN: Nor eye hath seen, nor ear hath heard, nor hath it entered into the heart of man what God hath prepared for them that love Him. — *St. Paul*

Nov. 9.   DEDICATION OF LATERAN BASILICA

This church is considered the mother and mistress of all the churches. The more recent structure is itself very old, having been rebuilt and consecrated by Benedict XIII in 1726; the original building had been erected in 324 by Constantine, only thirty years after his own conversion.

Grant that whoever enters this temple to ask blessings of Thee, may rejoice in obtaining all he asks. — *Collect*

What meaneth this most loving condescension and so friendly an invitation? — *Imitation: Book IV*

IDEAL: There is no other nation under heaven that has its gods so nigh to them as Thou, O Lord, art nigh unto us. What if all the Catholic churches in the world were to be closed for one week, and we could not enter for holy Mass even on Sunday? How terrible that would be. And yet, for all we think of our great privilege, the church might very well be closed for days and we should never know it.

TODAY: Thank God on your knees for the inestimable privilege of your faith; then, for all the wonderful blessings which come to you through that faith, the greatest of all being the holy Sacrifice of the Mass. There is no greater Act ever performed, even in heaven.

SLOGAN: My house is a house of prayer.

Nov. 10.   ST. ANDREW AVELLINO

Handsome, clever, wealthy, St. Andrew was very popular at the law school in Naples. After he was admitted to the bar, he practiced in the Church courts. Once in pleading a case he told a lie. Almost immediately after he came upon these words: "The mouth that lieth killeth the soul." He gave up his law business and entered the Theatine Order.

He entered manfully and cheerily upon the harder life, and set to work to better himself therein. He was a wonderful instance of self-control, long-suffering, lowliness, and hatred of self. — *First Nocturn: Fifth Lesson*

Man looketh on the face, but God seeth the heart. — *Imitation: Book II*

IDEAL: This was a lawyer who left the profession because he was lured into telling a lie one time in pleading a case. If a man with the education and the virtue of Andrew Avellino finds a lie so undesirable a thing, there must be more to it than merely a passing habit that "everybody permits himself once in a while."

TODAY: Do you ever tell little white lies? There is very much of the coward in a liar. Lying has very dreadful consequences, and usually very disagreeable associates. With lying and after it come stealing, unfairness, cheating, etc., until a man becomes either so ashamed of himself that he has not the courage to start over, or so hardened that he has no desire to do better.

SLOGAN: Oh, what a tangled web we weave
When first we practice to deceive!

Nov. 11. ST. MARTIN OF TOURS

One winter's day St. Martin met a beggar almost frozen. St. Martin had no money with him, but taking off his warm cloak he cut it in two giving the beggar half of it. That night our Lord appeared to Martin wearing the half cloak.

That happy man, St. Martin, the bishop of Tours, hath entered into his rest: to welcome him came forth the angels and archangels, the Thrones, the Dominations, and the Virtues. — *Gradual*

Many are His visits to the man of interior life, and sweet the conversation that he holdeth with him; plenteous His consolation, His peace, and His familiarity. — *Imitation*

IDEAL: The giving of half his cloak to a beggar has gone down in history so that everybody knows of it. Do you ever do more than merely *think* how lovely it is to be charitable until it hurts?

TODAY: Christmas is a bit more than a month away. Suppose you begin today to forego some luxuries you might lawfully enjoy and with the money saved buy some clothing or food or, better still, send the money to persons you know are needy. Don't let them ever know from whom it came. Don't ever tell anybody you did it. You'll remember the joy of Christmas of this year for a long time.

SLOGAN: Amen, I say to you, as long as you did it for one of these, the least of My brethren, you did it for Me.

Nov. 12.   ST. MARTIN, Pope and Martyr

Because of his energetic opposition to heresy, St. Martin was kidnaped and taken from Rome to Constantinople. Banished to a desert place, he died of sickness and starvation.

Dearly Beloved, if you partake of the sufferings of Christ, rejoice, that when His glory shall be revealed you may also be glad with exceeding joy. — *Epistle: St. Peter 4*

Son, cast thy heart firmly on the Lord, and fear not human judgment, whensoever the conscience gives testimony of thy piety and innocence. — *Imitation: Book III*

IDEAL: This is another St. Martin. This saint was martyred for speaking out his convictions when he felt he must do so or be guilty of treason to his faith.

TODAY: When you are in a group where either another person's character is being defamed or your own sense of propriety is aroused, what do you do? Do you join in and smile at it all, or walk away to show your displeasure? The same group will probably never indulge in the like again when you are present. You may even do something for them regarding their topics of conversation even when you are not present.

SLOGAN: Birds of a feather flock together.

Nov. 13. ST. DIDACUS, Confessor

Too humble to aspire to the priesthood, St. Didacus, or Diego, was a simple lay Brother in the Franciscan Order. His special devotion was to the Passion of our Lord. Oil from the lamp that he kept burning before a statue of the Blessed Virgin cured the sick.

Blessed is the man that doth meditate on the law of the Lord: His delight is therein day and night, and whatsoever he doeth shall prosper. — *Matins: First Antiphon*

Truly a lowly rustic that serveth God is better than a proud philosopher who pondereth the courses of the stars, and neglecteth himself. — *Imitation: Book I*

IDEAL: Like St. Francis of Assisi, this saint was too humble to aspire to the priesthood, so he remained a Brother all his life. Monsignor Benson says in one of his books "Very few, except the most mortified saints, fail to feel satisfaction at their growing importance." We all love to see our name in print, to think that the whole world is talking about us, that there never was a person quite as wonderful as we, even if it be in nothing more wonderful than driving nails.

TODAY: When somebody does better than you in a test, do you think and say, "Oh yes, if I had the time and the chances, and got all the breaks like so-and-so," or do you say "so-and-so has real talent and uses it too. If I studied like that, I would do better too"; which?

SLOGAN: Envy hath slain its tens of thousands.

Nov. 14. ST. JOSAPHAT, Bishop and Martyr

St. Josaphat gave his life for the restoration of unity in the Greek Church which had become schismatic (would not acknowledge the Pope) about 100 years before his becoming a bishop. He was born in Poland and is greatly venerated by the Poles, was a member of the Order of St. Basil, and was martyred by the very people he was trying so hard to help, in 1623.

Let us all rejoice in the Lord, celebrating a feast day in honor of the Blessed Josaphat. — *Introit*

Above all things, and in all things, do thou, my soul, rest always in the Lord. — *Imitation: Book III*

IDEAL: How like his Master this saint was, to give his life for his friends in the same sense that our Lord did, for what He termed his friends were really His executioners.

TODAY: Set your sights for doing the will of God each instant; put on blinders to shut out the vision to the right or left and then walk straight ahead in pursuit of your goal. The many annoyances which come to those who try to please the world will never come near you.

SLOGAN: Thy will be done on earth as it is in heaven.

Nov. 15. ST. ALBERT, Bishop and Confessor

Born in 1206, St. Albert became the teacher of the great St. Thomas Aquinas. He died in 1288, having devoted his life in great part to research in the various fields of theology and science. He is one of the many great glories of the Dominican Order.

The Lord filled him with the spirit of wisdom and understanding. — *Introit*

Let the eternal Truth please thee above all things. — *Imitation: Book III*

IDEAL: St. Albert is a good patron for teachers. He died in 1288, was canonized in 1934. His pupil, St. Thomas Aquinas, died near the same date and was canonized within fifty years of his death. Those things, as all things are, are within the designs of Providence, but it does seem a little bit as if teachers normally wait longer for some kind of recognition than their students.

TODAY: It made no difference whatever in the joy and happiness of St. Albert the Great that he had not the honors of canonization until 700 years after his death; nor does the esteem of men make a difference one way or the other to any of us. What does make a difference is the esteem and the regard of God. Work for it.

SLOGAN: And only the Master shall praise us and only the Master shall blame. — *Kipling in "L'Envoi"*

Nov. 16. ST. GERTRUDE

St. Gertrude wrote Latin with unusual elegance and force. As abbess she ruled her convent in sweetness and charity. She was one of the first saints to spread devotion to the Sacred Heart.

O God, who didst build up for Thyself a pleasant home in the heart of the holy virgin Gertrude: for the sake of her merits and prayers, do Thou wipe away from our hearts every stain of sin, nor refuse us a share in that happiness which is hers forevermore. — *Collect*

Verily, Thou art my Beloved, the choicest among thousands, in whom my soul is well pleased to dwell all the days of its life. — *Imitation: Book IV*

IDEAL: Another splendid saint like St. Teresa whose feast we had on the fifteenth of last month, as you recall, St. Gertrude was very highly educated. Best of all, she was, like St. Teresa, an intense lover of our Lord. He once showed her a crown of roses and one of thorns and asked her to choose. "I have no will but Yours," she said. "Will You choose for me?" What would you have done?

TODAY: Devotion to the Sacred Heart is particularly one of love for our Saviour's Passion, and then as a reparation. Young hearts are hungry for love, more than older ones. There is not a heart in the world where you will be so absolutely certain of never being deceived, where you will be loved in return with an infinitely satisfying love as the Sacred Heart of Jesus. If you have not a real enthusiastic love for the Sacred Heart, pray for that love today.

SLOGAN: Sacred Heart of Jesus, I implore that I may love Thee more and more.

Nov. 17. ST. GREGORY THAUMATURGUS

The prodigies and miracles which this saint worked earned

for him the title Thaumaturgus or wonder-worker. At his word a rock moved from its place, a river changed its course, a lake was dried up.

Amen, I say to you, that whosoever shall say to this mountain, Be thou removed and be cast into the sea, and shall not stagger in his heart, but believe, that whatsoever he saith shall be done; it shall be done unto him. — *Gospel: Mark 12:23*

It is better to supplicate the saints in devout prayers and tears, and with an humble mind to implore their glorious suffrages, than by a vain inquisitiveness to search into their secrets. — *Imitation: Book III*

IDEAL: Do you think the things this saint did were wonderful? You can work much greater miracles. It is plain to see that the saint himself had little to do with the actual moving of the rocks, or the drying up of the lake; God did that at the saint's prayer. If you remove from your own life the rocks of selfishness, and dry up the lakes of vanity and vainglory, you must do most of that yourself, assisted by His grace, of course. But your part of the task is not at all easy, as you know, if you have ever tried.

TODAY: Sometime today, when nobody is watching you, make a mark representing each of the virtues you have practiced since you began this reading in September. Then, in a parallel line, make a mark for each of the bad habits you have corrected. Will there be many marks? Or any?

SLOGAN: If a man shall succeed in a lifetime to destroy a single habit, he shall have done well.

Nov. 18. ST. ODO OF CLUNY

It was the ambition of St. Odo's father to see him occupy a distinguished place at court. But Odo's dream was realized when he became a Benedictine. His winning personality made him an efficient peacemaker between contending princes.

Triduum for the Feast of the Presentation begins today.

Good and faithful servant, enter thou into the joy of thy Lord. — *First Vespers: Antiphons*

All the saints, the higher they are in glory, the more humble they are in themselves, the nearer to Me, and the more beloved by Me. — *Imitation: Book III*

IDEAL: Do you think St. Odo was foolish to sacrifice a place in court and become instead a monk, to bury himself in a monastery? What would you think of a man who turned down the chance to become county sheriff because he knew he could run successfully for U. S. Senator? Odo gave up the chance for a place in a plain mortal's court for a place in heaven's court.

TODAY: They tell of St. Francis Xavier that the thought "What shall it profit a man if he gain the whole world and suffer the loss of his own soul" took such possession of his mind that he found no peace till he left all things to join the newly founded order of Jesuits. Give that thought some space in your mind today, and see what it does for you.

SLOGAN: What shall it profit a man if he gain the whole world and suffer the loss of his own soul?

Nov. 19.   ST. ELIZABETH OF HUNGARY

Charity to the poor was the distinguishing characteristic of this saintly queen. In the miracle of the roses God stamped the seal of approval on her love for the sick and unfortunate.

> Laud we the saint most sweet
> Shining in glory blest,
> Who bore a hero's noble heart
> Within a woman's breast.
> — *Lauds: Hymn*

Son, let not the labors which thou hast undertaken for My sake crush thee, neither let tribulation, from whatever source cast thee down; but in every occurrence let My promise strengthen and console thee. — *Imitation: Book III*

IDEAL: This lovely saint is known to every Catholic. You recognize her at once with the roses falling from the folds of her mantle.

TODAY: Read the life of this dear saint. You will say almost instinctively, "A saint just like my mother!" And she was that. She lived her life in exact fulfillment of her duties; that is all. She was a faithful wife, a dutiful mother, a good neighbor always ready to help the poor and needy, never allowing the fact that she was a queen forbid her to associate with those whom she might aid.

SLOGAN: Do the duty that lies nearest you.

Nov. 20. ST. FELIX OF VALOIS

St. Felix belonged to the royal family of France. Wishing to put aside any claim to the throne, he renounced all he possessed and retired to the desert. With St. John of Matha he founded an order for the ransom of captives.

The just shall spring as the lily: and flourish forever before the Lord. — *Gradual: Psalm 111*

Thou must become a fool for Christ's sake, if thou wishest to lead the life of a religious. — *Imitation: Book I*

IDEAL: Are you inclined to be amused at these saints who throw aside wonderful opportunities of being a king or of filling some other prominent position? Do you know who was the famous man in the baseball world before Babe Ruth? The only glory that will profit any famous personage in his position is God's love.

TODAY: Students who practice for speed in typing often write this line: "Write it on your heart that every day is the very best day of the year." Change that slightly to "Write it on your heart that nothing is worth a lifetime of effort but God's love and heaven."

SLOGAN: Nothing is worth a lifetime of effort but God's love and heaven.

Nov. 21. THE PRESENTATION OF THE BLESSED VIRGIN MARY

When only three years old the Blessed Virgin was presented in the temple by her holy parents. Tradition tells us that she remained here for some time in company with other young girls in the care of holy women.

Hers was the hidden treasure of modesty, hers the high standard of faith, hers the self-sacrifice of earnestness, hers to be the pattern of maidenhood at home, of kinswomanhood in ministry, of motherhood in the temple.

Whosoever, therefore, shall humble himself as this little one, he is the greater in the kingdom of heaven. — *Imitation: Book III*

IDEAL: Your love for our Lady has, no doubt, made you foresee the approach of this lovely feast.

TODAY: Say all your prayers, do all your work as you think our Lady would, and try to imagine her watching you trying to imitate her. If your little sister has ever been caught imitating your mother, you know how your mother loved to watch her.

SLOGAN: He that is mighty hath done great things to me.

Nov. 22.   ST. CECILIA, Virgin and Martyr

St. Cecilia is the patroness of musicians. Born at Rome, of an illustrious family, she consecrated her virginity to God when she was still a child. The house in which she lived and suffered martyrdom has been transformed into a beautiful church.

The musicians played, and the maiden Cecilia sang in her heart unto the Lord alone, saying: Lord, let my heart and my body be undefiled, that I be not ashamed. — *Matins: First Responsory*

Free me from evil passions, and cure my heart of all disorderly affections; so that inwardly healed and well purified, I may become apt to love, courageous to suffer, and steadfast to persevere. — *Imitation: Book III*

IDEAL: St. Cecilia is typical of the kind of woman who inspires those who admire her to become like her. She was good and holy, and became the inspiration for Valerian to become a Christian and give his life for his faith as she did.

TODAY: Everybody who meets you is better or worse for the meeting. You cannot go to heaven alone, nor can you miss going there alone; that is, you influence one way or the other those with whom you live. Think about this today, and tell yourself of what kind your influence must be.

SLOGAN: I am a part of all I have met.

Nov. 23.   ST. CLEMENT, Pope and Martyr

It is said that St. Clement was consecrated bishop by St. Peter whose successor he became. In order to bring relief to Christians who had been condemned to work in marble quarries, he caused a miraculous stream of water to flow from a rock.

And I looked, and, lo, a lamb stood on the mount with a river of water of life proceeding from under his feet. — *Lauds: Third Antiphon*

The Lord is my light and my salvation: whom shall I fear? If whole armies should stand together against me, my heart shall not fear. The Lord is my Helper and my Redeemer. — *Imitation: Book III*

IDEAL: You notice how readily God seems to hear the prayers that are said for others. So often, when we pray it is for some selfish interest of our own. We ought often to pray for others — for the sick, the dying, and those in distress and temptation.

TODAY: Life is rather difficult at its best. As long as we are all companions in misery on the way to heaven, why not give each other a "lift" occasionally along the upward climb? It will make the way far less unpleasant for ourselves.

SLOGAN: Who gives himself with his gift, feeds three: himself, his hungry neighbor, and Me.

Nov. 24.   ST. JOHN OF THE CROSS, Confessor

From bitter experience St. John learned what it meant to

be misunderstood by those of one's own household. He was an ardent co-worker of the great St. Teresa.

Christ once asked him what reward he would have for so much work; whereto he replied: "Lord, that I may suffer and be disesteemed for Thy sake." — *Matins: Sixth Lesson*

I have received, from Thy hand, the Cross; I will bear it, and bear it even unto death, as Thou hast laid it upon me. Truly the life of a good religious is a cross but it is also the guide to paradise. — *Imitation: Book III*

IDEAL: When you do some kindness for another and mean to make that other person very happy by surprising him with your little act of attention, when that person so helped interprets your action as "interfering in his affairs" — what is your reaction?

SLOGAN: In the Name of the Father and of the Son and of the Holy Ghost.

Nov. 25. ST. CATHERINE, Virgin and Martyr

St. Catherine was able to outargue the most learned men of her time and succeeded in bringing a number of them to Christ. Angels carried her body to the top of Mt. Sinai.

After her shall virgins be brought to the King: her neighbors shall be brought to thee with gladness. — *Gradual: Psalm 14*

I am He who teacheth men knowledge, and who giveth a more clear understanding to little ones than can be taught by man. He to whom I speak will quickly be wise and will profit greatly in spirit. — *Imitation: Book III*

IDEAL: You must know the life of this saint. You cannot appreciate some of the loveliest art pictures or certain lovely poems unless you know St. Catherine; most of all, you would miss knowing one of the most charming patrons of students.

TODAY: Get the *Catholic Encyclopedia* and read the life of St. Catherine of Alexandria. No more need be said; you will know what to do after you have read her life.

SLOGAN: Virtue and science.

Nov. 26.   ST. SYLVESTER, Abbot

Through the centuries, various holy men have instituted branches of the Benedictine Order. St. Sylvester established such a branch, the Sylvestrines who live by the rule of St. Benedict. St. Sylvester died in 1267 at the age of ninety years.

O most merciful God, who deigned to call Sylvester to a life of shining merit . . . when pondering upon the vanity of worldly things. — *Collect*

Son, walk before Me in truth. — *Imitation: Book III*

IDEAL: For all his living in the desert so much of his life, and perhaps because of it, St. Sylvester lived to be ninety years old. Perhaps you do not wish to live so long. In any case, it does seem to favor the truth that self-denial is conducive even to longevity.

TODAY: It is worth one's while occasionally to ponder for a moment or two seriously on just what it does profit a man to gain the whole world and suffer the loss of his own soul.

SLOGAN: What doth it profit a man to gain the whole world and suffer the loss of his own soul?

Nov. 27.   ST. MAXIMUS, Bishop
   (Feast of the Miraculous Medal)

A living example of his own teaching, this saint understood perfectly the art of leading others to love God and to do good. Forced to accept the bishopric of Riez, he overcame his repugnance and proved himself an excellent bishop.

There was not found the like to him, who kept the law of the Most High. — *First Vespers: Second Antiphon*

Thy abode must be in heaven, and thou shouldst look upon all earthly things as it were in passing. — *Imitation: Book II*

IDEAL: Here is another saint who became such by making

the best of things. He did not want to be a bishop, but when he realized there was nothing to prevent it, he was the best bishop he could be.

TODAY: When your teachers assign you some special task, it is because they have faith in your ability. They should know as much about that as you. Attack any task thus assigned as if you had as much faith in yourself as others have in you. Do your best; no one expects more.

SLOGAN: Do your best; angels can do no better.

Nov. 28.   ST. JAMES OF LA MARCA OF ANCONA

Educated at the University of Perugia, St. James was a private tutor. A visit to the Church of St. Francis at the Portiuncula decided his vocation. He became a Franciscan.

The just shall flourish like the palm tree: he shall grow up like the cedar of Libanus in the house of the Lord. — *Gradual: Psalm 91*

It is a great honor, a great glory, to serve Thee, and to despise all things for Thee. — *Imitation: Book III*

IDEAL: You will note much like St. Matthew about St. James. Each heard the call of God to a higher life, left everything, and followed the call.

TODAY: So often it happens that young people, who feel themselves called to a higher life, argue that they could not leave home, etc. What if they should die? Or, should they embrace the married state, would they go on living with their parents?

SLOGAN: He that loveth father or mother more than Me is not worthy of Me.

Nov. 29.   ST. SATURNINUS, Martyr

This saint was the first bishop of Toulouse. On his way to Church he was seized by heathens and asked to offer sacrifice. In consequence of his refusal he was tied to a bull and dragged through the streets of the city.

My hand shall help him and My arm shall strengthen him. — *Gradual: Psalm 88*

Oh, if thou couldst see the everlasting crowns of the saints in heaven, and in how great glory they now triumph, who appeared contemptible heretofore to this world. — *Imitation: Book III*

IDEAL: The account of this martyr's death is almost too gruesome for words. And yet, the saint's reasoning was philosophic: in a few hours it will all be over and heaven lasts forever.

TODAY: Will you try to keep that in mind today, particularly if you have something to do you dislike very much?

SLOGAN: Heaven is worth everything.

Nov. 30. ST. ANDREW, Apostle

This Apostle was always eager to bring others into notice. He died on a cross in the form of an X. For two days he hung suffering upon the cross preaching to those who came to visit him.

The Blessed Andrew prayed saying: O Lord, King of eternal glory, receive me hanging on this gibbet. — *First Vespers: Antiphon 2*

Then all the servants of the cross, who in their lifetime have conformed themselves to Him that was crucified shall come to Christ their Judge with great confidence. — *Imitation: Book II*

IDEAL: This is St. Peter's brother. You know a great deal more about his brother than about St. Andrew, and yet, it was Andrew who brought Peter to Christ the first time. He was that kind of man, always pushing others forward.

TODAY: Whenever you can give another the credit for work that has been done in partnership, do so.

SLOGAN: Honor to whom honor is due.

Dec. 1. ST. ELIGIUS

St. Eligius was a goldsmith in Paris. As a reward for his honesty, the king offered him a place at court. Fearing the temptation to loose living might prove too strong for him, he practiced severe penance and resorted to ejaculatory prayers. His charity for captives was boundless.

> Godly and prudent, meek and chaste past telling,
> Nought of ungoverned lust his living staineth,
> Whilst, in the members of his body dwelling,
> The soul remaineth. — *First Vespers: Hymn*

He whose taste discerneth all things as they are, and not as they are said or accounted to be, is truly a wise man, and taught rather of God than of men. — *Imitation: Book II*

IDEAL: Before any war in which our country joins, there is much preparation going on everywhere in the land. Ammunition being stored, guns being built, even bandages, etc., being prepared for the care of the wounded. Then, when the war actually begins, everything is ready. This life is a warfare and this saint had the good sense to get his ammunition prepared in proportion to the danger.

TODAY: You are due for a call up to the front at any time and you have no way of knowing exactly how powerful the enemy will be except from the experience of those who have met him previously. Say the *Our Father* just as devoutly as possible today and think of each good act as so much ammunition against future possible attacks.

SLOGAN: Lead us not into temptation.

Dec. 2. ST. BIBIANA, Virgin and Martyr

The parents of this saint were both martyrs. A wise and prudent virgin, St. Bibiana feared the loss of her innocence more than the deprivation of all her wealth. Tied to a pillar she was scourged to death.

Again the kingdom of heaven is like a merchant in search of fine pearls. When he finds a single pearl of great price, he goes, and sells all he has, and buys it. — *Gospel: Matt. 13*

He that loveth must willingly embrace all that is hard and bitter for the sake of his Beloved, and never suffer himself to be turned away from Him by any contrary occurrences whatsoever. — *Imitation: Book III*

IDEAL: In these days when so many girls make nothing of endangering their loveliest possession, purity of soul, this young saint stands out as a beautiful example of death rather than sin.

TODAY: The poet Young wrote a splendid line when he said: "Guard well your thoughts; our thoughts are heard in heaven." Keep that in mind always, and mind that if our thoughts are heard in heaven, certainly our deeds are known there.

SLOGAN: Guard well your thoughts; our thoughts are heard in heaven.

Dec. 3.   ST. FRANCIS XAVIER, Confessor

In the University of Paris this saint was making a name for himself as a brilliant professor of philosophy. He was an intimate friend of St. Ignatius who saw in the young man great possibilities for heroic self-sacrifice. The oft-repeated words of St. Ignatius: "What shall it profit a man if he gain the whole world, and suffer the loss of his soul," finally induced him to become a Jesuit. He became the apostle of the Indies.

The Lord guided the just in right paths, showed him the kingdom of God, and gave him knowledge of holy things, made him rich in his travails, and multiplied the fruit of his labors. — *None: Chapter*

For when the grace of God cometh to a man, then is he powerful for all things. — *Imitation: Book II*

IDEAL: Of course, you would be interested in Babe Ruth, in DiMaggio, in Edison, in Pasteur, and in Bing Crosby. What would you think of a young man who had all the skills of these several combined and was a teacher at the university besides? Francis Xavier was such a man, handsome, wealthy, athletic, brilliant, charming.

TODAY: Take just a few minutes' time to count up the good it would have done Xavier had he kept on making a name for himself. Then, try to count up the good it has done him and the world that he did as he did. Balance your columns and draw your own conclusions.

SLOGAN: What shall it profit a man if he gain the whole world and suffer the loss of his own soul?

Dec. 4. ST. PETER CHRYSOLOGUS, Doctor of the Church

ST. BARBARA, Virgin and Martyr

St. Barbara was brought up a heathen. Her father jealously kept her secluded in a lonely tower. In her enforced solitude she studied and prayed, took instruction by stealth, and was baptized. Upon learning what Barbara had done, her father ordered her tortured and finally beheaded. A flash of lightning killed the father. St. Barbara is one of the fourteen Auxiliary Saints.

Come thou spouse of Christ, receive the crown, which the Lord hath prepared for thee from eternity: for whose love thou didst shed thy blood. — *Gradual: Psalm 44*

If Jesus be with thee, no foe can harm thee. Whoever findeth Jesus findeth a good treasure — yea, a good above every good. — *Imitation: Book II*

IDEAL: Have you ever heard people bemoaning that they have no chance? Have you done it yourself perhaps? This saint had a pagan father who vowed Barbara would not learn of the foolishness of Christianity. She managed to learn all about it, to be baptized, and even to die a martyr at the hands of her own father.

TODAY: And you? What of your opportunities? And what have you to show up for them? There is no reason, you know, except that God was infinitely generous, that you were not born in the wilds of unexplored Africa. Resolve this minute never to envy other people's chances; to thank God for your special privileges instead.

SLOGAN: He that is mighty hath done great things to me.

Dec. 5.   ST. SABBAS, Abbot

St. Sabbas lived in Palestine in a cave on the top of a mountain at the bottom of which flowed the Brook Cedron. Fastings and austerities were conducive to the health of this saint for he lived to be ninety-four years old.

He asked life of Thee and Thou hast given him length of days forever and ever. — *Gradual: Psalm 20*

It is by resisting the passions, therefore, and not by serving them, that true peace of heart is found. — *Imitation: Book 1*

IDEAL: Fasting and prayer did not seem to shorten the life of this man, for he lived to nearly one hundred years. You have noticed that you feel better when you have denied yourself something at a meal, and it gives you the feeling of strength of character besides.

TODAY: Self-denial becomes a great deal easier when you make it a habit. Decide upon some little mortification you will practice always at meals. (This is Advent, you know.) For instance, when you spread butter on bread, you might always miss the whole crust with butter and no one would notice except God and your angel.

SLOGAN: Habits grow by unseen degrees,
         As brooks make rivers and rivers run to seas.

Dec. 6.   ST. NICHOLAS, Bishop

This saint never grew old. All his life he retained the bright and guileless manners of his youth. He once helped a destitute father by throwing a bag of gold through an open window and hurrying away.

Thou hast made him a little lower than the angels, Thou hast crowned him with honor and glory, and madest him to have dominion over the works of Thine hands. — *Second Nocturn: Psalm 8*

Be not ashamed to wait on others for the love of Jesus Christ, and to be looked upon as poor in this world. — *Imitation: Book I*

IDEAL: Santa Claus owes his name to this saint, as you know. Besides loving him as the originator of a very delightful custom, we would do well to know something more of his exemplary life.

TODAY: It is not so very difficult to do kind things for others when the whole world stands up in the bleachers to give us a cheer of praise, but to do things for others without anybody ever knowing, that is honest-to-goodness charity. Try to do a few acts of the latter type, and if you find it hard, do many more.

SLOGAN: Let not your left hand know what your right hand doeth.

Dec. 7. ST. AMBROSE, Bishop

St. Ambrose received a liberal education in Rome. As Bishop of Milan he knew no fear in defending the rights of the Church. He was the friend and consoler of St. Monica, the mother of St. Augustine, and had the joy of admitting her son to the Church.

O right excellent teacher, light of the Holy Church, St. Ambrose, blessed lover of Divine law, pray for us to the Son of God. — *First Vespers: Antiphon*

He that hath true and perfect charity seeketh himself in nothing, but only desireth God to be glorified in all things. — *Imitation: Book I*

IDEAL: St. Ambrose was tender in his encouragements to St. Monica when she fretted about her wayward son Augustine, but when the Emperor Theodosius took it for granted that he might retain his place of honor in the cathedral though guilty of a public misdemeanor, this tender Ambrose met him at the door and forbade him entrance.

TODAY: Do you say "Yes, yes" when everybody else says that, regardless of your real convictions? Don't sacrifice truth or honor or virtue to be a "good fellow." You win no man's respect by such conduct and, what really matters, you lose God's respect.

SLOGAN: They make clean the *outside* of the cup.

Dec. 8. THE IMMACULATE CONCEPTION OF THE BLESSED VIRGIN MARY
(Followed by Octave)

Having decided from all eternity to make Mary Mother of the Incarnate Word, God willed that she should crush the head of the serpent from the moment of her conception. He covered her with a mantle of holiness and made her soul, which He preserved from all stain, a worthy dwelling place for His Son. On December 8, 1854, Pius IX officially proclaimed the Dogma of the Immaculate Conception.

Thou art all fair, O Mary: and the original stain is not in thee. Thy vesture is white as snow; and thy face is as the sun. — *First Vespers: Antiphon*

O happy mind and blessed soul! which deserveth to receive Thee, her Lord God devoutly, and in receiving Thee to be filled with spiritual joy. — *Imitation: Book IV*

IDEAL: This is our Mother's greatest feast. And, oh, are you not proud of your Mother? Of course, you can never really appreciate the fact that our Lord gave her to *you*, His Mother to *you*. And today, while the angels surround her with songs of praise for her, their *Queen*, they are honoring your *Mother*, Queen of the Angels, but your Mother.

TODAY: It is hard to say words today; all one can do is to keep from shouting for sheer exultation and happiness at the glory that heaven and earth shower on your Mother, knowing all the while that amid the clouds of incense from angels' censers, amid the songs of saints and angels, your

Mother thinks of *you*, waits with love for your mite of praise.

SLOGAN: Hail Mary, full of grace, the Lord is with thee.

Dec. 9. ST. LEOCADIA, Virgin and Martyr
(St. Peter Fourier)

St. Leocadia was a native of Toledo in Spain. Because she refused to deny her faith, she was thrown into prison. When she heard of the martyrdom of her friend, St. Eulalia, she prayed to die. God heard her prayer. There are three churches in Toledo that bear her name.

> Double the palm of triumph which she beareth,
> Strove she to vanquish woman's fear of death:
> Quelled now the hand of death and hell appeareth
> Her feet beneath. — *First Vespers: Hymn*

It is a fearful thing to die; perhaps it will be still more dangerous to live longer. Blessed is the man that hath the hour of his death continually before his eyes, and daily putteth himself in order for death.

IDEAL: Today you have another example of a young woman who had the courage of her convictions. When the persecutors thought to frighten her by torture, they found there was nothing could terrify this Christian but sin.

TODAY: There is nothing in the world that is real misfortune except sin. All other things that seem misfortune end in less than a hundred years mostly. Sin and its consequences last through life and may extend into eternity. Think about it.

SLOGAN: Nothing is worth doing wrong for. — *Nancy in "Silas Marner"*

Dec. 10. ST. EULALIA, Virgin and Martyr

"All this you will escape if you will but touch a little salt and frankincense with the tip of your finger." This remark was made to St. Eulalia after she had been shown instruments of torture. Without hesitation she chose rather to sacrifice her life than to deny her God.

Virginity is not to be praised because it is a grace which is poured forth in martyrs, but because it is a grace which maketh martyrs. — *Matins: Fourth Lesson*

If thou hadst a great conscience, thou wouldst not much fear death. It were better to shun sin than to fly death. — *Imitation: Book I*

IDEAL: This saint was a friend of St. Leocadia whose feast we had yesterday. That is a test for the right kind of friendship, mutual inspiration to right.

TODAY: You call some people your friends, of course. Take just a second or two to think this thing out. Why are you a friend of so-and-so and not of so-and-so? You know the old adage: Tell me with whom you go and I shall tell you who you are.

SLOGAN: Birds of a feather flock together.

Dec. 11. ST. DAMASUS, Pope and Confessor

St. Damasus was a man of great learning, well versed in Scripture. Through his efforts the cemeteries in Rome, where rest the bodies of many saints, were beautified. He extolled the prerogatives of virginity in poetry and prose.

He established the usage which already prevailed in many churches, of singing the Psalms, both by day and by night, by alternate choirs, and of adding at the end of each Psalm the words, "Glory be to the Father, and to the Son, and to the Holy Ghost."

Love Him, and keep Him for thy friend, who, when all forsake thee, will not leave thee, nor suffer thee to perish finally. — *Imitation: Book II*

IDEAL: You note that St. Damasus was interested in the beautifying of the resting places of the Christian dead. Our body is the temple of the Holy Ghost and, hence, the Church respects it accordingly. Greater concern is due the soul, however.

TODAY: Have you ever stopped to think how very partial we all are to our body and our soul is scarcely thought of?

We eat three times a day, sometimes lunch between, clothe our body very luxuriously at times, gratify it in every way and are quite concerned always about its wants. Only God can satisfy the longings of our soul.

SLOGAN: Thou hast made our heart for Thee, O God, and our soul is restless until it rests in Thee. — *St. Augustine*

Dec. 12.   ST. VALERY, Abbot
(Feast of Our Lady of Guadalupe)

The chief aim of St. Valery's life was to draw near to God by penance and prayer. His holy example inspired a number of his friends to aid him in founding a monastery.

Well done thou good and faithful servant, thou hast been faithful over a few things, I will make thee ruler over many things; enter thou into the joy of thy Lord. — *Matins: First Responsory*

Above all things, and in all things, do thou, my soul, rest always in the Lord for He is the eternal rest of the saints. — *Imitation: Book III*

IDEAL: You have read so often in this book of the power of good example. The saint of today illustrates that power once more.

TODAY: Know that you can help in a very practical way to spread God's kingdom by leading a very good life. And you should know by this time that all you need do to lead a good life is to do each duty, one at a time, well.

SLOGAN: Nor knowest thou what argument thy life to a neighbor's creed has lent. — *Emerson*

Dec. 13.   ST. LUCY, Virgin and Martyr

At the tomb of St. Agatha, St. Lucy obtained a miraculous cure for her mother. In gratitude St. Lucy distributed all her wealth to the poor and consecrated her virginity to Christ. Denounced as a Christian she rejoiced to shed her blood for Christ.

In patience hast thou possessed thy soul, Lucy, bride of Christ: thou hast hated the things that are in the world, and art glorified among the Angels: thou hast shed thy blood, and conquered the adversary. — *First Vespers: Antiphon*

I am accustomed to visit My elect in two manner of ways; namely, by trial and by consolation. — *Imitation: Book III*

IDEAL: St. Lucy is a very popular saint among the Italians, as you know. Dante has immortalized St. Lucy in his *Divine Comedy*. But mere hat waving and loud singing in any saint's honor does not mean a thing if our life is such that the saint needs to blush at our demonstration.

TODAY: Whether you are Italian or not, do honor to St. Lucy by some attempt at imitation of her courage. If you are Italian, you have all the greater reason.

SLOGAN: Not everyone who says to Me, "Lord, Lord," shall enter the kingdom of heaven; but he who does the will of My Father in heaven shall enter the kingdom of heaven.

Dec. 14. ST. NICASIUS, Archbishop, and HIS COMPANIONS, Martyrs

In a futile effort to save Reims from destructive barbarians, St. Nicasius exposed himself to their fury hoping to save his helpless people. He was mercilessly beaten with clubs and finally beheaded.

This is he who loved not his life in this world, and is come unto an everlasting kingdom. And he is numbered among the saints. — *Matins: Third Responsory*

Drink of the chalice of thy Lord lovingly, if thou desirest to be His friend and to have part with Him. — *Imitation: Book II*

IDEAL: Our Lord said: "Greater love than this no man hath, that he lay down his life for his friends." When you are asked to do a favor that means great personal sacrifice, do you say: "What do I get out of this"?

TODAY: Watch for a chance today to do something for somebody who could not do anything for you in return, and be glad if he does not even thank you for your kindness. Be sure to make the good intention first.

SLOGAN: If you do good to them that love you, what reward shall you have?

Dec. 15. OCTAVE DAY OF THE IMMACULATE CONCEPTION

During eight consecutive days the Church celebrates the glory of the Immaculate Conception. During this season of Advent let us fix our eyes on the Virgin who is to give us Christ.

> Fair Lily, found among the thorns!
>   Most beauteous Dove with wings of gold!
> Rod from whose tender root upsprang
>   That healing Flower long since foretold!
>
> — *Matins: Hymn*

I am the Lover of purity and the Giver of all sanctity. I seek a pure heart, and there is the place of My rest. — *Imitation: Book IV*

IDEAL: On the calendar we keep the feast of the Immaculate Conception for eight days, but in our hearts, oh, in our hearts, we keep the feast unending, as do the angels and saints and our Lord in heaven.

TODAY: Let your heart beat faster at thought of our Lady's day; let the knowledge that she is soon to give to us the Saviour of the world make your love for Mary grow and make itself manifest in the increasing likeness of your soul to hers.

SLOGAN: Help me grow like thee, sweet Maid!

Dec. 16. ST. EUSEBIUS, Bishop and Martyr

Though this saint did not actually shed his blood for the faith, he suffered so intensely in defense of the purity of religious teaching that he is given the honor reserved for martyrs.

He was sent to Bethsan in the Holy Land, suffering hunger, thirst, stripes, and all manner of violence, but for the faith's sake he despised this life, and feared not death, but freely delivered his body to the tormentors. — *Matins: Fifth Lesson*

If thou wouldst persevere dutifully and advance, look on thyself as an exile and a pilgrim upon the earth. — *Imitation: Book I*

IDEAL: This man is classed a martyr and he did not even die for his faith, though he suffered much and would have died, had his persecutors been able more easily to accomplish that feat.

TODAY: You see how very much depends upon one's intentions. God looks upon our will and not upon our actual accomplishment. If you become the head of a company, then go bankrupt, you are a failure before men. If you are willing to die for your faith, actually willing, God gives you a martyr's crown, whether you actually give your life so or not. See the difference in working for God?

SLOGAN: Not what we do, but why.

Dec. 17. ST. OLYMPIAS, Widow

After the death of her husband, St. Olympias devoted herself to the care of the altar. She performed the office of sacristan for many years. She considered it the greatest of honors to dedicate her time to the immediate service of her God in the Blessed Sacrament.

Many daughters have gotten riches, but thou excellest them all. Favor is deceitful and beauty is vain; a woman that feareth the Lord, she shall be praised. — *Prime: Chapter*

I am He that in an instant elevateth the humble mind to comprehend more reasons of the eternal truth than if anyone had studied ten years in the schools. — *Imitation: Book III*

IDEAL: The Seven Great Antiphons begin today. You know there is no finer poetry in the liturgy of the church. Here is the first great antiphon: O Wisdom who camest out of the mouth of the Most High, reaching from end to end and ordering all things mightily and sweetly: come and teach us the way of prudence.

TODAY: These fine old patriarchs and prophets who wrote under the direct inspiration of the Holy Spirit always prayed for that light of Wisdom. Do you ever think of praying for light and success in your schoolwork at other times except just before an examination? You should.

SLOGAN: Drop down dews, ye heavens, and ye clouds rain down the Just!

(See Ember Days.)

Dec. 18. ST. GATIAN, Bishop

The Gauls among whom St. Gatian worked were extremely addicted to the worship of idols. St. Gatian was tireless in his efforts to convert them. Of caves he improvised chapels in which he said Mass and administered the Sacraments.

This is the faithful and wise steward, whom the Lord setteth over His family; to give them their measure of wheat in due season. — *Communion: Luke 12*

For the just man will not be troubled, whatever happeneth to him from God. — *Imitation: Book III*

IDEAL: Second Great Antiphon: O Adonai, and leader of the house of Israel, who didst appear to Moses in the flame of the burning bush, and didst give unto him the law on Sinai: come and with an outstretched arm redeem us.

TODAY: Note how these holy men prayed and sighed for a leader for the house of Israel. That Leader has come and, in spite of the four thousand years they waited, He chose rather to come at a time when *you* are living, and to live right next door to you, as it were.

SLOGAN: No nation has its gods so nigh as our God is nigh unto us.

Dec. 19. ST. NEMESION, Martyr

St. Nemesion was an Egyptian. Accused of being a Christian, he was inhumanly tortured, but no mere physical pain could deprive him of the heavenly joy that shone on his face; a joy that astonished both judge and executioner.

Lord, Thou hast set upon us the light of Thy countenance. Thou hast put gladness into my heart. — *Matins: Psalm 4*

And he who neither desireth to please nor feareth to displease men shall enjoy much peace. — *Imitation: Book II*

IDEAL: Third Great Antiphon: O Root of Jesse who standest for a sign of the people before whom kings shall keep silence, and unto whom the Gentiles shall make their supplication, come to deliver us and tarry not.

TODAY: Read that antiphon again, and then picture to yourself Him for whom the nations yearned coming to His people, born — in a stable.

SLOGAN: Behold thy King cometh to thee, lowly.

Dec. 20.   ST. PHILOGONIUS, Bishop
(Vigil of St. Thomas)

This saint was one of the most successful lawyers of his day. He was admired for his eloquence but much more so for his integrity and the blamelessness of his life. He was consecrated a bishop without having gone through the usual preliminary preparations.

Therefore by an oath did the Lord make him to increase among his people. — *Vespers: Antiphon*

They shall gain great freedom of mind, who for Thy Name enter upon the narrow way, and relinquish all worldly care. — *Imitation: Book III*

IDEAL: Fourth Great Antiphon: O Key of David and scepter of the house of Israel, who openest and no man shutteth, who shuttest and no man openeth; come and bring forth from the prison house the captive that sitteth in darkness and in the shadow of death.

TODAY: Now that Christmas is so very near, you must have something to present at the crib. Nothing would so please the Baby Christ as the soul of some stray sheep of His flock brought thither by your prayers.

SLOGAN: The shepherds said: Let us go over to Bethlehem.

Dec. 21. ST. THOMAS, Apostle

By nature slow to believe and somewhat inclined to look at the dark side of things, he had a most courageous and sympathetic heart. The words: "My Lord and my God," to which the Church has attached an indulgence, were spoken by St. Thomas when, after a week of doubt as to the Resurrection of Jesus, he was convinced by the Lord Himself.

Because thou hast seen Me, Thomas, thou hast believed; blessed are they that have not seen, and yet have believed.

A wonderful thing it is, and worthy of faith, and transcending all human intelligence, that Thou, O Lord God, true God and true man, art whole and entire under a small form of bread and wine, art eaten by the receiver and without being consumed. — *Imitation: Book IV*

IDEAL: Fifth Great Antiphon: O Dawn of the East, Brightness of the Light Eternal, and Sun of Justice, come and enlighten them that sit in darkness and in the shadow of death.

TODAY: Five days hence, and the sweet feast will be here. You have not forgotten that you were going to make some sacrifices for someone who could never find out who did it for them.

SLOGAN: My Lord and my God!

Dec. 22. ST. FRANCES XAVIER CABRINI, Virgin

This is our own Mother Cabrini, for she did become a naturalized United States citizen, who lived and worked and died in places that we can find not only in our geography but even on the road map and in our train schedules. That seems to bring her so much closer to us. She died in Chicago, December 22, 1917.

I became all things to all men that I might win the more. — *Gradual*

Love often knoweth no measure but groweth fervent above all measure. — *Imitation: Book III*

IDEAL: Mother Cabrini's sanctity lay where ours will be found: in the simplicity of her intention. She sought only God's will and the promotion of His honor and glory; and if she concentrated a little more on her fellow countrymen, that is all right, too. Nobody else, except God, of course, and our Lady, was paying them too much heed in this country as far as their souls were concerned at the time.

TODAY: Thank God for Mother Cabrini. She shows what marvelous good sense the saints have and what perfectly charming personalities they do have. Her very smile is a comfort in distress.

SLOGAN: All things bright and beautiful; all things great and small, the great God made them all.

Dec. 23. ST. SERVULUS

St. Servulus was a beggar. He was afflicted with palsy; so wretched was he that he could neither sit nor stand. He was carried to the entry of a church where he begged for alms. He bore his misery patiently for the love of God, sweetly and courageously, and thus became a saint.

The Lord loved him and beautified him: He clothed him with a robe of glory, and crowned him at the gates of Paradise. — *Second Nocturn: Fifth Responsory*

He is gone before thee, carrying His cross, and He died for thee upon the cross, that thou mayst also bear thy cross and love to die on the cross. — *Imitation: Book II*

IDEAL: Seventh Great Antiphon: O Emmanuel, our King and Lawgiver, the expected of the nations and their Saviour, come to save us, O Lord our God.

TODAY: Christmas is upon us. You will not forget what it is all about two days hence, will you? It happens so often that people are so excited about the lovely singing in church and their own wonderful surprises around the Christmas tree that the dear little Child is left stretching out His little arms to empty space before Him. But not with *you* in Church; He may depend upon *you?*

SLOGAN: I was in prison and you visited Me.

EMBER WEDNESDAY

The four seasons of the year begin with the liturgical periods known as Ember Weeks. Their importance was very great in the early days of the Church. The Ember Days are three days of fast and abstinence, Wednesday, Friday, and Saturday, intended to consecrate to God the various seasons in Nature, and to prepare by penance those about to be ordained.

Drop down dew, ye heavens, from above, and let the clouds rain the Just: let the earth be opened and bud forth a Saviour. — *Introit: Psalm 18*

Strengthen me with heavenly fortitude, lest the old man, the miserable flesh not yet subdued to the spirit, get the upper hand; against which we must battle so long as we breathe in this most wretched life. — *Imitation: Book III*

IDEAL: The priests who are ordained during these days will have the care of your soul in the very near future. We are apt not to pray for priests, thinking they are so holy and so very close to God, they do not need our prayers, but they do.

TODAY: Pray for priests today, for the priests who have labored long and for those about to take up the burden.

SLOGAN: Pray therefore the Lord of the harvest to send forth laborers into His harvest.

EMBER FRIDAY

The Mass of today sums up perfectly the whole spirit of Advent, which is, so to speak, the first act of the great drama of the Incarnation. . . . It might be called "The Expectation of Christ."

Stir up Thy Power, O Lord, *and come:* that they who trust in Thy goodness may the more speedily be freed from all adversity. — *Collect*

Now do I desire to receive Thee devoutly and reverently; I long to bring Thee into my house. — *Imitation: Book IV*

IDEAL: As far as the fasting is concerned, you are not expected to fast, from food, that is. But we must all, regardless of age, fast from offense of God.

TODAY: Why should there be mention of avoiding offense of God when we are so busy gathering up surprise gifts to take to Him when He comes down on Christmas into His crib within our own soul?

SLOGAN: O come, my sweet Savior, in this heart recline,
Thou knowest, my Savior, 'twill ever be thine.

EMBER SATURDAY

Saturday was the most solemn of the Ember Days because that was the day on which the Church ordained her priests in the great basilica of St. John Lateran.

O Lord, come, and make no tarrying: loosen the bonds of Thy people. And gather together into their own land them that are scattered abroad. Stir up, O Lord, Thy power, and come among us to save us. — *Matins: Third Responsory*

O happy mind and blessed soul! which deserveth to receive Thee, her Lord God devoutly, and in receiving Thee to be filled with spiritual joy. — *Imitation: Book IV*

IDEAL: Before you leave for the vacation over the holidays, look back over the year thus far gone, the part of the school year principally. Just how much good has this reading done you?

TODAY: Have you noticed how much effort some of the students have made to carry out the little suggestions in the daily reading? *You* have made the difference. Let no one outstrip you in the new year.

SLOGAN: Time and tide wait for no man.

Dec. 24. VIGIL OF THE NATIVITY OF OUR LORD

Were it not for the purple vestments and for fasting, one would believe it to be Christmas Day. There is a spirit of joyful expectation in the air.

This day you shall know that the Lord will come, and save us: and in the morning you shall see His glory. — *Introit*

Son, I came down from heaven for thy salvation; I took upon Me thy miseries, not of necessity, but moved thereto by charity; that thou mightest learn patience and bear without repining temporal miseries. — *Imitation: Book III*

IDEAL: This is Christmas Eve. In a few hours Christ will be born again in our hearts through Holy Communion. The Babe of Bethlehem will be with us.

TODAY: Don't forget that all we do today is done in preparation for the coming of the Christ Child. Our real happiness tomorrow will be measured, not by the gifts we have given and received, but by what we have done to make our poor hearts a fit abode for the divine Infant. When we do our work let us do it as though our Blessed Lady were our constant companion.

SLOGAN: In the morning you shall see His glory.

Dec. 25. CHRISTMAS DAY

The most holy night of Christmas is sanctified by a midnight Mass, recalling the temporal birth of Christ in His coming of grace. The early dawn is sanctified by the Mass of the Shepherds, bringing to mind the birth of Christ in our souls by grace. Then the third Mass in the full light of day reminds us of the eternal birth of the Second Person of the Blessed Trinity from all eternity in the Bosom of the Eternal Father.

And the WORD WAS MADE FLESH AND DWELT AMONG US: and we saw His glory, glory as of the only begotten of the Father, full of grace and of truth. — *Gospel of the Third Mass*

Make, therefore, the soul of thy servant joyful this day, because unto Thee have I lifted up my soul, O Lord Jesus. — *Imitation: Book IV*

IDEAL: The sweet attractiveness of childhood reaches its perfection in the divine Child. No wonder this same divine

Child, when He had grown to manhood, taught us that "Unless you become as little children you shall not enter the kingdom of heaven."

TODAY: There is all the difference in the world between being childish and childlike. Let us be good children today and thank our heavenly Father for that Gift of gifts, His only-begotten Son. Let us be unselfish children, content with what we have and willing to share with others to make them happy.

SLOGAN: Jesus, judge me as a child.

Dec. 26.   ST. STEPHEN, First Martyr

The Church was still in her infancy when Stephen was commissioned to organize the meals where the poor were fed in common. Brought before the Sanhedrin, he boldly upbraided the priests for their hardheartedness in resisting the Holy Ghost. He was the first of an endless line of Christian martyrs.

And casting him forth out of the city, they stoned him. — *Epistle*

Oh! if thou couldst see the everlasting crowns of the saints in heaven, and in how great glory they now triumph, who appeared contemptible heretofore in this world. — *Imitation: Book III*

IDEAL: The witnesses of the stoning of St. Stephen laid down their garments at the feet of a young man whose name was Saul. This same young man later become the great Apostle St. Paul. He was the first fruit of St. Stephen's prayer: Lord, lay not this sin to their charge.

TODAY: Those who love the Lord must be willing to suffer for Him. We may never be asked to do what St. Stephen did, but we can earn the same heaven by dying to ourselves in little things. Be glad today for the countless opportunities of suffering in all the little ways that a loving Providence offers us. If there are not enough to satisfy our love for the divine Christ Child, we know that we can do many little things that are known to God alone.

SLOGAN: Peace shall come on one day, which is known to the Lord. — *Imitation: Book III*

Dec. 27. ST. JOHN, Apostle and Evangelist

St. John was the favorite of our Lord because he was clean of heart. He was thrown by Domitian into a caldron of boiling oil, for which reason he is reckoned a martyr, though he was miraculously preserved from hurt.

Greatly to be honored is John, who leaned on the Lord's breast at Supper. — *Versicle: Second Vespers*

Write, read, sing, lament, keep silence, pray, bear adversities manfully, eternal life is worth all these and greater combats. — *Imitation: Book III*

IDEAL: St. John had the great privilege of caring for the Blessed Virgin after our Lord's ascension. He is the disciple of Love. There was one sermon he preached over and over again: My little children, let us love one another.

TODAY: We do well to let St. John preach to us today. The great lesson of his life: Purity; and the lesson of his sermon: Fraternal charity.

SLOGAN: My little children, let us love one another.

Dec. 28. THE HOLY INNOCENTS, Martyrs

When Herod found out that the Wise Men did not return, he became furious and ordered all the male children in and around Bethlehem to be put to death.

Praise the Lord, ye children, praise ye the name of the Lord. — *Gradual*

All is little and short which passeth away with time. — *Imitation: Book III*

IDEAL: Like a compassionate mother, the Church clothes herself in the garments of mourning as she recalls the anguish of the mothers of the Holy Innocents.

TODAY: Notice how the feasts nearest Christmas are those

of martyrs. When we can find our happiness in suffering for
Christ we have found the door to real contentment on earth
and everlasting glory hereafter. Let us make a special visit to
the Blessed Sacrament today and ask the Holy Innocents to
make our love for the divine Child simple and childlike
and strong in making sacrifices.

SLOGAN: In God we trust.

Dec. 29. ST. THOMAS OF CANTERBURY, Bishop and Martyr

St. Thomas was a great friend of the king of England until
the former was made bishop. His insistence on the rights of
the Church without compromise made him an enemy of the
king. He paid for his loyalty to Christ and the Church with
his life.

O God, for whose Church the glorious Pontiff Thomas fell
by the swords of the wicked: grant, we beseech Thee, that
all who implore his help may obtain a salutary effect of their
petition. — *Collect*

Mind what thou art about: labor faithfully in My vineyard:
I will be thy reward. — *Imitation: Book III*

IDEAL: The true friend is not the one who always says:
"Yes, yes." When there is question of doing right or wrong
we must be willing to sacrifice the dearest friendship to keep
the friendship of God.

TODAY: Let us be careful not to demand anything of our
friends that would in the least draw them away from God.
On the other hand, let all those who associate with us be
brought closer to the divine Child because of their friendship with us.

SLOGAN: Adversity tries friendship.

Dec. 30. ST. SABINUS, Bishop and Martyr

St. Sabinus had both his hands cut off and was then beaten
to death with clubs because he refused to deny his faith.

Blessed is the man who endureth temptation: for when he shall have been proved, he shall receive the crown of life which God hath promised to them that love Him.— *Epistle*

It is no small matter to lose or gain the kingdom of heaven. — *Imitation: Book III*

IDEAL: St. Sabinus isn't sorry now that in the time of temptation he had the courage to say "No." Had he succumbed, what a different eternity would have been in store for him.

TODAY: Hilaire Belloc has an essay on "The Tremendousness of Trifles." Read the essay today and draw your own conclusions.

SLOGAN: And the least shall be the greatest in the kingdom of heaven.

Dec. 31. ST. SYLVESTER, Pope and Confessor

St. Sylvester was one of the great popes who guided the Church during her troublesome times of persecution. He faced the danger of death to encourage Christians to be faithful when brought to trial for their faith.

Behold a great priest who in his days pleased God. There was not found the like to him, who kept the law of the Most High. — *Gradual*

Ought not all painful labors to be endured for everlasting life? — *Imitation: Book III*

IDEAL: This is the last day of the year. If you have been lovingly attentive to the voice of the Church in her liturgy, you have learned to know at least 365 of the friends of Christ. Of these friends of Christ St. John in the Apocalypse says that he saw a multitude which no man could number of all nations and tribes and peoples and tongues.

TODAY: Set aside at least a half hour today for taking spiritual inventory. Are you making the necessary effort to be one of the multitude St. John speaks of? Your conduct minute for minute decides eternity for you.

SLOGAN: Only one thing is necessary.

INDEX